FROM DONUTS... TO POTATOES

My 366 Day Journey on a Plant-Based Diet

ESTHER LeBECK LOVERIDGE

BALBOA.PRESS
A DIVISION OF HAY HOUSE

Copyright © 2020 Esther Lebeck Loveridge.

All rights reserved. No part of this book may be used or reproduced by any means, graphic, electronic, or mechanical, including photocopying, recording, taping or by any information storage retrieval system without the written permission of the author except in the case of brief quotations embodied in critical articles and reviews.

Balboa Press books may be ordered through booksellers or by contacting:

Balboa Press
A Division of Hay House
1663 Liberty Drive
Bloomington, IN 47403
www.balboapress.com
1 (877) 407-4847

Because of the dynamic nature of the Internet, any web addresses or links contained in this book may have changed since publication and may no longer be valid. The views expressed in this work are solely those of the author and do not necessarily reflect the views of the publisher, and the publisher hereby disclaims any responsibility for them.

Esther writes the way she talks. Any grammatical errors
or long sentences are reflected in this book.

The author of this book does not dispense medical advice or prescribe the use of any technique as a form of treatment for physical, emotional, or medical problems without the advice of a physician, either directly or indirectly. The intent of the author is only to offer information of a general nature to help you in your quest for emotional and spiritual well-being. In the event you use any of the information in this book for yourself, which is your constitutional right, the author and the publisher assume no responsibility for your actions.

Any people depicted in stock imagery provided by Getty Images are models,
and such images are being used for illustrative purposes only.
Certain stock imagery © Getty Images.

Print information available on the last page.

ISBN: 978-1-9822-4417-0 (sc)
ISBN: 978-1-9822-4415-6 (hc)
ISBN: 978-1-9822-4416-3 (e)

Library of Congress Control Number: 2020904385

Balboa Press rev. date: 03/04/2020

DEDICATION

This book is dedicated to all of you who have joined me in "Esther's Nutritional Journey" on Facebook. You have kept me motivated with positive feedback on how these posts have helped to inspire you. You have thanked me for my help, guidance and wisdom as we navigate our new lives together. Your success stories are my measure of success and I thank you from the bottom of my heart.

EPIGRAPH

"IT'S THE FOOD" by John McDougall, MD

FOREWORD

"Esther is a teaching example of my statement, "Everyone following the Western Diet or worse (low-carb) who makes a serious change to the starch-based diet as recommended in From Donuts to Potatoes will experience almost overnight benefits in their appearance, feelings, and functions." In fact, most people will be able to declare themselves "cured" of their chronic diseases and constant battles with too much weight."

— John McDougall, MD
Author, Internist, Environmentalist
drmcdougall@drmcdougall.com

"As I read your posts, look at your pics and watch your journey, I am led to believe you are like the original Esther in the Bible and have been put in this place and situation for such a time as this. You are encouraging many to choose foods that bring life!!
Thank you for your transparency and commitment."

— Mary Sanders LaVine

"I'd hate to see your words get lost in the land where the internet ends. It would be a shame if your words disappeared... a book would make them live forever. They are beautiful and uplifting and it will be fun to pass them along to the generations to come."

— Valerie Stewart

PREFACE

THE DONUT SHOP STORY

In 1987, I went to Baker Ben's Donut Shop on 28th and Broadway to take advantage of a coupon from my father. I thought it would be nice to take some donuts to work so I stopped on my way to the Secretary of State's Office where I was employed as an Office Assistant.-Receptionist in the Executive Office. I was hooked. The donuts were very good and I soon became a regular customer. I was able to get off Highway 99 at Broadway, get a donut and a cup of coffee and continue on down Broadway to 16th Street and head up to J Street to the parking lot without going out of my way at all. It didn't take Ben long to realize that I chose the same thing every day – a cup of coffee and a buttermilk bar and soon he had my donut all bagged and ready to go when I went into his shop.

One day, when I stopped for my "fix", I ate the buttermilk bar while driving to work. I parked my car in the lot and as I started to throw away the bag, I noticed something blue in the bag. I was surprised to see something in there and I soon discovered it was Ben's business card. On the back he had written a note saying that he'd like to get to know me and could we have lunch sometime? He asked me to give him a call.

Suddenly, the clock turned back and I felt like a teenager again. I just didn't know how to react in this situation. Basically, I didn't go back to the donut shop for awhile. Then I thought about the donuts and how I was missing them and Ben was missing out on a good customer. Perhaps the best way to handle it was to go back and pretend like I never got the "message". This time, shortly before Thanksgiving, was our real beginning. After I got my donut, I walked out of the shop, but unbeknownst to me, Ben exited through the back door and met me at my car in the parking lot. He asked me if I got his note, and I said "Yes". He asked me if I was single etc. and we exchanged information about our families and finally, he asked for my phone number and called me later that day and asked to take me to dinner on Saturday night, December 5th 1987

I was nervous about our first date and discussed my feelings with my brother Paul, my friend Sue Edelmayer and her mother Bess Paul at breakfast that morning at the Distillery on L Street. Bess suggested that when Ben arrived, I should invite him in and then go get my coat which would allow him a few minutes to check out my place. I followed her advice.

Ben took me to the Coral Reef and we had a wonderful dinner and had their famous Mai Tai's before and after dinner as we sat near the fireplace. Right off we really clicked and spent most of the evening telling each other about places we liked and wanted to share with each other. It was as though there wasn't going to be enough time to do all we wanted to do.

When Ben took me home, he asked me if he could take me out

for breakfast the next morning and I said "Yes". He had to drive from Valley Hi where I lived to his home in Fair Oaks and then come back again in the morning. It was probably at least 50 miles round trip and the following morning when he came to pick me up, he brought us some donuts from the shop. Tim, my older son, got to meet him when he came in from his night shift at Carl Jr's. Ben and I went down the river road to Isleton to a cute little café where we could watch the storm from the safety of the restaurant.

Stopping by the shop on the way to work became a daily experience and that made it easy to continue our routine of getting to see each other every day. We had dates on weekends, but workday mornings were enhanced by me riding with him as he made deliveries to his wholesale accounts. Jesus, an employee, would bring my coffee and donut to me while I waited in Ben's Suzuki until Ben loaded the trays of donuts in the back. After making the deliveries, we'd park in the fabulous 40's neighborhood and chat or nap for awhile. Ben would then head back to the shop and I'd go on to work.

And that's how it all began. Ben quips that the old card in the bag tricks worked every time!

We were married 32 months later.

1987

1989

30 years later

ACKNOWLEDGEMENT

I acknowledge John McDougall, MD for writing "The McDougall Program for Maximum Weight Loss which was my guide to converting to a plant based way of eating. He also designated me as a "Star McDougaller" and posted my success story on his website.

Other members of his team include Doug Lisle, PhD, who taught me that we are naturally drawn to the most calorie dense food in our environment, Dr. Anthony Lim who offered his support to me at the McDougall 3-day Intensive Weekend Program and Jeff Novick, MS, RDN who taught me all about nutrition. My personal physician

Dr. Rajiv Misquitta has supported my new life in every way possible and has been my greatest cheerleader.

Chef AJ has also been a big influence on addressing the issues of Food Addiction and I thank her for teaching me "If it is in your house, it will be in your mouth".

I want to thank the following people for giving me an opportunity to share my story:

Corinne Nijjer, for giving me two interviews on her podcast in Australia.

Terri Edwards, for connecting me to Woman's World Magazine for their August 5, 2019 issue.

The 5th grade children in the UK, who interviewed me by SKYPE so they could learn more about diabetes and obesity.

To Vicki Pepper, for inviting me to speak at her Kaiser program in San Diego, CA.

Linda Middlesworth, who asked me to share my story at "Get Healthy Sacramento Speaker's Series 2020", and

Al Schmidt, who arranged for me to tell my story at the VegFest 2019 in Sacramento, CA and on the Peggy Bean Radio Show in Nevada City, California.

I owe a big thanks to Mary Heutmaker Smith who contacted me and said she wanted to help me with this project and connected me to Balboa Press.

I also want to thank my very dear anonymous friend who gave me Dr. McDougall's book – knowing it was just what I needed. My life has been enriched through my husband Ben Loveridge. He has stood by my side every day for over 32 years. He loved my brain and my soul, not my ever changing body.

I am grateful to Rev. Phil Pierson for tying the knot on August 9, 1989 and for teaching us Unity principles which can be applied to our everyday lives.

And finally, I am indebted to Balboa Press for their sustained assistance in getting this book published.

INTRODUCTION

"I could never eat like you". "Oh, I could never give up cheese". "You mean I would have to give up my cocktail hour?" "I have given up red meat, but I do eat chicken". "My husband insists he needs animal protein". "I have kids and grandchildren who have to have their snacks" and the list goes on and on as we establish reasons or excuses for why we "can't" switch to a plant-based diet.

As long as we hold these beliefs close to our hearts, the struggle will continue. Conforming to these ideas doesn't bring any resolution to the issues of our health. We dig in our heels but still wish we could find relief from what is keeping us from being our best. We are torn.

It is a real dilemma. What is the answer? What is at the core of the problems we face? Do we continue to judge and condemn ourselves for being weak? Do we find other people to blame?

I search my mind for answers. I ache for all of you who are suffering. I wonder what it will take for you to find your answer. Many of you have watched the documentaries, webinars, been to seminars and collected many of the cookbooks searching for something sustainable. And yet, you have joined another group on Facebook looking for more help or picked up this book.

What can I offer that will be the key to your success? Is there something I can say that will turn on the switch that will change your life forever? What is the missing link to your personal success? If I knew what it was, I would tell you. I would love to set you all free from the pain and suffering. I would love for you to enjoy life to the fullest. I would love for this to be the final stop on your journey to finding answers.

What I come up with is just sending you love...the kind of love that says "You're okay" knowing that the key is making friends with what you are WILLING to do. That also requires accepting the consequences. Maybe it is just that simple.

ABBREVIATIONS

WFPB - Whole Food Plant Based
WOE - Way of eating
MWL - Maximum Weight Loss

JANUARY 1
WORD FOR TODAY: CHOICE

Countless choices are made each day. Our brains are such a gift to us. We can think, we can choose, we can change, we can move forward or not, we can share, we can learn from our choices and we can reinforce them as well.

Our internal guidance system will continue to lead us forward. Yes, sometimes we are stubborn and self centered and ego strong and insist on having our own way, but eventually our internal guidance system says "recalculating" and we still have the choice of finding our own way or submitting and listening to who we now call "Gabby".

There is no decision but what there can be positive outcomes. What if I had been on a Whole Food Plant Based eating program back in 1987 and didn't accept the coupon my father gave to me for Baker Ben's Donut Shop? Would I have met "Baker Ben"?

That one decision changed the direction of my life. Eventually my attraction was to him, although of course I loved his buttermilk bars too.

You have made the choice to join "Esther's Nutritional Journey". No one signed you up. You were not added because someone else thought you needed this group. It was your choice. It is your choice to glean whatever is helpful to you and inspire others. Maybe some of you will start your own group to share your success story. I encourage you to reach out and touch "Your World". The choice is yours.

_____

_____

_____

_____

FROM DONUTS...TO POTATOES

JANUARY 2

WORD FOR TODAY: MIND

This word brings to my mind several childhood instructions: Mind your manners. Mind your parents. Mind your teachers.

Is your mind open or do you have a closed mind? Maybe you have your mind set on something you want to accomplish. Maybe your mind is made up. Perhaps changing your mind is not anything you have ever considered.

Well, we are evolving, adapting to our environment and challenging the status quo in many situations. Thoughts that we held to be true as children are now surfacing in our minds and we get to re-evaluate and see if those same "truths" hold value today.

I was taught to clean my plate and I still do. However, if we can learn to stop eating when we are satisfied, does it really make any difference in the long run if we eat the last bite or throw it away or save it for later? We used to say "waste not, want not" and of course we were taught about the starving children elsewhere in the world.

How about counting calories? What about portion control? And then there is that old myth called moderation.

Yes. We can think. We can evaluate for ourselves what works for us. Isn't that just grand?

Nobody is the boss of you...unless you relinquish that role.

_____

_____

_____

_____

JANUARY 3
WORD FOR TODAY: BAG

What's in your bag? Do you carry around guilt, shame, fear of loss or do you have a mixed bag with helpful tools too?

The "tools" for success in your bag may include watching documentaries, reading success stories, reading inspirational books, surrounding yourself with positive people and certainly keeping your kitchen filled with compliant food.

Maybe you haven't switched to eating plant based food 100% but have decided to do the best you can. We are all different and it helps to remember the story about the tortoise and the hare.

Every bite you take is a step towards health or disease and those steps are cumulative.

The key is to KNOW that most of our chronic diseases are a result of eating toxic food...poison. A little "dab" may seem innocent enough but for many of us food addicts, a little is never enough and just takes up room in our bag.

Aim high and clean out your bag before you get carried out in one. You are worthy of the best. You are of value. This is your life.

_____
_____
_____
_____

FROM DONUTS...TO POTATOES

JANUARY 4

WORD FOR TODAY: LISTEN

In the early morning hours, when all seems quiet, I sometimes hear traffic, far away. Even farther away, is the sound of a passing train. Close to me is the sound of my husband breathing and I give thanks.

There is another voice that is worth listening to. It is the messages we receive from our bodies. Any discomfort we may experience is a voice speaking to us.

When I had pancreatitis and a gall bladder attack, I didn't listen. When I had GERD, insomnia, sleep apnea, constipation, arthritis, back pain, blood pressure creeping up and cholesterol rising, I just took statins and other medications. Prediabetes didn't even scare me because I was not diabetic yet. But when my knees cried out for help, when my love of traveling was threatened, I finally listened. My body finally had my attention.

Someone once said they were having trouble staying on their eating plan and I jokingly replied, "Would you like me to pray that more pain comes into your life"?

Pain is our alarm clock. It wakes us up or, we can roll over, hit the snooze button and go back to sleep

ESTHER LEBECK LOVERIDGE

JANUARY 5
WORD FOR TODAY: MEET

Many people are so convinced that meat needs to be a part of their lifestyle and they are right. It is just that they have misspelled it!

We must meet together, have a meeting of the minds, meet on common ground and meet the needs of one another.

Being a part of a community is a wonderful place to do all of those things and we had a great opportunity to do that yesterday at Esther's Nutritional Journey Luncheon to celebrate the success of everyone there. I met many from this group for the first time and it felt like we had been friends for a long time.

We are not alone. We are not the only ones striving to enjoy a whole food plant based lifestyle. We are touching the lives of everyone we meet - spreading the good news of how to be our best and heal our bodies from the ravages of meat.

We will continue to meet up together in the future. Share your ideas and suggestions and let's make it happen.

_____
_____
_____
_____

FROM DONUTS...TO POTATOES

JANUARY 6
WORD FOR TODAY: LIGHT

When we take a journey, it helps to travel light. Over packing weighs us down. And so it is in life.

Light can also represent information, knowledge and wisdom. My Grandmother Kearns was an old Quaker and when I was young and pondering a decision, she would ask me if I felt "light" about it. Lightness seemed to come when I found my answer and felt at peace.

In "The Healthiest Diet on the Planet", John McDougall, M.D. uses the traffic light to demonstrate what foods are good for us to eat. Foods listed under the green light are foods that are healthy, those under the yellow light are foods where one needs to slow down and of course foods listed under the red light mean stop - or don't go there.

I like the story of the camel going through the eye of the needle. I used to question how that could even be possible until I learned that the eye of the needle was only a gate and all weights had to be removed from the camel's back in order for it to fit through the narrow opening.

Sometimes there may be people in our lives who don't want to see the "light". They may be comfortable sitting in the dark which doesn't require as much action. I, too, was in the dark for over 72 years. I had no idea that following "The McDougall Program for Maximum Weight Loss" (John McDougall, MD) would lighten my path and show me how to live for the rest of my life.

I feel light.

_____

_____

JANUARY 7
WORD FOR TODAY: LIFE

A life may be something we save. Sometimes it is lost. Often it is shared and sometimes abused. What is life? Is it a gift that is given to us for a period of time and then it is up to us to decide how to spend it? Do we waste it, use it or watch it go idly by?

Life is fragile, often taken from us before we are ready to release it. When it is gone, where does it go? Does it come back or do we simply hope it remains in the hearts of those we have loved?

What I do believe is that it is never ending. There are many stops along the way but it does continue. We can make the most of it. We can love it, appreciate it and share it.

The question remains - how effective is our use of the gift we have. Can we enhance it, nourish it, let it grow and learn what it is all about?

Life is love in action. It is learning when we think we are teaching. It is the longing to know all we can. It is our undying spirit striving to quench its thirst.

FROM DONUTS...TO POTATOES

JANUARY 8

WORD FOR TODAY: SAY

What we say, what we declare to be true and when we speak our minds are all ways we testify to what we believe.

When I started "Esther's Nutritional Journey" on Facebook, I posted two questions for prospective members to answer. One question was "What do you want to learn from this group"?

The primary response has centered on wanting to lose weight. Improving one's health has also been the goal of many. There are those who say they want to stay on track with their eating plan and others say they want to reduce or eliminate the medications they are currently taking. Some say they want motivation, inspiration, and support in their own personal journey. I call it WISH - Weight, Inspiration, Support and Health.

Then there are those who are just plain curious about this old woman who decided it is never too late to turn one's life around and that has ignited their desire for hope.

It has been important to me to hear what you have to say. It is a baby step in achieving your goal. By actually writing down what you want to achieve from being a part of this group, you have taken the time to think about it and focus on what is important to you.

Any failure you have experienced in the past does not have to define you today. Today is a new opportunity to be kind to yourself and aim for your goals. You notice I did not say achieve your goals. That will come in time. The first step is to aim for your desired outcome and you have already started that by simply declaring what you want.

Say what?

_____

_____

JANUARY 9
WORD FOR TODAY: FAITH

When my former personal physician confronted me with the fact that I needed to lose 70 pounds before he could even refer me to Orthopedics for knee replacements (my knees were almost bone on bone), I had no faith in any diet and didn't know how I would ever be able to accomplishment that kind of weight loss.

I'm sure all of the different diets that I had tried in the past, surfaced in my mind as I tried to think about how to lose the weight again. I had tried Weight Watchers, Dr. Atkins, TOPS, Overeaters Anonymous, the Grapefruit Diet, the 600 Calories diet in Reader's Digest and there was also The Diet Center Diet where I'd go for weigh-ins. Back in the 70's, maybe late 60's, I was even given "diet pills". At some point when I was having trouble losing weight, I questioned whether or not I suffered from a low thyroid and was put on levothyroxin and continued that for at least 30 years until July, 2018.

At this critical fork in the road, it was through a close friend that I received my answer. She had been reading about a plant based diet in an effort to stem her own rising blood sugar levels. She did not want to get Diabetes. I had never even heard of Dr. John A. McDougall much less the concept of eating a whole food plant based diet. She gave me a copy of his earlier work - "The McDougall Program for Maximum Weight Loss". That's just what I needed - Maximum Weight Loss. I did not want to fool around. I wanted to get down to business and reduce the stress on my knees. I wasn't

FROM DONUTS...TO POTATOES

even opposed to having my knees replaced if that is what it would take. What I didn't like is that at that point in time, I did not have a choice.

Did I have faith in Dr. McDougall? Probably not at first, but as I read his book, listened to podcasts and learned how we can cure or reverse food borne illnesses, my faith increased. I had tried everything else. What did I have to lose (besides the 70 pounds)?

What a life changing experience. It is hard to describe the relief I feel from being free from past food addictions and to know I will never gain weight again as long as I focus of the four food groups: vegetables, fruit, grains and legumes. It is so simple. Eat when hungry and stop when satisfied. Keep it simple. Do I have faith in the work of Dr. McDougall now? Yes.

_____
_____
_____
_____

JANUARY 10

WORD FOR TODAY: PANIC

Life is a series of stressful events - situations which create an opportunity for us to learn. When something stressful happens, we can go into a state of panic - fear the worst and default to our most common response - grab something to eat.

Does eating the food solve the problem? Does eating a handful of what we used to see as the remedy to stress help? No. The situation remains the same - stagnant until we choose to use the situation to go into a thinking mode and come up with a solution.

ESTHER LEBECK LOVERIDGE

When we were getting ready to deplane in Cambodia, we were given documents to fill out so that we could obtain a visa upon arrival at the airport. I knew we would need three visas for this trip, one of which (Vietnam) we had already obtained by going to San Francisco, CA. The other two, we were told, could be gotten on site. We were instructed to bring extra passport photos for these other two countries. We did that. We were prepared. The problem was that I put those photos with copies of our passport in the luggage that we checked in and as I sat there on the plane, I became concerned that we would need to complete the visa process in customs, prior to getting our luggage.

Did we panic? No, but it was a concern. That's when I reminded Ben not to worry because Fred Rogers (Mr. Roger's Neighborhood on TV) used to say, "Whenever there is a problem, look for the helpers".

Did we reach out for a cookie while we proceeded to get off the plane? No, we went to one of the helpers (before we got to the bank of official government custom officers) and told him of our dilemma. He touched my arm and assured us that there was no problem - they could capture our photo from the photo in our passport. We learned that there was a real solution - we paid the $3.00 for this service and we were once again in a peaceful state.

There are not very many situations to which there is no answer. So when we are tempted to reach out for the drug of food, we can engage our brains and come up with a real solution and resist hitting the panic button.

Think first, don't panic, and then tuck the learning experience into your reservoir of successful solutions.

_____

_____

_____

_____

FROM DONUTS...TO POTATOES

JANUARY 11

WORD FOR TODAY: REWARD

A reward is often offered when something is lost and we want it back. When we accomplish a task, we often get rewarded. But how we choose to reward ourselves can promote good health or even set us back from the very goal we wanted to accomplish.

Today, I made it to the top of Angkor Wat in Cambodia. It required, first of all, a desire. When we saw the long line of visitors waiting to climb the steps, we didn't know if we would have time before we would need to catch up with our guide. When he realized how important it was to us to get to "Nirvana", the top, he said he'd make the time to allow us to do it.

Determination was also a factor. The steps looked pretty steep but the challenge was not diminished. It was really important to me because when we went to the Great Wall in China, I only went far enough to be able to say "I was on it". With my at this point 125 pound weight loss, I was determined to have a different experience this time.

Step by step, we inched our way to the top. We took advantage of the support of others who offered us a hand or a shoulder to brace ourselves on as we made our journey.

The reward was the panoramic view from the top but even more rewarding was the ability to move my body in ways I could not have done almost 30 months prior.

Hard work, setting goals, sticking to a plan and following through were other steps taken before these today.

Day by day...step by step and support from others all lead to victory.

_____

_____

JANUARY 12

WORD FOR TODAY: CONTRASTS

We see contrasts wherever we look. People wear different style clothing, some fill them out more than others, and some people seem to be affluent while others seem to struggle in life.

On our journey, contrasts pop out at us at every turn. Yesterday we left our hotel by bus, and then went from stopping by the rice fields where we saw how people were cutting the rice stalks by hand to taking an ox cart ride in the country. We then took a boat ride down the river to see the floating fishing villages where people may never walk on land. We flew to Bangkok, Thailand on a two prop plane where we had to walk out to the plane and climb the stairs and finally arrived at the opulent hotel here in Bangkok, Thailand where the lights glitter like Las Vegas, the people look rich and the views of the river from the Terrace Restaurant made me feel under dressed.

Someone once said we do not have to compare ourselves with anyone. We do not have to compete with anyone else - the only one to compete with is who we were yesterday.

Each day brings new opportunities to strengthen our resolve to be our best. I do not insist on everyone following what has worked for me. I can only attest to what I did, that it worked for me and that maintaining my weight loss has never been easier. I will continue eating this way for the rest of my life. It is the food I was meant to live and thrive on. It has cured me of everything I can think of. I feel whole and ready to take on a new adventure today in Bangkok.

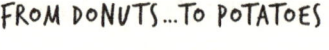

FROM DONUTS...TO POTATOES

_____

_____

_____

_____

JANUARY 13

WORD FOR TODAY: RECALCULATE

There are times when we must recalculate what we are doing. We continue on a healthy journey, but sometimes slip off the road. We don't always know we have gone off track until our bodies speak out to us.

In my case, I need to make some adjustments on this trip to Southeast Asia. My feet are experiencing some swelling. Yes, I know it is warmer here but I think the real culprit is eating out 3 meals a day at bountiful buffets and I have been eating lots of vegetarian dishes which means they do not necessarily know about our preference of eating no oil and they certainly may use copious amounts of salt.

So, what is my next move? I am going to eat more raw vegetables when we are having a meal at a hotel buffet. When lunches and dinners are included in this tour, I cannot order off a menu. What I can do, is use that opportunity as a tasting experience. I don't have to eat the whole thing. I have been cleaning my plate at every meal. Of course things are tasty - I never use salt at home so that old caloric density thing kicks in and I dive into the food like a starving prisoner.

What I have noticed is that my policy has basically been - no animal or dairy products. That is pretty easy, but put some vegetable tempura or some cashews in a celery entrée in front of me and I am off to the races, which reflects my rich food addiction.

This journey is wonderful. I love every moment of this experience but I am going to pay attention to the message my body is sending me. Thank you, body, for not remaining silent. I hear you.

_____
_____
_____
_____

JANUARY 14

WORD FOR TODAY: DIFFICULT

There are people who appear to be difficult to get along with and we often face challenges. We pass difficult tests and learn hard tasks. Our accomplishments are sweeter in direct correlation to the level of difficulty.

Just because something is hard to do doesn't mean it isn't worth doing.

Going WFPB (Whole Food Plant Based) is hard. We are taking on the task of breaking long held and entrenched habits. We are bucking addictions and traditions. We are resisting foods which we are actually advised to eat by some doctors. We visit unfriendly restaurants and sometimes feel like we are from another planet.

BUT...joy comes when we advance and pass each test that comes along. The turning point is when we start to feel the benefits of eating this way. It is difficult to convince someone of how great they will feel before they get there. It has to come from experience, not suggestion.

FROM DONUTS...TO POTATOES

Drug pushers want prospective "customers" to just "try it". Obtaining good health is a longer process. It requires many tries. There is no magic pill or quick fix. It is a daily challenge with equally fantastic results.

_____

_____

_____

_____

JANUARY 15

WORD FOR TODAY: RESPECT

There is a special way that people in Southeast Asia show respect to one another. It doesn't matter how many times you greet someone in a restaurant, hotel or even when doing a transaction in a store or public place. They take the time to see you, clasp their hands in front of their chests and slightly bow their heads. These interactions cause us to slow down and see one another.

Yesterday, we experienced a special welcoming ceremony when seniors and one young lady came to our hotel and welcomed us into their community by bringing food, drink and flowers and lots of blessings.

We sat in a circle around the room and over time, each person, while on their knees, came to each of us individually and tied a cotton string around our wrists as they quietly said a blessing for us. It was a very special ceremony and I was deeply touched. These people are so kind and loving and show respect every chance they get. We have so much to learn.

As I think about all of you who have joined my journey, I want to think of you individually with stories that have yet to be told. We all have had pain in our lives and through this community, I hope to respect all of you, no matter where you live on this planet or whatever your customs, religion or traditions. We are all one and love binds all of us together as we seek to continue to be our best and strive for better health. The weight loss will take care of itself as we release all that has held us in bondage to food. Be free. Be well. Be respected.

_____

_____

_____

_____

JANUARY 16

WORD FOR TODAY: AFFLUENCE

How do we measure affluence? I guess it is done in as many different ways as there are people to do it. Maybe it starts with collecting marbles as a child. I remember collecting them and some were definitely worth more than others. And then my girlfriend and I used to collect the little charms that we would get out of gum ball machines. Somewhere along the line I collected a few story book dolls (some of which are still stored away in a box).

So when do we have enough stuff to represent the success of our lives? Or does stuff even represent the part of us that is eternal and will be passed on to our children and grandchildren? What do we really want them to know about us and our life experiences or would we just be happier if the next generation even wanted our stuff?

FROM DONUTS...TO POTATOES

On this trip to Southeast Asia, I have been impressed with the lives of the Buddhist monks.

Life is very simple, food is simple, clothing is simple, and their needs are simple. I used to see them in San Francisco wearing their orange garments and thought they were a cult. I judged them without knowing anything about their lifestyle or their desire to learn about being kind. When we can dismiss one another, we do not even have to think about them or consider them. They are just "different".

How does all of this relate to our excesses in our food choices? Instead of collecting stamps in a book to cash in for merchandise, we collect food experiences in exquisite restaurants and think we need to eat everything that is offered or even available. I mean, why is it there if it is not for us to enjoy? We think we live in a rich country and we do...but the richness of what is available to us is also our downfall. Our bodies tolerate the excesses for a long time but later in life, our greed for rich foods exceeds our body's ability to keep up and illnesses seem almost insurmountable.

The good news is that it is never too late to make food our medicine, not our demise. Keep it simple and explore your world, your family and your community. Be creative. Take a walk, smell a flower, observe the sky and look into the faces of all you meet. Connect.

_____

_____

_____

JANUARY 17

WORD FOR TODAY: ALONE

While we are on this whole food plant based way of eating, there are times when we may feel alone. We may feel isolated at parties where we once felt like we were in the "groove" with others. Even in our own families, we may feel like the "odd man out". Well, it is because we often ARE the only ones who have seen the light as to what is best for us.

Sometimes, we are the leaders of the future. How else can changes be made?

I want to remind myself that really, I am never alone. That is because inside my head, I have lots of voices keeping me company. I can tap into them at any given moment for support and reassurance that the journey isn't easy, but it is possible to stay the course.

Sometimes I hear Chef AJ tell us "If it is in your house, it WILL BE in your mouth". And of course Dr. McDougall is always there saying "It's the Food" and "The fat we eat is the fat we wear" and "Starch is the solution". Dr. Doug Lisle keeps me company too. He tells me to strive for excellence, not perfection. My dear friend is always there saying when we know better, we do better and then I know from my childhood that there is no temptation that is greater than we can handle. We just have to look for the way to escape it.

Being alone is a great time to own what you want in your life. It is time to resolve to be your best. It is time to know that it is okay to be alone. That just may be where our growth occurs.

_____

_____

_____

_____

FROM DONUTS...TO POTATOES

JANUARY 18

WORD FOR TODAY: LONGING

Recently, I have been longing to hold a baby. It has almost been the cry of my heart - an actual aching. Well, I do believe that what we think about, we bring about and my "cry" has been answered. On this trip to Southeast Asia, I have had the opportunity to hold 3 babies. In a way, I was surprised that the parents were not reluctant to share. They seemed pleased to have someone love on their baby and appreciate the newness of life.

The last baby I held was very heavy and I was surprised at how solid he was. I didn't hold him for long because once he reached out for his mother, I knew that was where he felt safe.

What are your longings? What do you dream about doing? Do you wake up and decide to make this day different? Are you open to new experiences that bring joy into your life?

There are no coincidences. We are all here together to bond in what we believe is our path to wholeness. We may eat different food, different quantities and frequency but we are drawn together to learn the answer to our own lives. I believe we all have a longing to be our best.

Sometimes, we just aren't sure about the process and past attempts and seeming failures may make us feel skittish about whether or not a whole food plant based diet will work for us.

Never mind past attempts. This is a new time. We know more about health than ever before and it is just time to work on our commitment. Keep watching the health related podcasts, success stories (yes, they are real) and check out Dr. McDougall's website www.drmcdougall.com. So many answers to your questions can be found by using the search bar.

Emerge yourself; strengthen yourself layer by layer until you satisfy the longing of your heart.

JANUARY 19

WORD FOR TODAY: MEDICATE

When I started reading "The McDougall Program for Maximum Weight Loss" in July, 2016, I was on several prescription medications. I was taking statins for high cholesterol, had been taking levothyroxin for my low thyroid for over 30 years, took Ambien when I couldn't sleep and used 800mg Motrin when my "back went out" from time to time and was taking one of the heavy duty pain medications to mask the pain in my "almost bone on bone" knees. I had also been taking a lower than therapeutic dosage of lithium for 30 years as insurance against having a manic episode.

And that was just the prescribed medications. In the past, I also took over the counter medications for constipation, low iron, vitamins, and glucosamine for my joints.

As I lost weight, I think the first medication to go was the heavy duty pain medication for my knees. Through following the MWL program, I have lost 6 inches off each knee. Shortly thereafter (December, 2016), my doctor said I could quit the Lithium. I'm not sure when the statins was removed or when I stopped using Ambien but I do remember it was July, 2018 when I did an experiment to see how I would respond without the thyroid medication.

For my thyroid, I had been taking 112 units, then it was lowered to 100 and finally down to 50 and I wanted to know if I still needed it at all. I didn't think so and I asked my doctor at Kaiser if I could do a test to determine that. I asked him to tell me what would be the worst thing that could happen. He said I might gain some weight and have less energy and I was willing to take the risk. I have actually lost even more weight and have more than enough energy. My labs, 6 weeks later, showed my level was at 5.59, slightly higher than the normal range. I discussed this with the doctor at Dr. McDougall's 3 Day Intensive Weekend in September, 2018 and he said he would not put me back on levothyroxin at that level.

After two years of following the MWL program, I was medication free. I do take a vitamin B12 tablet once a week. Instead of rushing to a sleeping pill when I am "Sleepless in Sacramento", I meditate. I use that wakeful time to give thanks, to listen to my body, to do some breathing exercises, to think about words to share with you, to sing to myself and to rest. I don't worry about lack of sleep. I trust my body will have all it needs.

Good Morning, Vietnam.

_____
_____
_____
_____

JANUARY 20

WORD FOR TODAY: FAREWELL

The time has come for our journey in Southeast Asia to come to an end as my journey to sustain my good health continues.

Our group has jelled in a beautiful way. We have learned so much from each other and yes, I have had a chance to tell my story over time and two of the other 5 couples have been added to our group.

Everyone wants to be healthy - it's just a matter of desire and timing for minds to be opened to new ways of succeeding.

As we all fly home tomorrow, memories of a great trip will continue to remind us of the joy of traveling, meeting people from all over the world and learning that customs and traditions may reflect differences but all in all, we want to be our best.

It is possible to travel and eat healthy, nutritious food. I hope my food entries show you how it can be done. It does take preparation (letting your tour company know that you live on a restricted diet - vegan/vegetarian) and then sticking to it while others eat what you used to enjoy.

If you need more hints on how to eat this way and travel, check out Esther Loveridge's drastic weight loss secret video on YouTube.

Farewell to Cambodia, Thailand, Laos and Vietnam. Beautiful people live, love and laugh in all of these places. Children grow up, people work, babies are born and the taste of joy is spread on so many faces.

_____

_____

_____

_____

FROM DONUTS...TO POTATOES

JANUARY 21
WORD FOR TODAY: RIPPLE

No stone is cast into the water without affecting a change in the water. Circles or rings of energy spread out from where the stone came into contact with the lake, river or stream.

As I write, I am being contacted by Tola Lay, our waiter at one of our hotels. Who would have dreamed that making that connection would be a continuing "ripple" of that experience?

And then there was Hiro, the Japanese man I met while we took in the rays of the sun while sitting out on the deck of a boat, and then there was OJ who joined our group after a brief encounter at the airport.

And of course I will always be thankful for the connection with my new "sister" who shared her life story with our group as we sat in her home for dinner.

Jim and Sean from our traveling group have made an impact on me and I am glad we will be able to stay in touch through this nutritional journey and the traveling experience.

Ripple is more than an inexpensive wine. Ripple is what we do every day. Ripples in the water of our life's experience affect us and we are changed forever.

_____
_____
_____
_____

JANUARY 22

WORD FOR TODAY: REFLECTION

There are lots of ways to reflect on our lives. We often look back but what if, instead of looking back, we looked into a mirror and saw our reflection as of today? What does the current image show us? It may show us an accumulation of choices.

After all, it is just a reflection of our bodies. Our minds and our spirit do not get reflected and that too needs to be taken into account as we check ourselves out to see how we are doing.

Our state of mind must be measured in other ways. Are we at peace or is our total worth determined by what we see in a mirror?

Balancing all aspects of ourselves is important. When I see wrinkles in the mirror, I remind myself that in my mind, many wrinkles have been ironed out as I see my value in helping others, having a clear mind and being at peace with myself.

There are consequences to the choices we have made in life. We may have abused our bodies in numerous ways - feeling invulnerable to the ravages of poor food choices. But, the good news is that it is never too late to nourish ourselves and restore ourselves to the best health possible.

The best is yet to be. If you have lost your way, go forward and leave the past behind.

Create a joyful journey and your reflections will be positive.

_____

_____

_____

_____

FROM DONUTS...TO POTATOES

JANUARY 23
WORD FOR TODAY: GROOVE

⋈

Ah, it feels good to be back in my batch cooking groove. When we got home last night from our Southeast Asia trip, the first thing I made was a batch of Quinoa because it only takes one minute to cook after the pressure in the Instant Pot is obtained.

We got up at 2:00 a.m. Ben has the laundry in process and I made a double batch of steel cut oatmeal, a batch of brown rice and now the Mayocoba beans are in the Instant Pot. Our refrigerator is nearly empty, but we still had some citrus fruit left and of course the frozen blueberries. I see us going to the farmer's market tomorrow for our fresh vegetables and potatoes and sweet potatoes and I'll be back in business again.

I feel full of energy this morning and may even head back to the gym at 7:30 to see my friends and get in a swim, time in the hot tub and the sauna.

Grooves let us perform activities without having to think and make big decisions. That's why I love cooking simply. Cook and eat - that's my idea of making it a no brainer. Some habits or routines are beneficial. Don't be afraid of grooves that free up time to do fun things. Get the food made and then explore your world - wherever it is.

_____

_____

_____

_____

JANUARY 24

WORD FOR TODAY: DELETE

I was working on a handout for my presentation at the SacTownVegFest on Saturday and realized it was too long so I had to delete some of the text.

Text is not the only thing we need to delete from our lives. I have deleted animal and dairy products. Some people have a hard time deleting cheese and of course some people don't think there is a need to delete anything. After all, so many options exist for our consumption.

It could be that you even choose to eliminate some folks from your inner circles if the opposition to your goals becomes troublesome.

When some things are deleted from our lives, it is not always necessary to fill that gap.

Sometimes a void is a good thing but sometimes, we want to delete faulty thinking and replace that with positive steps we want to take to realize our goals.

Let what doesn't serve you go and retain what brings you joy.

_____

_____

_____

_____

FROM DONUTS...TO POTATOES

JANUARY 25
WORD FOR TODAY: UP

We can be up and we can be down and being only half way up is neither up nor down. I think that idea can be applied to how well we stay on whatever eating plan we have chosen. The most uncomfortable place to be must be when we fall off the wagon and are in that in-between place of not being in control and not enjoying our indulgences either.

Peace can come when we make a decision to be our best and even when there are moments that we fall short of our goal, we nevertheless make the most of the situation and get right back up on the program. When we "stray", we don't have to stay in "no-man's land" for an indefinite period of time. We can choose to make that digression as short lived as possible and learn what we can about what in our environment has seduced us.

Keeping a clean environment is the best predictor of success. When in doubt, throw it out is a good rule to follow while eating a plant based diet because if we keep it around, it will eventually end up in our mouths. My friend says, "When we know better, we do better".

Give yourself a break from any past criticism and pat yourself on your back for each wise decision you make. You make hundreds of decisions a day. Be true to what works for you and when you learn new techniques, face up to it and make adjustments.

Rise up and enjoy your day.

_____
_____
_____
_____

JANUARY 26
WORD FOR TODAY: SACRIFICE

When a baseball batter bunts a pitch, he may choose that action in order to advance a team member already on base and in line to make a run. It is called a "sacrifice". He is forfeiting the pleasure of getting a hit himself in order to help the team.

Parents often sacrifice their own pleasures or acquisition of stuff in order to advance the education or experiences of their children.

Many women have sacrificed a career in order to be a homemaker. Some people sacrifice their own achievements in order to care for an elderly parent or a sick child.

Sacrifice can have its own rewards but it can also be a way to embrace victimhood.

When we give up one desire in order to achieve a higher goal, we can feel committed to our values.

Giving up toxic food has many benefits - but depending upon how we view that choice, we could feel sorry for ourselves - you know, "I'm on a diet and I can't have that". When we see our sacrifice as the price we pay for sustained health, our perception changes.

Do you give into the desires that set you back or are you willing to make a commitment which actually eliminates the idea of sacrificing? It becomes an investment in your best self.

Take time to identify your priorities.

_____
_____
_____
_____

FROM DONUTS...TO POTATOES

JANUARY 27

WORD FOR TODAY: AFTERGLOW

After the excitement simmers down, after a big event, we often experience the "afterglow".

It may come after an especially heartfelt conversation with someone, sometimes it comes after a special trip, maybe even after a satisfying meal or a little time of intimacy with someone you love.

The afterglow isn't the event. It would not happen if the experience had not preceded it. It is secondary but it is important.

As important as it is to a sense of well-being, the afterglow is not the place we stay. We enjoy it for awhile and then take the next step in our journey.

Constantly moving ahead in our lives is important. Progress leads us on but in the meantime; don't forget the joy of the afterglow. Bask in its warmth and then move on

_____

_____

_____

_____

JANUARY 28

WORD FOR TODAY: OUTREACH

We used to hear the slogan "Reach out and touch somebody". It may have been a telephone company commercial, but if you could touch someone's life, whose would it be? Who do you hold close in your heart with whom you'd love to share the story of healthy eating and miraculous results?

Outreaching may include stepping outside the box of our usual habits. It may include trying new vegetables that we have never been introduced to. On our recent trip, I learned about the uses of tapioca in Thailand. Eaten plainly, it was not the most delicious food I have tasted, but if I were hungry and could grow it, it would become a regular staple. (The local people dip it in a mixture of salt and sugar and of course we all know that that enhances any food and usually leads to over consumption for food addicts).

My close friend, reached out to me in July, 2016 when she gave me "The McDougall Program for Maximum Weight Loss" book by John McDougall, M.D. Little did she realize the ripple effect that her gift would have on my life. Maybe Robin, my friend at the gym, did know what could happen when she suggested I start a group on Facebook. The point is we do not need to know the outcome. We just know that when we reach out to others, we strengthen ourselves as well. When we teach what we know, we continue learning.

Reaching out to family and friends requires tact and patience. Months ago, I might not have been interested in hearing the words of Dr. McDougall. Today, I want a megaphone. I want to shout it from the rooftops. I want the world to know that healthy choices extend lives, reduce inflammation, eliminate disease and enable us to thrive. What is there not to share?

Sometimes I am guided to tamper down my exuberance but on the other hand, that moment of sharing may be the only chance I have to let someone know there is a solution and starch is the solution.

Extend your outreach as you are able.

_____

_____

FROM DONUTS...TO POTATOES

_____

_____

JANUARY 29

WORD FOR TODAY: DELIVER

Early this morning, I heard the Sacramento Bee hit our porch and I knew the news had been delivered, at least the news that is contained on those pages. But there is more news that doesn't get reported each day.

Years ago, my youngest brother was delivered from alcohol addiction. Now that is good news

How did he do it? Well, I asked him because I knew I had a similar addiction - sugar. He had a profound explanation. We didn't know about the work of Doug Lisle, Ph.D. back then who explains that decisions are made on a cost-benefit analysis. In other words, we have to compare the cost and the benefit of the decisions we make. My brother simply told me that when the picture in his mind of the fun of drinking was outweighed by the picture in his mind of lost health, income and family, he decided to do something about it. He lived many years after that.

In the U.S. many people attend services where The Lord's Prayer is recited. Prayers can be effective and they can be a ritual. I am thinking about the phrase which says "And deliver us from evil". I like it when I heard that evil is simply LIVE spelled backwards.

It's not the work of a boogie man or some powerful force. It is choosing to go back to our old habits and ways of thinking instead of reversing the process and going forward with the new knowledge we are gaining as we learn how to put healthy food into these beautiful bodies and live to the fullest.

ESTHER LEBECK LOVERIDGE

Temptations are just that - temptations. They have no power over us when they are not sitting right there in front of us. We may be drawn to them from time to time - that is normal. It does not mean we are weak. The best measure of success is to reduce toxic food from our environment. You know, out of sight, out of mind.

I want to deliver good news. My youngest granddaughter was delivered on January 29, 2007.

_____

_____

_____

_____

JANUARY 30

WORD FOR TODAY: IDENTITY

Who am I? That is a question I attempt to answer. Sometimes I describe myself by relationships to other people. My identity may also come from employment, hobbies, beliefs, education, community or nationality, personality and even by what food I choose to eat.

Just as there are so many cells in our bodies, there are hundreds of ways to describe ourselves. But the question remains? "Who am I"? How do I identify myself?

Am I who I think I am or what others think I am? Why is it that sometimes I see myself one way and others view me differently? Is there a contradiction? What do I accept as true?

What I have learned is the importance of recognizing the best in other people. When we cease judging one another and accept each other for the gifts each of us has to offer, we build the "cells" of our collective body. It is our very differences that give us strength and endurance.

As we get in touch with the best within us, we have courage to share our gifts, know that we are worthy...just as we are. We do not have to do anything to get love. We are love.

It is worthwhile to be aware of how we choose to complete the sentence: "I am ___."

_____
_____
_____
_____

JANUARY 31

WORD FOR TODAY: PROCLAIM

Have you ever felt like you would like to go tell something on a mountain?-

When we have good news, we want to proclaim it -tell it on the mountain as it were. We want the whole world to hear the news.

That's how I felt when I told my story on January 26, 2019 at the "SacTownFegFest 2019"

Through the efforts of the Panel Moderator, Al Schmidt, it was recorded and now the story can be shared whether I am on a mountain top or sitting at the computer.

What good news do you have that is worth proclaiming? We know good news travels fast because we all want to be inspired and encouraged - especially when we are going against the grain and making big life changes.

ESTHER LEBECK LOVERIDGE

Claim your own journey and then proclaim it in your own world. People are waiting to hear it.

_____
_____
_____
_____

FEBRUARY 1
WORD FOR TODAY: STRATEGY

I have a suggestion for people who are struggling with staying compliant. It is a new strategy - at least in my way of thinking.

If eating a healthy diet is important to you and you are willing to put some energy into it, I am going to suggest keeping a food journal with a different strategy. What if you only wrote down what you ate every time you made a healthy choice? At the end of the day, you could look at your journal and say, "Hurrah - look at all of the times I made a good choice".

Let any less than perfect choices go unnoticed. Do not focus on them - they were just experiences where you had an opportunity to learn.

I keep a weight journal and I only post new low weights. Each time I look at it, I smile at my progress on the graph. Sometimes there are just a few days between postings and sometimes there may be a "plateau" but visually, I smile because it shows I am going in the right direction.

Punishment does NO good. We know how to do that very well. What we need is a new strategy to keep track of the positive choices we are making in our lives. We need to be our own cheerleader - not an accuser.

_____
_____
_____
_____

FROM DONUTS...TO POTATOES

FEBRUARY 2
WORD FOR TODAY: URGENCY

Urgency is a bit different from being anxious. When I think of being anxious, it is usually because I sense that I am out of control mixed up with some worry.

Urgency, on the other hand, is a compelling force to get something done. It is like passion or zeal. It has to do with maybe having a time limit.

We all have a time limit in this lifetime. At 75, and being full of good health and feeling the best I ever have, I think celebrating my 100th birthday is very doable. BUT, there are circumstances in life that shorten our lives besides disease. People even have died in a synagogue, church, mosque or school for goodness sake. So, where does my urgency come from?

It is a product of having found the answer to my lifetime of not only dieting but reaching that age when poor food habits were catching up with me. And now that I have found my answer, how can I morally keep it to myself?

When we choose to love others as much as we love and protect ourselves, we ache when others hurt and are in pain - especially since so much of those ills are reversible. What drug can promise that?

So, when my exuberance to spread the good news seems like I am over the top, it is because I am over the top at wanting to help anyone who is willing to wake up and smell the roasted vegetables.

_____

_____

_____

_____

FEBRUARY 3
WORD FOR TODAY: ADVOCATE

It is not only by our words and speech that we advocate what works for us...it is our behavior.

We have come to realize that our actions speak so loudly that others can't hear what we are saying.

Learning what we are willing to stand up for is a process...maybe it is called maturity. As a teenager, it seems like it was so important to blend in - to go along with the crowd - to be accepted and be a part of the clique.

But then, something drastic happens. It may be a spiritual conversion, a medical life saving event or even a time when we lost someone so important to us that we woke up and decided to make some changes to our lives.

At that moment, we may take on a new direction. We may be weak at first, we may struggle, but when we are convinced that the change makes us a stronger person, we learn how to form a new clique or village for strength and support as we try our wings in a new flight pattern.

I never thought I'd be a "demonstrator", a "rebel" or an "activist" but then it happened...I found my answer and although it may not be for everyone (at least at this time) what I do know is that no one's health has ever been reduced by eating a whole food plant based diet. The side effects are tremendous and it is a "no brainer". I think I can now be called an "advocate" for better health.

_____
_____
_____
_____

FEBRUARY 4

WORD FOR TODAY: PEACE

Peace may come after a battle, after a storm or anytime conflicts gets resolved.

After achieving peace, do we go back and try to re-visit the divisions that existed before or can we accept the terms of the peace agreement and go on with our lives?

On my journey, I have come to the conclusion that there are foods that no longer serve me.

Can I accept that or is there a part of me that wishes I could still enjoy the tastes of the past?

Those thoughts may surface from time to time, but I can honestly say I do not want to re-introduce foods that led me down the slippery slope. My palate is clean and I want to keep it that way. Usually those foods have no merit anyway. Often there is no nutritional value in them and if they should awaken the ghosts of the past, my peace would be disturbed.

Peace comes at a great price. Lives are lost in battles. Lifetime injuries result and when the war is over, I want to let peace reign.

_____

_____

_____

_____

FEBRUARY 5
WORD FOR TODAY: HOME

Home is where the heart is but what does that mean?

Well, I'm sure it means many different things for each person. To the person returning home from overseas service, it means coming home to loved ones.

For those who spend a long day at work, they may long to come home, relax and settle in.

And for some of us, it is finding a place of like-minded people where we can share ideas, have our resolutions supported, get encouragement in following our path and feel safe.

My heart is at home since I have found a place where my new lifestyle is supported, honored and valued. In this place, I am able to think about how I want to spend the rest of my life. It is the place where my soul is nourished and where I feel like I can advance as I learn more and more about how to sustain a healthy life. My body has found its sweet spot and my heart is happy too. I am home.

_____
_____
_____
_____

FROM DONUTS...TO POTATOES

FEBRUARY 6

WORD FOR TODAY: TALK

We have heard it said that talk is cheap. We often want action but how does action start before either reading words or hearing them speak either from outside of us or from within?

Perhaps excessive "talk" weakens one's impact. My brother has often said that when we are selling something, it must be done in a certain amount of time and if we continue after that amount of time, we are buying back our own product.

When I was in the 6th grade, Mr. Victor Brownell was my first male teacher. He has passed, but in my autograph book, he wrote "You will grow up to be a fine person if you learn not to emulate other women by talking so much". I talked a lot in school and must have been disruptive!

Now, I still want to talk - I want to spread the word about how I have re-gained my health. It is a miracle to me - at this age to be off all medications and even not needing my glasses anymore! Who wouldn't want to spread the "gospel of health"?

What I am also learning, is the joy in silence. Those early morning hours before I arise remind me that my Grandmother Kearns, a devout Quaker, had learned the benefits of sitting in the silence.

The best advice comes from within. It is only accessible as we sit quietly and listen.

_____

_____

_____

_____

FEBRUARY 7
WORD FOR TODAY: FAST

Some people eat fast, and then there are "fast talkers". Often people eat "fast food" and many try to live in the fast lane.

What is so good about fast? We gain weight over a long period of time and then think we should be able to lose it fast.

Some people have gone on the water fast to clean out toxins and then there are those who have gone on a religious fast.

Some Evangelical Christians follow a partial fast in which meat, wine, and other rich foods are avoided in favor of vegetables and water.

During Ramadan, Muslims fast. Jewish people also fast during holy days. Although I am not a big supporter of fasting per se, I was somewhat surprised when I realized that a whole food plant based diet is what Daniel (in the Book of Daniel) ate in order to prove to the King that eating this way made him stronger than the King's men who ate the rich food.

So, it looks like I am a believer in the Daniel's Fast - not for three weeks but for a lifetime of good health, improved vitality and a clear mind.

It worked over 2,500 years ago and I have demonstrated that it is still a good guide for healthy living today. Fast? No, but it is sustainable.

_____
_____
_____
_____

FROM DONUTS...TO POTATOES

FEBRUARY 8
WORD FOR TODAY: ATTACHMENT

Want to let go and be free? Wish you could fly with an eagle? Ever think of where helium balloons go when you let go of the string attached to the end of your finger?

Explore. Come along with me as we learn how to let go of attachments which keep us moored to the boat dock of the past.

We are meant to go, to move, to expand, to investigate, to learn and to be free.

What do you want to be free from? What is holding you back in your life's journey? What or who tells you "No, it is not possible"? What little voice is in your head that doesn't want you to be your best? If you became your best, would there be attachments that would change?

Is pleasing others something you hang onto in order to feel included or loved? Where does honesty fit into your profile? When pleasing others is in conflict with your own direction or conviction, let honesty rule.

If there is a food that you say you cannot give up and you believe it is unhealthy, think about the attachment you have to it and what it means for you.

Be free.

_____

_____

_____

_____

FEBRUARY 9
WORD FOR TODAY: ABOVE

Sometimes we say a certain task is "above our pay grade". It is also easy to feel like others in our social circles are "above" us, but that is not possible.

No one is above another. It is my hope that my behavior is "above" what it was yesterday.

As we strive to be our best, we look above past performance and in the present moment become aware of how we can improve ourselves.

When we look at the tapestry of our lives, we often see the underside - the side where strings hang down and the weaving looks all messed up. But if we look above, we can see the weaving of our lives is making a beautiful tapestry.

Look up. Be above the fray. Know your aspirations and goals will lead you above all expectations.

Above all...share love.

_____
_____
_____
_____

FROM DONUTS...TO POTATOES

FEBRUARY 10

WORD FOR TODAY: COMFORT

We talk about wanting to be in our comfort zone. We eat food that we think brings us comfort. We like to be with like-minded people because there seems to be less stress when we are with others who think like us.

Peace of mind also brings us comfort. Solutions to problems add comfort to our lives. Getting rid of pain certainly makes us feel more comfortable.

When we dull our senses with drinks like "Southern Comfort", it is only a temporary relief. Even once the drug of rich food wears off, we no longer feel comfort - the pain, emotional or physical, rears its ugly head once again.

Comfort can be sustained when we find the solution to our food born diseases...it's the food. Our minds become clear, we make better choices and pain in joints is relieved and, a wonderful side effect is weight loss.

For so many of us, losing weight is the biggest motivator, but I can attest to the fact that after a certain amount of weight loss, I realized that the total picture is really about health and the weight just seems to find its own comfort zone.

_____

_____

_____

_____

ESTHER LEBECK LOVERIDGE

FEBRUARY 11

WORD FOR TODAY: DEMONSTRATE

I looked up the word demonstrate because I wanted to know more about some of its definitions and it simply means to show the existence or truth of something by giving proof or evidence.

Aha, that is good. Now I can claim to be a demonstrator! There haven't been very many times in my life when I joined a march or publicly stood up or out for something. It was always easier to just blend in with the crowd.

But now, things are different. Not only do I now KNOW that this way of eating is the best for me, I have "proved" that it is my solution since I have put it to the test, made my body my living laboratory and can publish the results. It has been fun acting like a scientist, working in the lab of my own kitchen and documenting the outcome of the experiment.

The proof is there for anyone who wishes to examine it. I have lost 130 pounds, sustained each loss since July 13, 2016 and have nurtured my body to the point that all medications are a thing of the past and that even includes my eye glasses. No longer does my driver's license require corrective lenses.

We used to say the proof is in the pudding. Now I cite Dr. John McDougall's who says "It's the Food". I challenge everyone to create their own test and publish their results. Be a demonstrator.

_____
_____
_____
_____

FROM DONUTS...TO POTATOES

FEBRUARY 12
WORD FOR TODAY: WALLS

I got to thinking about walls and how they can be seen as protective devices but they also create divisions in our communities. Even in our homes we have walls which separate us from each other. Rooms get designated for certain purposes and if you are like us and have a "living room", it may only be there for limited purposes.

Today it is common to live in gated communities where we have codes which let us enter - then we drive to our homes, activate the garage door opener and enter our secluded area - rarely sitting out on the porch anymore to engage with unmet friends and neighbors.

Walls give us a sense of being safe and protected but we need to examine the walls which also keep us imprisoned in our own cells of false beliefs.

Thinking we need to eat animals for protein or drinking milk from cows for strong bones can also be seen as walls which keep us in prisons of poor health. How can we break down those old ideas/walls and be free to regain our safety (health)? Walls come tumbling down once we repeatedly challenge them.

Examine your walls. Are you safe or imprisoned?

_____
_____
_____
_____

FEBRUARY 13
WORD FOR TODAY: POWER

Power is a useful tool. Electronic or battery operated tools give us a boost in accomplishing great things. We no longer have to rely on just our own personal strength to get a job done.

And so it is with the power we have within us to accomplish our goals and aspirations. At first, we may not think we are capable of creating a new body, a new mind set or achieving what we want in life, but as we exercise that power and realize it is there for us to use, we get stronger in believing it is possible.

It all starts in the mind and we are capable of renewing our minds and eliminating thoughts which limit us. We can break through those chains and be free to explore and see what new ideas will enable us to be our best.

You can say to this mountain (faulty thinking) be removed. Be gone. I no longer need you to block my progress. You are in the way. I release you. Let freedom ring!

_____
_____
_____
_____

FROM DONUTS...TO POTATOES

FEBRUARY 14

WORD FOR TODAY: VALENTINE

First thing this morning, Ben presented me with his hand-made valentine. "I love you more than yesterday". It can't get any better than that.

It is so true that all of us are moving forward in our lives - being better than we were yesterday. There is no one else to compete with. We are on our own journey and being more loving, more caring, more supportive and more giving than we were yesterday is our measuring stick.

What else is there but love to share on this day when we often ask special people to be our Valentine?

A valentine can be a tribute to someone or some writing expressing uncritical praise or affection.

Today I do not ask you to be my valentine. I want to be your valentine and see the best in you, know you have the capability to achieve all you want, reach your goals and feel the love that we share.

Happy Valentine's Day

_____
_____
_____
_____

FEBRUARY 15
WORD FOR TODAY: SOURCE

There is a lot of talk these days about the source of our food and the source of our ideas and information.

I was thinking about my source for following "The McDougall Program for Maximum Weight Loss" and it is the author Dr. John McDougall himself. He has been educating us about the "Healthiest Diet on the Planet" and telling us that "The Starch Solution" is the answer to our dietary needs.

After having this wonderful information tucked away in our brains, it is easy to forget that the source of so much information lies at our fingertips. All we have to do is Google his name or go to his website http://drmcdougall.com for an encyclopedia of information. The search bar on the website is a valuable tool for accessing information about any disease or condition of the body for which I am concerned. It is also the pathway to many videos, recipes and help AND IT IS FREE.

Although the source is free, there is work and energy required to put his facts into practice in our lives. As they say, "There is no free lunch". It takes commitment and practice to accomplish our new healthy lives but the payoff is tremendous. It is life saving.

FROM DONUTS...TO POTATOES
FEBRUARY 16
WORD FOR TODAY: ADDICTION

Wow - that is a big word, not only in terms of the number of letters, but what it means to all of us.

Addictions are what we tend to think "other" people have. It is so easy to identify people who have gone overboard in certain behaviors or what they put in their bodies: drugs, alcohol, cigarettes but what about those of us who self-identify as Food Addicts? How do we overcome our food addictions when we must eat in order to survive?

Addiction is a complex condition or a brain disease that is manifested by compulsive substance use in spite of the harm it causes us.

I'm sure we have all told ourselves, "I shouldn't eat this, it gives me indigestion, heartburn, makes me constipated, or raises my blood sugar and then I will have to take more meds to counteract it...but I WANT IT". We then say, "I'll accept the consequences and deal with them later".

Food addictions, like many other ingested or inhaled substances, can best be overcome through abstinence. That is another big word and one most of us do not want to hear.

But how do we get rid of addictions? The simplest answer is to clean up one's environment but the motivation to do that may only occur when the negative effects of eating unhealthy food outweigh the pleasures we obtain when we indulge.

To addicts, "moderation" is a deadly myth.

_____

_____

_____

_____

ESTHER LEBECK LOVERIDGE

FEBRUARY 17
WORD FOR TODAY: COINCIDENCE

A co-incidence can be two or more things happening at the same time, seemingly by chance, or not?

As I look back at the beginning of this journey, I recall two incidences that happened at nearly the same time.

Ben told me that I would have to write my own obituary so one night, back in 2016, I got out of bed in the middle of the night and wrote it.

Nothing seemed so special about that...weird, maybe, but not special. Then, two weeks later, I was given a book - "The McDougall Program for Maximum Weight Loss".

One incident was a review of my life and the next incident was the beginning of my new life. Little did I realize when I wrote the obituary that a totally new path would lay before me?

Was it coincidence or divine order? We get to choose.

_____
_____
_____
_____

FROM DONUTS...TO POTATOES

FEBRUARY 18

WORD FOR TODAY: SOLUTION

It is amazing how we have all faced challenges in our lives. Problems crop up from time to time - giving us a chance to look for a solution or an answer. Once the answer comes to us, the problem just seems to dissolve.

Sometimes we just can't get our head around how easily that happens. Once we listen to what our bodies are trying to tell us and we take appropriate action, we wonder why in the world we ever worried or fretted about that condition.

Why did we hang onto the problem as though it was giving us a focus in our lives? Once we found what we thought to be a solution, why did we go back to what created the problem in the first place, forgetting that we already knew the answer?

Do we really like repeating the same mistake over and over while expecting a different result? Once we really know the solution, we can let it go - forever. That lesson does not have to be repeated over and over.

There is no failure in taking a class. There is always something to learn. The joy is in moving forward, letting that lesson go and advancing to the next step in our recovery and journey.

Look for the solution - don't magnify the problem.

_____

_____

_____

_____

FEBRUARY 19
WORD FOR TODAY: RESIST

It is so easy to go along with the crowd. It takes energy to decide what is best for us and to implement it into our daily schedule. Taking time to think takes energy.

When we come to a new understanding of something, we can no longer hide in the dark. We can't pretend that we do not know the outcomes of certain behaviors. We are now informed.

But how do we build the muscles it takes to be strong? It is like any other new behavior we want to try on for size to see how it fits our lifestyle. We take baby steps and often fall down and have to learn how to resort to crawling for awhile. Then we find something we want and the fastest way to get there is to stand up and move forward.

If we want strong bones and muscles, resistance training can be helpful. What do you want to resist today? It may be sitting on the couch; it could be not making a batch of food so that you are prepared and don't get caught off guard. It could be resisting the old haunts by choosing a healthier place to eat. It may mean setting boundaries of with whom and where you want to spend your time.

Be the leader of your own life.

_____
_____
_____
_____

FROM DONUTS...TO POTATOES

FEBRUARY 20

WORD FOR TODAY: SURRENDER

It is interesting that today, I am thinking about the word surrender when just yesterday, I was talking about the word "resist". It would almost seem that there could be a contradiction between those two concepts and yes, there are often contradictions in life but not always.

We must resist falling into traps that lead us down a path to nowhere and to continued poor health; however, on the other hand, we must surrender our old beliefs before we can adopt new, life-giving ones. When we give up former, outdated and misinformed ideas, we make room for new concepts which have been proven to be successful and valid.

Many of us have learned prayers from our childhood one of which includes the phrase thy will be done. How can we say that as long as we are holding onto our own stubborn ways?

When I surrender foods that are harmful to me and take up healthy ones - you know, the ones that grow, I am resisting and surrendering at the same time.

There is no conflict in working towards being our best as we understand what that is.

Each day brings new strength, additional resolve and the knowing that the best is yet to be.

_____

_____

_____

_____

ESTHER LEBECK LOVERIDGE

FEBRUARY 21

WORD FOR TODAY: TICKET

"Ticket? Ticket please" the conductor might call out as he passes down the aisle of the train. A ticket is required to reach your destination.

What was my destination and did I have the proper ticket? I knew I wanted to be free of knee pain and the doctor said the "ticket" could be knee replacement(s) but I was not even eligible to buy the "ticket" with my insurance. Another price was involved that I hadn't even contemplated and that was losing 70 pounds first.

There is a price to pay when we want to take a trip. Sometimes, someone else pays the price for us. In my case, my friend purchased my ticket to success by giving me Dr. McDougall's "The McDougall Program for Maximum Weight Loss" book. But, in order to utilize the value of the ticket, I had to apply the required principles.

When I was 14, I had the privilege of going to Disneyland. Back then, a book of tickets were sold with rides categorized from A to E. The A tickets were for the kiddy rides but what we really wanted was the E tickets to the most exciting rides there.

And so it is that now I am on a constant E ride: After deciding that whole food was my "ticket", I have Energy, Enthusiasm, Excitement, and want to "Evangelize" the world. Hop on...it is never too late to catch the train to renewed health.

FROM DONUTS...TO POTATOES

FEBRUARY 22

WORD FOR TODAY: STAND

Stand up and be counted. Stand up for what you believe to be true. Stand up for your ideals. Stand up in the midst of the crowd which seems to be heading in a different direction.

Is this an easy life? Yes, but not necessarily at first. It is easy to experience isolation, ridicule, and criticism, but then, what in life has been easy when we work towards being what is best for each of us?

People have died because of their religious, political or scientific opinions. What we face as we go upstream and encounter the onslaught of divergent thinking, the nearly constant lure of commercials and parties or gatherings supporting poor health is difficult but with a strong resolve to give our bodies the best fuel, we will make it.

We will be strong. We will teach. We will encourage. We will make mistakes. We will recover and continue our wonderful, live-giving journey.

I am glad you are all aboard.

_____

_____

_____

_____

FEBRUARY 23
WORD FOR TODAY: ACCEPTANCE

I don't have to accept that. Yes, that is true. None of us need to accept what is not true for us. As we learn and grow, we change. Sometimes, other people don't like the changes we make in our lives, our bodies or our food choices.

But change is inevitable. We all evolve. We all grow into our best and that can alter relationships. It can make some people uncomfortable. Many of us have a hard time accepting the changes in another or perhaps even accepting the fact that others choose not to change even in the face of danger to their health.

That too, is their choice. We all learn through different time tables. Timing is crucial to making changes in our lives.

Perhaps the AA Program best summarizes it when we are admonished to change what we can, and accept what we cannot change (and recognize the difference) as we work towards being serene.

_____
_____
_____
_____

FROM DONUTS...TO POTATOES

FEBRUARY 24

WORD FOR TODAY: COMPETITION

When I think of competition, it is easy to think in terms of winners and losers but does it have to be that way?

Do we value ourselves in terms of how we measure up to others? If someone loses 10 pounds in a month, does that make them a better or more "successful" person? How about those times when we measure our progress by the scale and it just won't budge? Are we disappointed? Sure, but do we view ourselves as a failure?

I have been learning that competition with others is a downward spiral. There will always be those who have more money, a nicer house, a better wardrobe etc. but what is really revealing to me now is how I compare with who I was yesterday. That is a big difference. Being more productive, loving, and committed to helping others than I was yesterday is something I can compete with and win.

There are many voices in this whole food plant based way of eating and we are all part of the same choir. We each have our own part to sing, our own words to write, our own voice to proclaim as we spread the joy of finding renewed health.

We are a part of a big, growing symphony, and the music is compelling.

FEBRUARY 25

WORD FOR TODAY: IDENTITY

Who am I? If I lost a leg due to diabetes, lost my eyesight due to a stroke, lost a breast due to cancer or even lost 1/2 of my weight, would I still be me?

What about if I just changed my hair color, or got a perm, added some new eyelashes or added long nails to my fingers, would I still be me?

What is it that determines who I am? What if I hadn't gotten married had children, a career or a certain talent? Would I be a different person then?

How much of my identity is determined by my outward appearance? How much by my spiritual nature or my intellectual capabilities? When I get down to brass tacks, regardless of all descriptions, I am a creation, an expression of God's love just being manifested in this body - regardless of its appearance or shape.

Changes are only a part of our transitions as we move through life. We still exist. Be yourself and express your best.

FROM DONUTS...TO POTATOES

FEBRUARY 26

WORD FOR TODAY: DIVE

There are many things I'd like to dive into - the universe is holding so many secrets, formulas and magnificent order that I don't understand.

I used to dive into sweets. This morning, I kind of dived into the last scrapings on the spatula from the jar of peanut butter that my granddaughter was putting on her toast. I tasted it, let it swirl around my tongue, felt how greasy it felt and then decided I had enough. I did not need to swallow it and I actually spit it out. Yes, it is different spending a week away from my compliant kitchen.

I switched from tasting the peanut butter to the turnips and beets I roasted this morning. I have a new favorite - it is the skinny roots of the beets that are actually delicious and very crunchy. I never would have thought to leave them on, roast the whole beet and turnip and then experience the crunch. Now those veggies are something I will dive into this morning.

I will also slip into the bonds of the warm hot tub as we go to another gym location which is closer to my son's home.

Immerse yourself in your heart's delight. Drown out disappointments, relish each new experience and top it all off with love and joy as you dive into a beautiful new experience.

_____
_____
_____
_____

FEBRUARY 27
WORD FOR TODAY: FUN

Fun for one is not fun for all. I remember having a practical joke played on me and it was not fun for me but was it fun for those perpetuating it? You bet! They laughed and had a grand old time. I got over it, ha.

Cooking was never fun for me. I had to think of a kind of meat and then think up food to go with it. Those decisions got very old; however, baking was another matter because everyone loved sweets.

So, now that I am eating so simply, what is fun? What is fun for me is using my Instant Pot and doing batch cooking. Nothing fancy, just cooking up a bunch of food so I am prepared. Pulling items out of the refrigerator and re-heating them is easy and fun.

If eating rich and decadent food has been your fun, you may have to search out new ways to have fun. Maybe it will be getting some enjoyable exercise. You might want to explore a new hobby. Getting together with people of a like mind is also fun when we realize we are not alone on this journey.

We need fun (healthy dopamine hits in our brain) to sustain a healthy eating habit so get your fun on and enjoy life.

_____
_____
_____
_____

FROM DONUTS...TO POTATOES

FEBRUARY 28

WORD FOR TODAY: TEMPERANCE

Temperance, it is said, is putting moderation into practice.

Years ago, there was a temperance movement which focused on the abstinence of alcohol.

We don't use that word much anymore. In fact, I had to look it up because I thought it had something to do with being tolerant. As it turned out, it has nothing to do with tolerance but with abstention.

As we focus on the kinds of food and beverages that lead to a healthy body and a clear mind, it might be good to revive that word and know that when it comes to food or alcohol addictions, moderation will not work. We need to know about temperance and not be deluded with the idea that moderation is the key to everything.

Toxins poison our bodies and temperance will help us achieve our goals.

_____

_____

_____

_____

ESTHER LEBECK LOVERIDGE

FEBRUARY 29

WORD FOR TODAY: LEAP

Have you ever had the chance to leap for joy? Did you ever leap into a relationship and discover that perhaps you could have given the decision more thought? Maybe you were told you were too young but decided to leap anyway.

On February 29th, we get a chance to experience a day that is free to us every four years. I know, it is really a day to equal things out, but to us non-scientists, it feels like a freebie so the question remains, "What do you want to do with this special day?"

As it turns out, everyday is a new day to leap out of bed, decide how we are going to be able to help someone with a smile or an encouraging word or maybe just clean the toilets.

Maybe it is a day to take stock of your cupboards and refrigerator to make sure that all non-compliant foods have been removed.

One thing we do not want is to have desires for unhealthy food leap into our mouths. It is amazing how easily that can happen if they are available. Keep a clean kitchen, have a clear mind.

_____

_____

_____

_____

MARCH 1
WORD FOR TODAY: HAPPINESS

Wow - now that is a word that many seek to find and one which can elude people as they search for what they think is the longing of their soul.

Are we able to be happy regardless of our circumstances? Or do we think happiness resides just over the hilltop - perhaps in another place, another time or another season?

Maybe happiness for many is a change in their environment, a reduction of their weight or an improvement in their health. It could also require for some an adjustment in relationships.

But...maybe it is none of the above. Happiness may simply be a state of mind, regardless of where we are or even with whom we live. What is the happy place for one may not be the happy place for another, but what I do know is that it is possible to experience it. It is real. It is within us. It is in accepting who we are and knowing that the best is yet to be.

_____
_____
_____
_____

FROM DONUTS...TO POTATOES

MARCH 2

WORD FOR TODAY: REVERSE

At first, I was thinking about reverse in terms of going backwards, but then I realized that going in reverse doesn't have to mean going back. It can simply mean changing one's direction.

With that in mind, I thought about how going forward with a whole food plant based diet also includes going in reverse.

So how do we go forward and in reverse at the same time? I can now tell you. By going forward with a healthy diet, I have reversed the direction of my labs results. Instead of my cholesterol, blood pressure and pre-diabetes markers going up, they have reversed their direction.

Going forward and going in reverse is not mutually exclusive... nor does it lead to being stuck somewhere in the middle.

Be forward thinking and reverse your diseases.

_____

_____

_____

_____

MARCH 3

WORD FOR TODAY: MOVE

Action, lights, camera...well, at least action. I have heard it said that if we don't use it, we lose it. To thrive, we must move.

Moving doesn't have to be all that strenuous. It can be just a few more steps than we walked yesterday.

I have been asked if I had to exercise in order to lose my weight. Well, I do like to swim laps and have done so for up to an hour several times a week, but, now, if I have a chance to spread the good news of a healthy diet and what it can do for one's body while I am soaking in the hot tub or relaxing in the sauna, that is the path I take. That is how I choose to spend my time.

Am I suffering? No. Will I pick up swimming again? Probably but right now, I don't want to miss an opportunity to spread the word. In the meantime, I move around in the hot tub and sometimes jog in place while waiting for the microwave to re-heat some food.

It feels good to move - to stretch and to ease stress so move at your own speed and smile while you do it. There is a time for everything.

_____

_____

_____

_____

MARCH 4

WORD FOR TODAY: CONSUME

We can consume ideas and thoughts or they can consume us. Yesterday I heard an acronym for Lent. Yes, Wednesday is Ash Wednesday and many faiths observe the 40 day period prior to Easter as a time to sacrifice something (seems like it is usually an unhealthy food, kind of like a New Year's Resolution).

But the word I heard yesterday resonated with me: Let's Eliminate

FROM DONUTS...TO POTATOES

Negative Thinking. Now that is something I can be conscious of all year long and what a good idea to be keenly aware of it now.

So, am I going to also give up some food for LENT? No. What I think about seems to be more important to me and for the most part, nothing that I put into my body needs to be eliminated.

Except: Yesterday, while cleaning out a cupboard, I found my caramel apple topping. It used to be my favorite treat. I consumed part of it yesterday - just fell into the trap of something over 3 years old! Good news: I didn't eat it all. I put it under the faucet, cleansed the container and eliminated it down the disposal. It will not be here during LENT or ever again.

_____

_____

_____

_____

MARCH 5
WORD FOR TODAY: SIMPLE

Simple Simon was a pie man because well, I don't really know why. Maybe it was because he hadn't heard of Dr. McDougall and how we could reach the height of our health by eating starch and not fat.

And then there was Jack Sprat who ate no fat. He was starting to learn.

Little Miss Muffet sat on her tuffet eating her curds and whey because she didn't know about the ill effects of consuming dairy.

Maybe Jack in the Bean stalk had something going - at least he got his exercise.

The point is, it is so easy to be simple and eat from our four food groups: Vegetables, Fruits, Grains and Legumes and reverse so many food borne diseases and be in the best of health. It is never too late.

___

MARCH 6

WORD FOR TODAY: WHAT

Recently, I watched an interview with Chef AJ where they were talking about the simplicity of eating a whole food plant based diet. It really doesn't matter HOW much we eat (i.e. counting calories or portion control), or WHEN we eat (i.e. time of day or how often), nor does it matter WHY we eat (i.e. emotionally eating). Interestingly enough, it is WHAT we eat that is our concern.

When we eat from the four food groups: Vegetables, Fruits, Grains and Legumes (beans), we satisfy all of our needs for good fuel.

Now we can get all religious about some of the other issues, but keeping it simple is such a strong message and clearly one that we can live with for the rest of our lives.

Yes, we can add spices and jazz up our food if we so choose, but it's the food. We cannot out exercise a bad diet nor can we eliminate our food addictions by playing with them. Poison is poison and restricts our body from doing what it does best -HEAL.

What's on your plate?

FROM DONUTS...TO POTATOES

MARCH 7
WORD FOR TODAY: TRANSITION

Ah, we are all in a state of transition. We are all one. We all want to not stagnate, but to grow in knowledge, grace, love and health.

Yesterday, by the pool, I saw a butterfly on the ground, flapping its wings and I presumed it was trying to dry off so it could fly again. He didn't accept my help - he probably had faced this situation before and knew what to do to change his condition.

We too, like the caterpillar and the tadpole, get to gradually transition into a new being with every new thought that comes into our brains. We can dismiss the thoughts as impossible or we can embrace them with delight - knowing that we can become the person we once dreamed about.

As we renew our minds, new possibilities surface and we can put our dreams into reality with every step we take.

Transitions can be a slow process, or sometimes, miracles occur and we change our direction overnight. Be keen to your heart's' desires, write them down and see them materialize right before your own eyes.

MARCH 8

WORD FOR TODAY: DOPAMINE

What tickles your fancy? What activities do you engage in that bring you pleasure? What affects your brain and makes you feel real good?

Some say it is high caloric food. Some say sex. Some say "when I give to others". Some find pleasure in hobbies, addictions and drugs. Some even get it from a religious experience.

So, the question remains - if we crave certain foods and are not satisfied until we get them but also realize they are not healthy for us, what do we do to get to that pleasurable state without indulging?

Most answers are not very enticing at first, but once we understand that it is normal to seek pleasure, it is possible to explore other areas of our lives and come up with other ways to have that same sense of pleasure.

For me, communicating with others about how to be their best is a real boost for me. Sometimes, it is listening to good music. Sometimes it is cleaning out a cupboard. Sometimes it is just by checking things off my "to-do" list.

Sometimes it comes to me when I count my blessings and give thanks for a body that has found a better way.

FROM DONUTS...TO POTATOES

MARCH 9

WORD FOR TODAY: GATHER

I heard that a rolling stone gathers no moss, but all of us following a whole food plant based lifestyle like to gather.

We like to meet, we like to greet. We like to talk, we like to walk.

When we get together, we gather recipes, fun ideas and most of all learn to improve our lives and enjoy it to the fullest.

We gather at restaurants. We meet at VegFests. We watch good documentaries and learn how to eat the healthiest food.

Today, some of us will have the opportunity to gather at Loving Hut in Elk Grove to hear each other's success stories, reinforce our resolve to be our best and enjoy some good food as well.

Gather your positive thoughts for a fun weekend wherever you meet to greet those you love.

_____

_____

_____

_____

MARCH 10

WORD FOR TODAY: DRAFT

Oh, yes, we are back to choices. Have you ever been drafted to serve on a committee you never intended to serve? Have you been drafted into the military at a time when you had other plans?

How about being drafted into a religion by marriage - just to make it work? Or, maybe, you were drafted into a college that wasn't your first choice.

How did you manage to reconcile what you wanted with what you got drafted to do? Maybe you went along with someone else's "program" just to keep from making waves or maybe you resisted their "draft".

The alternative, of course, is to be a free agent - to get to make our own choices in life. After all, we are the ones who get to live with the consequences.

Moving towards what we want to claim for our lives gives us freedom from the "draft" and the ability to move into the choice column.

Today we get to choose how we want to spend our lives. The military draft has been eliminated but what about the other drafts that can snag us?

_____

_____

_____

_____

MARCH 11

WORD FOR TODAY: STRUGGLE

When we feel like we are still in a struggle over anything, it simply means that we are a work in progress and are moving ahead.

If we gave up, it wouldn't be a struggle would it? My struggle is in keeping this space a commercial free zone. It is not a big struggle, but one of which I am conscious.

Your struggle may be having someone in your life who continues to "tempt" you even though they know you are in a struggle for your life. Why is it that anyone would want to sabotage your progress? Who knows? However, the point is that it is us who need to continually strengthen our resolve to be our best as defined by us.

Will the fight ever be over? I can't promise that it will be, given the many voices in the crowd, but what I can promise you is a big pot of joy every time you take that next step forward.

Feel the joy, embrace it, love it and know that with every step you take, you are reinforcing your determination to succeed.

_____

_____

_____

_____

MARCH 12

WORD FOR TODAY: WILL

Will, is an interesting word. Sometimes we back off from a commitment by saying "I will try".

I kind of laugh at myself when I tell people, "Isn't it interesting that when we get married, we say "I will", not "I will try"?

Yes, it is true that sometimes we bite off more than we can chew. We get overwhelmed, over committed and over involved in things that really don't matter in the long run.

But when it comes to saving our lives, it is easier to get serious. I know people who have decided that chemo therapy is important to their survival and agree to commit to the treatment. Then I also know people who have committed themselves to kidney dialysis and they don't "try" to make it to their appointments. Their life depends on it.

Sometimes, we put our heads in the sand when we pretend that most of our diseases are not caused by the toxic food we ingest. We are what we eat. How can we be anything else?

Choose life if you will.

_____
_____
_____

MARCH 13

WORD FOR TODAY: CLEAR

Most people have set goals to achieve what they want in life but has the way been made clear?

Have obstacles been removed, distractions eliminated and the road been made smooth?

We cannot jump from point A to point B without preparation. It takes thoughtful planning - just ask any civil engineer.

Wanting to become healthy after years of faulty thinking about what makes up a good diet is a process. We must challenge what we thought would work for us and learn that repeating the same process over and over without getting long term success will only deepen the rut we are in.

I read "The Starch Solution", "The McDougall Program for Maximum Weight Loss" and "The Healthiest Diet on the Planet" all written by Dr. John McDougall, but I would not have found my way clear if I wasn't convinced that a whole food plant based diet was the answer.

My mind became clear, my purpose became uppermost and I daily work to keep my road to success clear of anything or any thought that would keep me stumbling along.

Be clear about what you really want.

___

MARCH 14

WORD FOR TODAY: IGNORANCE

For many years, we have heard the phrase "Ignorance is Bliss", but is it bliss? Or, by chance, is being ignorant only delaying the requirement of taking corrective action?

Once we know something to be true, it is harder to ignore the facts. If we are responsible people, knowledge often requires action. If we don't want to deal with change, then maybe we do think we are happier by keeping our heads buried in the sand. But, true happiness resides in being free from false perceptions.

Ignorance may keep us in the dark and we may feel safe in our comfort zone, but when we bring situations into the light, we can deal with what needs to be done, do it and feel the joys of success.

Find solutions. They are within.

MARCH 15
WORD FOR TODAY: STRATEGY

What is your strategy for winning at the game of life?

Sometimes we simply make up our mind to do something and do it. However, there are times, in the beginning of a new endeavor (or diet) when we may need additional reinforcement.

With that in mind, I see we have some time until Easter. If saying "My doctor said" or "I am allergic to" hasn't worked for you or maybe a New Year's Resolution takes too long, why not consider LENT as a time to experiment with eliminating meat, dairy, oil or all three?

Surely your friends and family might question you, but I can tell you they will be less threatened than if you told them you were going to give up all three forever!

Caution: If you have not already eliminated those three things from your life, be prepared to because you just may feel the best you have in years.

Let's Eliminate Negative Thinking (and toxins).

FROM DONUTS...TO POTATOES

MARCH 16

WORD FOR TODAY: MEDITATION

Last night, we were invited to attend a time of meditation in a Vietnamese Buddhist Temple.

It is interesting what goes through one's mind when sitting in the silence for 30 minutes. No music, no one speaking, no one directing anything.

So, what did I think about? Well, it seemed like I was able to pray for just about everyone I knew in 30 minutes. Sometimes I was tempted to peek to see what others were doing but mostly I just embraced people I love in my mind and hoped that by being silent for 30 minutes, just maybe I would learn (listen).

This is a busy world. We are connected to our devices, watch TV, listen to music and often don't remember just what it is like to be in our own space and investigate what silence feels like.

Getting out of our comfort zone can be a learning experience.

_____
_____
_____
_____

MARCH 17

WORD FOR TODAY: CROWD

Sometimes, the path of least resistance is to follow the crowd.

Sometimes, opportunities come where we are given the chance to crowd in when we know someone who has been waiting in line.

And then there is the crowd that we hang out with. They may be a healthy influence or they could even represent the way we used to think and not be supporting of our new way of life.

But what I really want to talk about is how we can let good thoughts and good food crowd out what is not serving us. Perfection is not required but the more we can replace unhealthy food with that which will rebuild us, the greater will be our success.

As old thinking crowds into our consciousness, we have the choice to say "No"; you do not belong to me anymore and replace that space in our minds with positive choices. Choices we want to continue to make to improve our lives.

Find your happy crowd and let the rest go.

_____

_____

_____

_____

MARCH 18

WORD FOR TODAY: IMAGINE

Imagine loving yourself as much as you love your children and grandchildren, what would that feel like? Would you be anticipating the times you get to share? Would you be thinking of the joy in each other's eyes as you met? Would you be imagining how good the hugs would feel?

Maybe you'd be thinking of a special activity you could do together. Maybe it would be sharing some of your own childhood

FROM DONUTS...TO POTATOES

memories. Maybe it would be fun to spend time in the kitchen together, take a walk or maybe even sit in the silence.

Whatever it is that draws you closer to them, you can do to draw yourself closer to your own inner child who still needs to be nourished, loved and cared for.

Remember, you are still that little person whose needs may not have been met in the past, but you can imagine taking care of that small inner child now.

Respect your body, mind and soul and give it the best possible nourishment you can. It depends on you.

_____

_____

_____

_____

MARCH 19

WORD FOR TODAY: BELIEVE

I BELIEVE
I get all the protein I need from plants.
I get all the calcium I need from plants
Milk is something from which to be weaned
Oils are toxic
Alcohol is toxic
Sugar and salt affects my appetite
It is not why, how much or when but what I eat that matters
Abstinence is easier than moderation
Exercise is helpful
Water is a beverage

Whole food is superior to processed food
Eating well allows weight to find its happy place
Our home environment is the best predictor of success
Community is important
I must share what I have learned

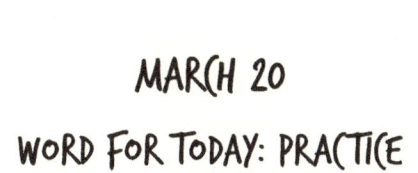

_____

_____

_____

_____

MARCH 20

WORD FOR TODAY: PRACTICE

I have heard it said that "Practice makes perfect", but does it?

What about if we are practicing something that has been initiated by another? What if our parents provided music lessons for us when we had no desire to learn? What if we 'practice' or repeat old thoughts in our heads about how valuable or invaluable we are? And what if we practice old habits that do not lead to health?

We could be further along in our journey if we practiced what we believed and were honest with ourselves. Do we really want to improve our health or is it just something we say so we feel like we are making progress?

When we take the time to better know ourselves, identify what we want in our lives and determine what it will take to get to our goals, we stand a better chance of getting there.

Practicing mindful eating is a good way to start. Practice and improve what YOU want in your life.

FROM DONUTS...TO POTATOES

_____
_____
_____
_____

MARCH 21

WORD FOR TODAY: BENEFITS

What is the benefit package if I accept your employment offer?

Yes, benefits are a big part of our portfolio. We all want health insurance, a fair retirement and maybe even a profit sharing plan.

What I have been thinking about is the benefit package (unexpectedly, I might add) I received after following "The McDougall Program for Maximum Weight Loss". What I was expecting was the following:

Weight loss, being able to fit into clothes I had saved for 20 years, not needing an extended seat belt on an airplane, getting to shop for clothes in any store, being able to get down on the floor, and finally, having the choice of having my knees replaced.

What I did not expect was the following: Eliminating all medications (lithium, levothyroxin, sleeping and pain pills and statins). What I didn't even dream about was having my eyesight improve to the point that at my age, I no longer need to wear glasses for driving, eliminated the need for knee replacement and eye surgery.

But the greatest benefit of all was peace of mind. I have found the answer to a lifelong battle of excess weight and the struggle is over. No more roller coaster rides - no more yo-yo dieting, no more internal fights about how to eat. The answer has been discovered and now I own it. It is mine. No one can take it from me. I am alive and well and I love it.

MARCH 22

WORD FOR TODAY: ENSURE

Ensure or insure? That is the question.

We have had auto and homeowner's insurance for 30+ years with no claims. The insurance gave us a sense of protection against any unforeseen calamity.

We have had health insurance for the same period of time but of course we have had to use it. We have had medical emergencies i.e. ruptured appendix, gall bladder removal and have used it for routine regular checkups.

But there is a difference between having an insurance policy to protect something and choosing to ensure something to make sure it happens.

When we eat a whole food plant based diet, we are choosing to ensure our health. We are making sure that we will have the best health possible. Sure, something unforeseen could happen, but we now know how to ensure our health.

We are in the driver's seat. Ensuring our health is up to us.

MARCH 23
WORD FOR TODAY: PRECIOUS

What is precious in the sight of one person may not be a treasure to another but I think life is precious to all of us on a whole food plant based lifestyle. Actually, life is precious to all...especially when one is in danger of losing it.

For some reason, we often don't appreciate our "treasures" until we are in danger of losing them. Then we hold tight and panic at the thought of no longer having them (or it) at our disposal.

When pain comes into our lives, we can embrace it too as a teaching tool. Something is amiss, out of order or in disease - either physically or psychologically or maybe even financially.

Health is a precious commodity and pain is the alarm button we ignore, turn off or try to snooze through. The time comes when the pain must be addressed - listened to and remedied if we want to protect what is precious to each of us...life.

MARCH 24

WORD FOR TODAY: PATIENCE

What color is patience? I think it must be green. It is something I want to keep in my heart, like the green grass of home. Sometimes, my grass is withered, brown and looks dead, but when I pay attention to it, I have the strength to water it and revive it.

Patience is something that my family has had with me for over 50 years as I struggled with my weight. They have watched me go up and down the scale between 140 and 282.

More central to my own happiness was thinking I could manage my weight but didn't - at least not long term. Each time I went on a diet, I succeeded. I was motivated, willing and determined but just never caught on to the idea that when I got to my goal (or at least got closer) adding back the very food that caused me to gain weight resulted in failure once again.

Why were so many years spent without waking up and learning this lesson? I think it was because I had never heard of a whole food plant based diet, food addiction and that obtaining good health supersedes appearance. It is a continuing way of life - one that leads to sustainability and happiness.

Patience is required for each of us as we take baby steps to change our environment and our eating habits. Taps on the back must come from within with every positive choice we make.

_____
_____
_____
_____

FROM DONUTS...TO POTATOES

MARCH 25

WORD FOR TODAY: PEACE

I wear these cute tennis shoes with the words "Teach Peace" written on them.

This morning, I was thinking about the power of peace in our lives and I came up with this acronym: Plant Eating Achieves Copious Energy.

Truly, when we eat a plant based diet, we are doing the best for our bodies, our environment and our planet. We are obtaining our food in a peaceful manner and cherishing what has been grown for us in nature.

Peace comes when we give up drama. It comes when we find our answer and are at rest in what we know is true for us.

Peace is felt after a big storm - a storm of misinformation. There are many ideas (winds) out there, but when we finally understand the way to health, vitality, longevity and happiness, we can relax. We have found the solution...it's starch.

_____
_____
_____
_____

MARCH 26

WORD FOR TODAY: VOICE

Everyone has a voice. Some sing better than others, some people have a strong voice and do not need a microphone and some of us just have a non-descriptive voice but have something to say, nevertheless.

We all have a story - whether or not it has been written. Our very lives tell stories about what we have overcome and what we have relished in our lives.

Some voices are soft and often silent - others seem to boom out, wherever they are.

The important thing for me to remember is that I have one mouth but two ears. Perhaps I am supposed to listen twice as often as I open my mouth.

Listening is a great way to learn. It is good to be still and listen to the voice within.

_____

_____

_____

_____

MARCH 27

WORD FOR TODAY: MINDFULNESS

How to be mindful in all we do is quite a challenge.

This morning, we decided to be mindful about our food and decided to sit at the table and slowly eat our oatmeal together.

FROM DONUTS...TO POTATOES

We can be mindful about how we talk and mindful of nature all around us. It is with a thankful heart that we can be mindful of our health.

As we continue our journey, we can be mindful of what we put into our bodies. When we pay attention, we are more aware of what is easy to stuff into our mouths when we are on the go.

Taking the time to think about our food, what it tastes like and how well it is going to nourish us is a good thing.

Take time to chew. Digestion really starts in our mouths. By thoroughly chewing our food, we give the enzymes in our mouth time to start the process. By slowing down, we also give our brain more time to tell us we have had enough.

Is your mind full?

_____

_____

_____

_____

MARCH 28

WORD FOR TODAY: SURRENDER

Surrender does not mean giving up. It does not mean admitting defeat. Surrender is not necessarily forever, but it can be.

When I think of surrender, I think of releasing what has not served me well in my life. In terms of advancing the whole food plant based diet, it means laying down my arms (weapons) which used to give me a false sense of security.

Those weapons were animal and dairy products, and then another weapon I used to depend on for survival was oil. Some of the smaller defenses I had in my arsenal were avocados, nuts, seeds, olives and soy products. Surely they were not harmful but neither did I need them if I was going to be a non-addicted soldier in this fight against disease and obesity.

Now that I have surrendered to embracing my vegetables, fruits, grains and legumes, I have found peace. I have free will. I can pick up one of the "guns" again and get back into the fight or I can continue living peacefully with all.

_____

_____

_____

_____

MARCH 29

WORD FOR TODAY: SUBSTITUTION

There are so many substitutions out there - even in the dietary sector. There are fake meats, fake cheese, fake ice cream, fake sour cream, and fake desserts.

By fake, I mean we often do not want to live without our favorite addictions so we look for substitutes. What will give us a thrill? What will give us the "rush" we used to experience when we ate high calorie dense foods? What, if anything, will squelch the thirsting of our "souls"?

We can choose the non-animal and non-dairy foods now as substitutes for what we used to eat. It is what some vegans do and it definitely is kinder to our animal friends.

However, are these substitutes really healthy food? Do they

FROM DONUTS...TO POTATOES

increase the fat content of our food? Is sugar still a component? How about excess salt?

What I do know is that there is no substitute for vegetables, fruits, grains and legumes. These are the building blocks of our future. They are what have allowed me to stay on track.

Spread the love - there is no substitute for that either.

_____

_____

_____

MARCH 30

WORD FOR TODAY: FEED

At Costco, they have cat food, dog food and at animal stores, one can get feed for any type of pet. I remember going to the feed store to get seed for our adopted rooster.

And then, there is food for our minds. What do we continually feed ourselves? It has been said that we "reap what we sow" which brings up the question "What are we sowing"?

When I was a child, my mother let it be known "I so wanted a 'lady'". My father bragged that he had three boys and a tomboy. All my two older brothers wanted were to have a sister so they could be relieved of the nightly chore of washing and drying the dishes.

Early messages from the adults in our lives may have sown seeds of value and unfortunately for some, seeds of doubt, inferiority, and even messages like "You will never amount to anything".

We get to be our own farmers. We are the ones who get to plant seeds of self worth. For every step we take towards our goals, we get to think about that accomplishment and pat ourselves on the back. That is how we nourish the healthy seeds and let the negative ones die out. We feed those little seeds of faith by weeding out criticism, judgments, and condemnation - of ourselves and others because what we feed others, also feeds us.

Spread the fertilizer of love all over your mind and watch the healthy seeds grow into their fullest expression.

MARCH 31

WORD FOR TODAY: RENEWAL

It is through the renewal of our minds that we are able to make changes in our everyday lives.

Sometimes, I post something on my Face Book page but it doesn't show up immediately and I wonder why. It is then that I realize that I must hit the "refresh" button and then, like magic, it appears.

I remember the I Dream of Jeannie TV Show where in the twinkling of an eye, Jeannie could change the entire situation.

So it is with us. In just a moment's time, we can adjust our view of the world and redirect our paths.

Yesterday is gone. We are in a new moment and we get to write what we want to happen today on the blackboard of our minds. Yes, young people, we used to have blackboards in every school classroom.

FROM DONUTS...TO POTATOES

What we wrote yesterday might have been cleaned off by the school janitor, ready for a new day of instruction and learning.

Blink your eyes and open them to new possibilities today. Envision what you want in your life and renew your spirit in alignment with your goals in each new moment.

_____

_____

_____

_____

APRIL 1

WORD FOR TODAY: OPEN

We sang a song in church this morning about opening our eyes. This morning, it was the first song on our lips as we sang together in bed. It is my new theme song.

As we open our hearts, eyes, ears and mouth to share the love that has blessed us, we will revive relationships and magnify peace in the world.

Be your own light. Know that darkness and ignorance dissipate as we shed truth and light on our lives.

It is so easy to dig into our "positions" and not listen to others. Our truth evolves as we learn more.

When we walk in the moccasins of another, we walk differently. When we listen to music, we hear differently. When we listen, we have the opportunity to hear the plight of others and respond. When we open our mouths, we can share our truth. I am open to learning all I can.

_____

_____

_____

_____

FROM DONUTS...TO POTATOES

APRIL 2

WORD FOR TODAY: PERSONIFICATION

Yesterday, someone wrote to me and said, "I love peanut butter". I have been thinking about how to address that stumbling block to losing weight. It is not that it is a "bad" food but it could be something to inhibit one's success in losing weight.

Maybe your stumbling block is something else - some people say they could never give up meat, chocolate, extra virgin olive oil, alcohol, cigarettes, ice cream or cheese.

But what if I used personification with peanut butter? What if I talked to it like it was a lover? I could then speak to the peanut butter and tell it of my love. I could say, "I love you so much. I think I'll take a jar of you for a nice ride in the car...or, would you like to sit on my nightstand while I sleep...or do you want to come to work with me? Is it silly? Maybe it is.

How many of us have loved someone but knew we could never live with him or her? What about those who have been abused by someone they love? Do they continue to put themselves in jeopardy by staying in the relationship? That is an option.

What if we are our own abusers? Maybe the time has come to get real with what is assisting us on our journey and what is holding us back from successfully reaching our destination.

_____

_____

_____

_____

APRIL 3

WORD FOR TODAY: STANDARD

I received an e-mail from a dear friend who gave this diet her best for three days. She was struggling - not feeling good and concerned that if she stopped eating this way (100%) that she would be a disappointment to me.

It was then that I realized that my exuberance and dedication could be construed as a "standard" to which someone else would have to measure up.

I want to say we all handle food, stress and strong habits differently.

There is nothing to be ashamed of when we take baby steps to improve our lives. We are all on our own journey. I would love to run a 5K like my niece. I would love to paint like another niece. I would love to be as smart as some of my friends. I would like to teach the world to have the best health possible. But...all of these desires require preparation, education and motivation.

It is my hope that this way of eating isn't construed as something that someone needs to accomplish overnight. I continually tweak my steps.

I encourage all of you to own what is real for you. Be the best you can be (as determined by you) and continue to grow as you are willing to make improvements in your life.

I'm here to support you.

_____

_____

_____

_____

FROM DONUTS...TO POTATOES

APRIL 4

WORD FOR TODAY: LEAD

It is said we can lead a horse to water, but we cannot make it drink. But, if we lead the horse to the water, the probability of it drinking when it gets thirsty will increase.

And so it is when we lead our lives by example. We are a role model for whatever it is we choose to do even if we don't recognize it. When we lead people to the waters of health and vitality, they may not be thirsty...but they will know where it is.

All of my life I only knew about fad diets. I had heard about the Seventh Day Adventists not eating meat or using alcohol and how they lived longer but somehow, never thought about adopting their lifestyle. About as close as I got to abstaining from liquor was when I was young. Then there are the Latter Day Saints who also take considerable effort in protecting their health. We have also read about Daniel's Fast in the Bible thousands of years ago where he ate the McDougall way and found favor with the king even while abstaining from the food from the king's table.

With all of these examples, it still didn't register with me to think about making like choices until I read The McDougall Program for Maximum Weight Loss by Dr. McDougall. It is interesting how finding a program to lose weight captured my attention more than healing my body.

I was fortunate. I learned that by putting my health first, my body would automatically find its happy place. Where he leads me, I will follow.

_____

_____

APRIL 5

WORD FOR TODAY: HUNGER

We often ask the question "What are you hungry for"? Of course we are usually thinking in terms of what to eat. In our present life, choices exist into the hundreds of foods. We have an abundance of fruits, vegetables, grains and legumes to choose from but unfortunately, it has not always been these foods that we were thinking of when we try to answer that question.

By nature, we are attracted to calorie dense foods to give us the "hit" we want. I bet it is rare that any of us have ever experienced real hunger.

Sometimes, it is not even food that we are hungry for. We might really just be wanting to be a part of a group, hear from family members, get a hug, have someone appreciate us, have more of whatever it is that gives us a temporary sense of relief from the everyday stresses of life.

Where or what gives you that hit of dopamine in your brain - your pleasure center in your brain? When you get it, is it ever enough or does it take a stronger dose of whatever it is to offer relief?

Having one's real hunger drive satisfied is just one of the benefits of following a plant-based diet. Hunger is easily satisfied when we eat plenty of starches. No more counting calories, points or monitoring portions. Eat when hungry, stop when reasonably full and for me, I eat a lot and never suffer from feeling miserably stuffed.

FROM DONUTS...TO POTATOES

Let hugs, community, learning and making good choices be your hit for the day.

_____

_____

_____

_____

APRIL 6

WORD FOR TODAY: DABBLE

I have dabbled in many things over the years, but when I read "The McDougall Program for Maximum Weight Loss" book by Dr. McDougall, I dove in.

How can we really evaluate anything in life unless we give it our all?

Scientists are very careful when doing experiments to make sure that the conditions are not contaminated and those events which could compromise the validity of the testing are eliminated.

I have dabbled in many diets. In fact, I have actually immersed myself in many of them. I was a good student and followed each program to the best of my ability. Because I followed their protocol, I was successful...for a time. Fortunately I was not able to sustain those unhealthy programs which finally led me to a program that works.

Dabbling can be fun. It can give us an opportunity to test something to see if it works for us. But dabbling must not be equated to immersion if one is to define the success of a program.

Some of us want to test a program by seeing how much of the old ways we can retain and still be successful. That's a choice, but it is not a test.

APRIL 7
WORD FOR TODAY: SOAR

In this journey called life, there are many paths we all take. Like people of years ago, sometimes it feels like we have been going in circles - wandering in the dessert if you will, wondering when if ever we will get to the Promised Land.

Storms come, obstacles rise and detours seem to be abundant. It is easy to fall into the pothole of thinking life should be easy and without challenges.

Sometimes we take a path and it leads to nowhere. Why is it that we often keep going back to square one and taking that same path again? Is it because we are familiar with it? Is it because it is the path of least resistance or perhaps because we have never looked up to discover another way?

As we let go of things that have encumbered us (addictions, toxic friendships, self doubt about our value and inner strength), we can soar above the clouds of despair, see the sun is always shining and experience peace.

FROM DONUTS...TO POTATOES

APRIL 8

WORD FOR TODAY: RECOMMENDATION

I have successfully reached my goal weight by following "The McDougall Program for Maximum Weight Loss". I continue to maintain my weight at or below my goal weight of 130.

I now experiment, once in awhile by adding some of the foods not allowed on that program until one has been at goal weight for six months: avocado, nuts, seeds, olives and soy - healthy foods but not allowed on the MWL program because of their high fat content.

If you want to know about the program, it is free.

Google drmcdougall.com and go to the search bar and type in Volume 4 Issue 1 and select "pushing your set point". He even includes a few recipes. You can read it, print it out and share it.

The program is free. It is what I recommend. It is what I follow. It has allowed me to give up all medications, avoid knee replacements, avoid eye surgery and give me a full life at 75.

APRIL 9
WORD FOR TODAY: RESPECT

Respect for someone means that we lean towards understanding how they got to where they are. There is no judgment about whether or not they are on their "right" path. Each of us is right where we need to be this moment to learn the lesson that is at hand.

As I have progressed on this journey, I realize that in my zeal I want everyone to be free from disease causing food, free of addictions, rid of medications and feel the wonderful energy - even like I have at the age of 75.

When I pause, I remember that just 33 months ago, I was at the same place many of my friends are - completely unaware of the connection between food and our health.

So, what is the answer? We can lead by example, we can share our stories but we must continue our love for others, knowing that it is up to them to be open or not. Freedom must be for everyone to be their best - not to just emulate us.

Regardless of the question, love is the answer.

FROM DONUTS...TO POTATOES

APRIL 10

WORD FOR TODAY: STEALING

Stealing is something I would not have said describes my behavior, but just maybe it does.

Sometimes my zeal to spread "the word" overtakes me. Spreading good news is a good thing. But when my need to share my story affects the timeline of another, I have had to revisit that word. I might be stealing a part of their self esteem.

Sometimes we rob someone of joy by speaking negatively of another. It is also possible to rob ourselves of a bit of happiness by putting ourselves down when we receive a compliment.

Giving our resources, time and energy to others keeps us from being self centered.

Time is a precious commodity and I want to use it wisely on my journey.

Ah, the baby steps of learning.

_____

_____

_____

_____

APRIL 11
WORD FOR TODAY: TRANSITION

Many transitions occur as we move through life. In school, our grandchildren have actually had a ceremony when they transitioned from Pre-school to Kindergarten and from Kindergarten to first grade. After that, it is usually about the sixth grade before another transition is publicly recognized.

Some transitions seem to happen overnight. We may get married, have a loved one pass from this life to another or it may be as simple as accepting a new position in our work.

Sometimes changes happen in the twinkling of an eye. We get inspiration, motivation and energy to create our own transitions to places we never dreamed possible.

Whether our growth is gradual or spread out over time, we get to be the creators of our new life. We get to decide how we want to live, how we want to eat and how we want to honor our bodies.

What affects one of us, affects all of us. We are all connected and everything we learn is spread among all of us.

We are the world. We are in transition.

FROM DONUTS...TO POTATOES

APRIL 12

WORD FOR TODAY: CONSISTENT

When we are learning a new behavior, consistently practicing it allows the behavior to become a new habit which in turn, means we do not have to even think about it so much.

For instance, if a person has oatmeal and blueberries for breakfast and eats that same meal consistently, choices are reduced and efforts are eased.

Time and effort is important when changing behavior. If something is hard to do, if it takes a lot of energy and time, we are less likely to want to engage in that behavior.

Some people say they could never (fill in the blank). What they may really be saying is (1) I don't want to change or (2) that would be too hard i.e. take too much time and energy.

New behaviors may have to be implemented for awhile before we see the benefits but once the benefits become evident, it certainly is easier to stay consistent and see the results grow.

_____
_____
_____
_____

APRIL 13
WORD FOR TODAY: TOGETHERNESS

When we all pull together, how happy we'll be.

I think what many of us are missing is a sense of community.

I love technology and science and all of the wonderful tools at our disposal. (I wouldn't be sitting here writing this if that were not the case). However, as in all things, balance is important in our lives. I hear seniors complain that their grandchildren spend too much time connected to their devices, but I think as seniors, we may often be guilty of the same thing. How much time do we spend in front of the TV which may inhibit real conversation? We have visited people who leave the TV on during a visit! Is that any different from the young people wanting to stay connected with their friends on their hand held devices?

The point I am making is that we are not islands, separate and alone. The opportunities exist to give of our energy and resources to others. Personally, I hardly ever entertain people. What is that all about? Well, I do know what it is about. It is about fear. Fear of not knowing what to serve, will my home be pleasing enough, clean enough etc. It is time to let go of fear and embrace love. They do not live well together.

_____

_____

_____

_____

FROM DONUTS...TO POTATOES

APRIL 14

WORD FOR TODAY: MESSAGE

What kind of message are you sending to your world? We are all messengers at some level. Some of us whisper, some come up with songs to share and some speak their truth from a pulpit or use a megaphone while standing on a street corner.

Some messages are sent by text and some are delivered in person especially when someone has died.

It is true that I have felt like an evangelist at times - wanting to share my story of "salvation" with everyone - even to those who might prefer to turn a deaf ear.

What is kind of funny to me is that people don't seem to turn off their TVs when the drug companies send us messages incessantly on the evening news. They extol the virtues of their products which falsely imply healing when maybe they are only offering a band aid while also warning of possible dreaded side effects. Who will counter these messages with the truth of healing which comes from eating a plant-based diet?

Are we then the ones that must be silenced or is our lesson to learn to be sensitive to those who are drawn to hear? Timing may be the key but holding back is a challenge when we see suffering and when living by example seems too slow.

Regardless of the question, I know the answer is love.

_____

_____

_____

_____

APRIL 15
WORD FOR TODAY: CREATE

I'm not sure if I have used this word in prior posts, but we are constantly creating what we want in our lives and so, even if I have, it bears repeating.

On Facebook, we can be creators. We can create events, create photo albums and create new friends.

Yesterday, at the luncheon for "Esther's Nutritional Journey", we all got to meet Barbara from Vancouver and we created a new personal addition to the group. Our connections spread all over the world and we are creating solidarity among so many who want to be their best while eating healthy food.

We can create a new spirit within all of us by the renewing of our minds. When we know better, we do better and the result is profound. We have the power. We have the will. We have the determination to be our best and to share the good news wherever listeners exist.

Have fun creating life experiences which bring you and others joy.

_____
_____
_____
_____

FROM DONUTS...TO POTATOES

APRIL 16

WORD FOR TODAY: NON-NEGOTIABLE

So, recently, I woke up with two words - "Try" which has already been discussed in relationship to Try vs. Do (or commit) and the second word which I want to talk about today is "Non-Negotiable".

If something is non-negotiable, it can be limiting or it can be freeing.

When I was growing up, we had certain religious habits which were non-negotiable. However, when it came to food, the sky was the limit. It is interesting that for some religions, eating some foods is non-negotiable. For instance, most Jews I know do not eat pork, Seventh-Day-Adventists abstain from meat and Christians I grew up with used to abstain from alcohol.

About 21 months ago, when I decided to eat WFPB (Whole Food Plant Based), animal and dairy products became non-negotiable for me. Did that restrict me or free me? Maybe it did both. Since I made a clear cut decision it actually freed me from even having to choose between so many foods. Limited choices are freeing - it takes less time to select the healthiest food from the vegetable, fruit, legumes and grains list.

When eating out, it is easier to just ask for what I want instead of grazing through the multiple mostly non-healthy choices on the menu. If someone has chosen not to drink alcohol, that decision doesn't have to be made at every social gathering. That is freeing. The decision has been made and the issue has been settled.

_____

_____

_____

_____

APRIL 17

WORD FOR TODAY: VALUE

What is on the top of your value list? Perhaps, whatever it is, that is what is driving your success or lack thereof in this period of time we call life.

I am coming to believe more and more that what drives me is my need for a strong spiritual connection. Everything else seems to fall into place as I realize who I am, what I am worth and how I can best nurture myself to be all I can be.

I can chase dreams, I can chase good times and good food, travel, nice home, good friends or I can learn to be happy regardless of the emotional or physical state I am in.

Peace of mind is a valuable commodity. It doesn't come to us automatically. It comes when we can be in the flow of life and know that no matter what we do, we are okay. We have bodies that want to be healthy.

I noticed the other day how quickly a burn formed a blister so the sore spot would be protected. For years, I abused my body, gave it junk for fuel and expected better results.

Now I am the feeder of my soul, body and mind. I have a choice.

_____
_____
_____
_____

FROM DONUTS...TO POTATOES

APRIL 18

WORD FOR TODAY: CONTINUE

When we are on the road to success, all we have to do is continue in the way.

Yes, there are often bumps (learning experiences) and detours (distractions) but if we keep focused on our destination (goal); we have the opportunity of getting there by continuing in what we know to be true.

Last Sunday, I got lost. I was on my way to pick up Barbara to go to church with us prior to attending the group luncheon. I wasn't really lost - I did get to the destination I had entered into my GPS so was I really lost or simply misinformed about the correct destination?

We must have our destination (goal) in mind if we expect to get there. If we follow unhealthy suggestions for our lives, we will arrive at an unhealthy state.

Clarity is important. What we want to achieve we must first imagine and then manifest it in our lives.

Messages come to us in a timely manner. Fortunately, Barbara sent us a message and we had a successful day.

_____
_____
_____
_____

APRIL 19

WORD FOR TODAY: MOMENT

Are we in the moment or are we fast forwarding to events, responsibilities and concerns over the future?

Perhaps we dwell in the past and wonder why we haven't obtained success on all of those previous diets that could not be sustained and we kept getting back on the band wagon when in fact, we had never found the right band.

This moment is all there is. The past is gone and the future doesn't matter. It is now that we have the chance to love the one we are with even if that only one is us. When we love ourselves and decide that no one else is going to put the fork to our mouths, it is up to us to choose what we want on the end of each bite.

Sure, change is a challenge. It requires resolution, belief in what you are eating, determination to be your best in spite of any toxic environment in which you must live.

It only takes one person in a household to make a difference. Change may not always be 100% but someone has to lead in the parade of good health.

_____

_____

_____

FROM DONUTS...TO POTATOES

APRIL 20

WORD FOR TODAY: CONFLICT

We can see the pros and cons of so many choices we make each day and sometimes, a conflict of opinions or ideas gives us an opportunity to stop and think.

Last night, we enjoyed a dinner with our visiting friend and fellow group member Barbara from B.C. Her friend Cheryl had joined her for a week in Sacramento so we got to meet her too. (Thanks for the delicious meal).

Anyway, we discussed some of the issues about following a WFPB diet when being invited to the home of people still eating the old SAD diet (Standard American Diet). Yes, it can be uncomfortable as we take a stand for how we eat. We may even feel like we are being rude by wanting to stick to a meal plan that is healthiest for us.

That perceived rudeness is false. If an alcoholic chooses water, he/she is not considered "rude" but is actually praised for being "on the wagon".

Dr. Lisle suggests saying things like, oh, this is just an experiment I am doing - it seems to be working for me and my doctor is happy with my progress.

Always eat before such occasions, offer to bring something to share and have something to eat at home when you return. Let others love you on your way to success.

_____

_____

_____

_____

ESTHER LEBECK LOVERIDGE

APRIL 21

WORD FOR TODAY: RISE

Many people around the world will be celebrating Easter in all of its various traditions, beliefs, customs and celebrations.

Every day in our life is a new day to rise to the occasion that lies before us. We rise out of bed. We raise a cup of cheer. We raise our forks and we raise the expectations of our performance.

When we are misinformed about the healthiest diet on the planet, it is like we are in a dark cave. We survive, we breathe, we live but is that the same as coming out of the cave into the sunshine and fresh air of a new beginning?

Just as seeds are planted early in the year, it takes a combination of the right elements for them to spring into their fullness.

We all have the seeds of good health within our bodies. We get to nourish those seeds and imagine the fulfillment in our lives as our ideas; dreams and plans take root and emerge once again.

Rise today to be your best.

_____

_____

_____

_____

FROM DONUTS...TO POTATOES

APRIL 22

WORD FOR TODAY: MIND

Hello seniors (and everyone else). How is your mind working? Are you claiming more and more "senior moments" as you struggle to utilize your mind's wonderful capabilities?

Have you ever considered the power of the mind as you clean up your act and start eating a healthy life-producing lifestyle?

Whether you have suffered from depression, mind fog, mindlessness or anything less than the best, realize that we are what we eat and if we want a clean system, it means giving ourselves the best fuel possible.

We don't accomplish that by going on a diet, then on a binge or by restricting valuable complex carbohydrates. We are what we eat. Food is our medicine.

I used to see a plaque somewhere that said "Take time to be holy". How in the world do we get holy? Well, a big step is to get quiet, sit in the silence and listen to our bodies. We must disconnect from mindless chatter, redundant TV and any distraction which does not give us the time to listen.

It is normal to be healthy. Anything less than being healthy is an alarm to wake up. You know the answers. It is within you. Honor your mind, body and soul. Be your best.

_____

_____

_____

_____

ESTHER LEBECK LOVERIDGE

APRIL 23

WORD FOR TODAY: PEACE

Peace comes when we have done all we can do, let go of the past, even relinquish what might lay ahead and enjoy the quietness of the moment.

This moment in time is all there is. This is the time to cherish our bodies - regardless of its condition of health, size or age.

To accept ourselves as the product of many choices we have made throughout our lives is simply that. It is acceptance.

Love, happiness and joy do not have to wait until we reach a certain goal. It is here now.

As we become aware of new choices to make, we address those changes with patience, love and compassion, knowing that we are novices in any new endeavor and making changes will take a lot of practice.

When we know better, we do better. Practice your art and your cooking and your shopping with tender loving care - looking for the best possible nourishment for you and your loved ones.

Be well.

_____
_____
_____
_____

FROM DONUTS...TO POTATOES

APRIL 24

WORD FOR TODAY: GAP

How big is your gap? A gap just may be a small degree of separation. It could be the one inch which prevents you from being able to zip up your pants all the way.

But when we are disgusted with ourselves for allowing our excess weight to get out of hand, self loathing can enter our minds. We condemn ourselves for not being strong enough to resist temptation. We then magnify it to where we see nothing good in ourselves. Negative self talk seems to run rampant as we start a collection of all of our shortcomings.

It's almost like when we were kids and collected marbles. Now the temptation when talking with our friends is to see how many pills we take as a badge of honor. Maybe our best friends have seen a collection of medical advisers who are helpful and try to guide them on their way. We look for a magic pill. We search for information outside of ourselves and many of us have spent years gathering information to the point that we failed to put any of it into practice.

We can feel so good about reading, studying and learning but what do we do about the gap between what we know and how we perform? Can studying be a form of procrastination?

Self help books abound telling us how to feel better about ourselves yet the gap continues. Maybe each of us has a different formula for bringing us closer to our authentic self. There may not be one single formula for all of us but today I'm thinking for anyone who is depressed and thinking they can't switch over to a plant based diet, what would it take to change your direction of thinking from negative to positive?

Maybe you can take time to think about it and choose one thing you're going to do today that will give you the opportunity to be proud of yourself at the end of the day. It may be as simple as making your bed.

Choose something you can do. Build on that by adding more things to your list that you can do and hopefully you will soon learn that you can do what you want to do.

Instead of making a "to do" list, try making an "I did" list. Be your own best cheerleader.

_____

_____

_____

APRIL 25

WORD FOR TODAY: FLOW

When traveling, be in the flow after planning and preparing the best you can.

Unforeseen events occur out of your comfort zone. Be adaptable. Some surprises may turn out to be miracles. Love doesn't insist on having its own way. Surrender to the river as you enter uncharted waters. Be open.

Pack lightly and be organized.
Inform airlines and tour guides of your dietary needs.
Ask for help on what food meets your criteria.
Bring food to carry you through rough spots.
Keep a light attitude and meet new friends.
Wear a half smile at all times (Buddhists will know what I mean).
Enjoy being a guest in someone else's country.

FROM DONUTS...TO POTATOES

APRIL 26

WORD FOR TODAY: RISK

How much of ourselves dare we risk in exposing who we are to our friends, let alone to the public on Facebook?

Does rejection play a part in how vulnerable we are? Maybe we want to fit in with a group so badly that we only tell others the parts of ourselves that align with their agenda, ideas, expectations or beliefs.

If I tell you who I really am will you still love me is a question we all grapple with.

In the end, we are wondrous creations and being congruent with our daily lives brings us into alignment so that we can be our best.

My brother Robert A. Lebeck taught me that if we always tell the truth, we won't have to remember what we said. How nice is that?

To risk being honest with ourselves just may be the first step. Do you have a desire to change your life? Do you worry about what others will think of you? Or is giving you the very best expression of yourself the best gift of all?

You are loved and the best is yet to be.

APRIL 27

WORD FOR TODAY: RELIEF

Years ago, I worked in the Corporate Division of the Secretary of State's office in Sacramento, California. We would be on the phones all day long and could not leave our post for a coffee break or lunch without having someone relieve us. The person who relieved me was named Rosa so I had a T-shirt made up which stated "How do I spell relief? ROSA."

Back then, we would see advertisements on TV which promoted Rolaids as the relief medicine.

But now I wear a T shirt I got at Dr. McDougall's 3 days Intensive Weekend. It has his website on the back but on the front it simply states "It's the Food".

Recently, I was so concerned over the lack of health in my dear hospitalized niece. I felt helpless until she told me she was ready to listen to information about a plant based diet. She wasn't lying. She has responded and rebounded in a remarkable way. Relief has come.

I don't care what your issue is. A plant based diet has only positive side effects: it doesn't matter when you eat or why you eat or how much you eat as long as you pay attention to WHAT you eat. Eat vegetables, fruit, grains and legumes. It is that simple.

Coming to the realization that many diseases are food borne diseases is my new relief. We are what we eat - it cannot be otherwise so when we are sick, it is imperative that we address what we are putting into our bodies.

The biggest relief for me since discovering the benefits of eating

FROM DONUTS...TO POTATOES

a plant based diet is freedom from desire - the kind of desire that kept me thinking about where to get my next fix.

How can one measure peace of mind? What can compare? To know that the battle is over and that you actually won is the best relief of all.

Is the road to recovery smooth? Of course it is not. There are habits to break etc. but the payoff provides the best relief ever.

RELIEF: Real Energy Living Inside Everyone Forever.

_____

_____

_____

APRIL 28

WORD FOR TODAY: PAYOFF

There is usually a payoff for everything we do. We work, save money to buy a house, travel, raise a family and get an education but somehow, when it comes to health, maintaining the status quo is enough.

Enough is fine too. Let's just get honest with ourselves. If only taking the minimum medication will get us through, maybe that is good enough.

Sometimes there is social pressure to look a certain way so we think we need to conform for the sake of acceptance when in fact, the way we are just may be good enough.

Who wants to struggle by going on a diet? Who wants to give up the abundant array of foods now available in the world? What incentive is there if enough is okay?

When the payoff for maintaining the current state of affairs is exceeded by a health crisis, we generally choose to do something about it. At that point it becomes real and the payoff in continuing our way of life becomes declining health. Maybe we don't care. Maybe we tell ourselves it is to be expected in old age. Maybe we accept the pain, the depression, the weight, being immobile. But again, maybe we don't.

_____

_____

_____

APRIL 29

WORD FOR TODAY: GREED

Passing up non-compliant food is not easy, but what makes it even harder for me is if I put additional value on what I am abstaining from.

For instance, on a plane ride, we were offered every imaginable drink - FREE. That really taps into me wanting to get the most for my money so when I pass up Champagne or any other beverage I place high on the value list, I can get caught in the trap of thinking I am not getting my money's worth if I choose water.

The place I want to get to and stay is realizing that when I choose water, although it is the least expensive drink being offered, n terms of health and a clear mind, it is the most valuable for health and weight loss success.

Eating a WFPB diet means giving up previously conceived values which we had put on food or drink in order to choose what is best for us in the long run.

FROM DONUTS...TO POTATOES

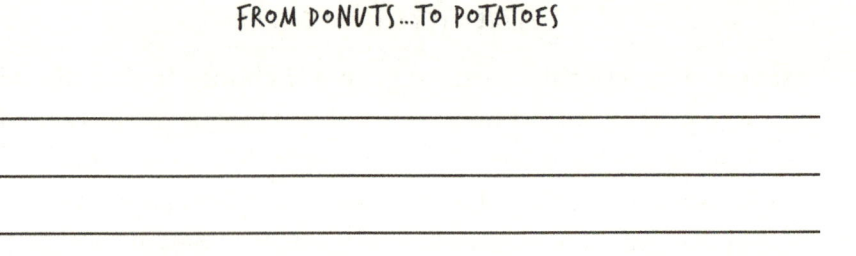

APRIL 30

WORD FOR TODAY: RAIL

We can "rail" against something or we can use rails to help us be safe.

Stairs have rails, some bathtubs have rails, cribs have rails and hospital beds have rails.

My rails are potatoes - all kinds. They keep me safe from runaway cravings. They keep me satisfied. They keep my brain fed. They give me energy and also provide comfort.

I also like rails on staircases. They support me as I pull myself up a long flight of stairs and also provide added insurance against possible knee weakness.

This group is also a rail for me. All of you who respond to my postings give me energy. There is a lot of support here and I am enjoying the camaraderie. Thank you for going on this journey with me.

MAY 1

WORD FOR TODAY: CRAZY

So, in this busy world, what is a simple definition of "crazy"? I have heard it said that crazy is doing the same behavior over and over again while expecting a different result.

If we bang our head against the wall until it bleeds and then keep banging our head against the wall (eating non healthy food), we are demonstrating crazy behavior.

I think somewhere in the Bible it talks about that actually being sin - you know - something like if you know better and you keep doing it, it is sin or more simply - just missing the mark. It will not send you to hell but it can certainly keep you in hell on earth.

So, how do we cure "crazy"? We can be crazy in love with someone to the point that we may violate ourselves in the process. We can be crazy about certain foods. I always chuckle when someone says, "Oh, I could never give up cheese, meat, ice cream, soda or oil". Perhaps those items are red flags to pay attention to.

Life is one big learning curve. We won't cure all of our mistakes at once. We will not be perfect but once we raise our consciousness to what is harming us and if we value ourselves, we can choose to do something about it.

Choose life.

_____
_____
_____
_____

FROM DONUTS...TO POTATOES

MAY 2

WORD FOR TODAY: PURSUE

It is important to pursue our goals, but first, they must be identified. We can set goals in steps. I remember my first goal was to get rid of all of my medications and lose 70 pounds. As that weight loss goal was reached, I re-evaluated what would be the next possible step. My doctor recommended that I get down to about 160. When that was realized, I thought, why not get down to 143 like Mr. Fred Rogers?

It seemed I just zoomed past that and so I changed my mind to 141 which would be 1/2 of my all time high of 282 in 2011. The next goal was 139, my wedding day weight in 1963 which I hadn't weighed since. As of this writing, I have hit 135.5 and that seems okay for me, but I actually have gone down to between 127 and 130.

We used to say that one's weight should be 100 pounds at 5' and an additional 5 pounds for each additional inch. Who knows? The point is that I have pursued healthy eating and the weight is continuing to adjust to what will be good for me. And, yes, as of July 13, 2018, I can claim part of my original goal which was to be prescription free.

Pursuing our dreams or goals takes action. Yes, we can dream about it but it does take practice, planning and preparation. Chase after your goals. Seek answers. Find solutions.

The importance of a target determines the amount of energy we will put into the pursuit.

_____
_____
_____
_____

ESTHER LEBECK LOVERIDGE

MAY 3

WORD FOR TODAY: HOARD

I am still dealing with the concept of hoarding - why I do it and how to release the need to collect beyond my needs.

We attended a farewell reception at the hotel at Bled Lake in Slovenia. Our tour continued for two more days in Venice, Italy but not everyone in the group would be going there.

The reception was lovely; photos were taken with our tour manager and bus driver. Our guide gave each of us a parting gift of a personalized size bottle of cherry liquor. The thought of giving our gifts to someone else that would really enjoy them did not cross my mind. I wanted the gift. But why was that so?

It's that old greed thing popping up again. After reflecting on it, I decided to leave them for the hotel maid.

And then...there were the peanuts at the reception. I fell into them like butter melting on a hot grill. Once again, upon reflection, I do know that it is easy to gravitate to the most calorie dense food in our environment but it doesn't mean we must. For me, I am continually becoming aware that when it comes to nuts, abstinence is easier than moderation.

Dr. McDougall tells us that the fat we eat is the fat we wear. Nuts, seeds, avocado, olives and soy products all fall into the category of healthy food but the fat content is too high for those following the Maximum Weight Loss Program. For me, they trigger "more".

I'm always learning.

FROM DONUTS...TO POTATOES

MAY 4

WORD FOR TODAY: ABBEY

We were fortunate to get to experience sleeping in the Abbey in Venice, Italy. Okay, so it may not be an abbey now, but at one time it was and if only the walls could speak to us today what would they say?

Ben actually woke up in the middle of the night and said he heard "angels" singing. Who would ever have guessed that this would occur loud enough for him to hear it?

He has never claimed to have heard angels before so this was a once in a lifetime occurrence.

Anyway, the bedroom was so cute, complete with a crystal chandelier and a Jacuzzi big enough for two. In the lobby, there was a nice sitting area where several of us sat in the afternoon - some arriving before the afternoon thunder shower and some, as seen by their wet clothes, arriving afterwards!

We had a remnant of our tour continuing here in Venice for the last two days. We had tea or coffee and croissants in what would have been a dining room in the old days as we discussed healthy eating!

One of the travelers was a former employee of Weight Watchers and subsequently Jenny Craig. It has worked for her and she is a lifelong member of Weight Watchers. She agreed that it is important to eat a healthy fresh diet.

Another couple from Florida wanted to join "Esther's Nutritional Journey" on Facebook and I am always willing to help everyone become their best.

Angels come in all sorts of forms. The ones Ben heard last night were actually coming from my iPhone where I sometimes listen to hymns in the middle of the night. They are supposed to put me to sleep, but since I know most of the words, I sing along. I think sometimes rest works just as well as sleep - but again, that is just me.

___

MAY 5

WORD FOR TODAY: TRAVEL

It has often been said "No matter where I travel, there is no place like home".

If you want to travel or simply experience a different perspective in your life, travel can be as simple as taking a walk in your own neighborhood with a camera and noticing the little things in life that are often taken for granted.

We are thankful that we got to go to Croatia, Bosnia, Montenegro, Slovenia and Italy. It was proof, once again, that through the healing powers of eating a whole food plant based diet I was able to not only keep up with the group but climb so many steps and walk everywhere. What a difference from 3 years ago when we went to Ireland and I could barely walk to the departing gate at the airport.

Life is good and I am thankful that I have found the answer to good health and energy.

FROM DONUTS...TO POTATOES

MAY 6

WORD FOR TODAY: ENERGY

Wow - where is this energy coming from? We landed at the airport 12 hours ago! We were driven home by our good friend Charlie Cassell after travelling for 23 hours and almost immediately, I began cooking.

As you might guess, the first was a pot of potatoes followed by a pot of brown rice and a big pot of Mayocoba beans. I got the suitcases emptied (last time it dragged out for about 2 months), went through the mail, fixed a phone issue, slept for 4 hours and this morning made a batch of oatmeal and a pot of "Dump Soup" and I'm almost done with the laundry.

It does feel wonderful to be home where food selection is a no brainer and memories of a wonderful trip abound.

My feet and ankles are still swollen from all of the time sitting on the airplane (and more salt than my usual intake) my knees are a bit stiff but no pain after hundreds of steps taken on this trip.

I am thankful beyond measure for my wonderful traveling buddy, for shelter, food, and all I need. I am blessed with health and renewable energy. "It's the Food"

ESTHER LEBECK LOVERIDGE

MAY 7

WORD FOR TODAY: INSIGHT

If you have read my success story "Esther: Her New Life" in Dr. McDougall's newsletter at drmcdougall.com you will know that through following "The McDougall Program for Maximum Weight Loss", my health has been restored. In December, 2018 I learned that in addition to the mentioned benefits, my eyesight has improved to the point that my doctor said "With your eyesight, you no longer need to wear glasses".

Having improved eyesight and avoiding surgery for a macular pucker in my eye, is exciting news. Yes, I still have cataracts, macular puckers and an inherited condition called pseudo exfoliation but given enough light, I can see and read without glasses.

What might be even more important than eyesight is insight. Many blind people live productive lives and of course all of us who have worn glasses enjoy clearer sight. But what, I ask, about insight which can continually improve our lives every day?

Insight is the product of listening to our bodies and allowing our minds to lead us in a new direction. We can stay in a rut and repeat unproductive behaviors or we can learn new habits and enjoy a more successful life.

Without insight into why we do what we do, we will continue to follow unhealthy practices and wonder why life hasn't improved.

_____

_____

_____

_____

FROM DONUTS...TO POTATOES

MAY 8

WORD FOR TODAY: DARE

I remember playing the "I dare you" game as a kid. Then the pressure in the game escalated to "I double dare you".

Recently I heard a song which challenged us to be strong enough to stand alone, have a purpose and let that purpose be known.

This song resonated with me on my whole food plant based journey. I have definitely had times where I stood alone and speaking my truth has not always been easy. But realizing I have a purpose like none before this experience is exciting. It requires tact when making my purpose known and I continually am challenged to be sensitive to others.

But, being sensitive does not mean being silent. It means we must know that other people have their own issues with which they are dealing and we can listen and be helpful; however, our truth may be just what they need to know to enhance their own journey.

Learning when to speak out and when to hold our tongue is a skill, but dare to be you. Dare to tell your story. Dare to ask for healthy food. Dare to pursue your purpose. Dare to speak openly about it. Dare to spread the good news of regaining a healthy body. Dare to be truthful. Dare to stand alone if necessary.

_____
_____
_____
_____

MAY 9
WORD FOR TODAY: TUMBLEWEED

I just purchased a CD to support my high school classmate Phil Stewart. One of the songs on this compilation of cowboy songs is an old favorite about tumbleweeds.

As I listened to the words, I wondered about the benefits of being a tumbling tumbleweed. There are benefits to everything in life. The tumbleweed may be lonely, but free. The cares of its past are left behind. It gets to just drift along, roll along and live life effortlessly.

But there is also something to be said about having roots, taking charge of our lives and making decisions that help us and all of those around us.

We can drift or we can become conscious of where we want to be and how we are going to get there. Making plans, preparing and working towards goals has its benefits too.

_____
_____
_____
_____

FROM DONUTS...TO POTATOES

MAY 10

WORD FOR TODAY: SPREAD

Spread can be something we put on bread, it can be an accumulation of tasty food in a buffet line, it can be a covering on a bed and it can be the concept of sharing or spreading good news.

I am excited that I have been asked to respond to questions proposed by a group of 5th graders in London, UK. We will be on SKYPE at 6:00 a.m. (2 p.m. in London) on Monday morning.

These bright students are working on a project which they initiated themselves. They want to talk about obesity, sugar and diabetes and will be directing those questions to me. I am not a doctor or a nurse or even a nutritionist by trade, but am willing to share my story with them. What really excites me is that this new generation has, on their own, raised questions that concern them and the health of everyone.

I am thankful to Ana who joined "Esther's Nutritional Journey" several months ago and is putting this "across the ocean experience" together for all of us.

By spreading our stories, we can strengthen our resolve and encourage others to do the same.

_____
_____
_____
_____

MAY 11

WORD FOR TODAY: TURN

On our journey, we can make turns that "turn" out to be beneficial. Sometimes we think we have taken a wrong turn, but if it is a learning experience, is that not a good turn?

It is easy to judge ourselves on the turns we have taken in life. We can be our own worst critic but we can choose to love ourselves in all of our manifestations as we continue on the road toward health and vitality.

I got turned onto the book "The McDougall Program for Maximum Weight Loss" in July, 2016 and my friend Cherie Larkin advises us to look out of the windshield of life instead of the rear view mirror.

We are the drivers on this journey. No one else force feeds us with ideas or food. We get to claim the map we want to follow, make adjustments as we go along and reach the destination we want with freedom to enjoy the ride.

U-turns are allowed.

_____
_____
_____
_____

FROM DONUTS...TO POTATOES

MAY 12

WORD FOR TODAY: UNITE

There is power in unification. It has been said that it takes a village to raise a child...we are not alone. No one is an island.

Sometimes we isolate ourselves unnecessarily, but there is also value in being alone, taking time to know ourselves, what we value and what we want in life.

But when we, individually, can unite our thoughts and our actions, we discover a power we may never have felt before. It has also been said that one cannot serve two masters, or a divided person is unstable in all ways.

So, how do we unite our minds into a single purpose, goal or aspiration?

We start by first of all, being honest with ourselves about where we are on our journey and where we want to end up. Once that has been identified, we need to eliminate any negative thinking or behavior which is contrary to what we have identified. What we think about...we bring about.

Be single minded, unite yourself with like-minded people, surround yourself with positive energy and know the power within.

_____
_____
_____
_____

MAY 13

WORD FOR TODAY: ANTICIPATION

Planning and thinking about a future event can be exciting. Some say that the anticipation is about as good as the actual event. I guess it all depends on what one expects the outcome to be.

This morning, I will be on SKYPE with a group of 5th graders in London and it will be interesting to hear all of the questions they have come up with regarding sugar, obesity and diabetes.

It is my hope that they will be inspired to be their best. Just coming up with their questions is a great start.

It is also important to "be in the moment". Sometimes we rush from one event to another, one goal to another and one activity to another.

Learning to be in the present, to be in the here and now is also important. It is all too easy to rush past precious moments in search of the next thing.

_____

_____

_____

_____

MAY 14

WORD FOR TODAY: WATER

We are made up of mostly water. I think the planet is mostly water and ordering water in a restaurant is a beverage. I remember when I

FROM DONUTS...TO POTATOES

was a single mother teaching my sons to order water when we went out for a meal and that was a great money saver too.

It can be ordered at any temperature and with or without lemon.

How much do we need to drink? I have heard it said that the color of our urine is a good indicator as to whether or not we are drinking enough water. A weak color is a good goal.

Sometimes I think I am hungry when in actuality I may just need to be re-hydrated. Yesterday I kept a cup with slices of lemon in it in the kitchen and just kept refilling the cup. The smell of the lemon was very refreshing.

We water our lawns, our plants and flowers and need to water ourselves.

_____

_____

_____

_____

MAY 15

WORD FOR TODAY: SHOCK

This morning, I wanted to make more salad dressing. I like the 3:2:1 ratio of balsamic vinegar, Dijon mustard and lemon or orange juice so I poured the vinegar into my dressing bottle but the shock came when I took a new jar of mustard out of the frig, opened it and discovered a layer of oil on top! I stuck my finger in it and sure enough, it was oil!

How could that be? Have I been duped all of this time thinking mustard was oil free? I stuck the knife in it and it was so thick I couldn't mix it up.

It was then that I took the time to look at the label. Had I purchased a different kind of mustard?

Suddenly everything fell into place once I realized I had mistakenly opened a jar of Tahini. Serving size is 2 T at 190 calories, 79% FAT.

Yuck.

Anyone want a new bottle of tahini? I bought it over 2 years ago when I was a newbie and didn't know.

Life is good again.

_____
_____
_____
_____

MAY 16

WORD FOR TODAY: HIGH

And when you're up you're up and when you're down you're down, but when you're only half way up, your neither up or down!

Someone once said it is better to be hot or cold than lukewarm. What is really important to me is to be honest about wherever we are. There is a season for everything. Sometimes we are grieving and need to be comforted. Sometimes we get so high we forget that others are suffering. And when we are low, we could forget that rising is possible.

This has been a great week for me from visiting with the 3 fifth graders in London via Skype to having Jennifer from the hot tub report her success in losing 40 pounds so far this year to hearing from Vicki Pepper that 45, the maximum allowed, will meet to hear

FROM DONUTS...TO POTATOES

my story in San Diego at Kaiser Permanent's Wellness Program on Friday night.

On another personal level, we will get to witness the university graduation of our granddaughter on Saturday. We are so proud of her and her lifetime of accomplishments so far.

Whether you are high or low or somewhere in between, know the best is yet to be.

_____

_____

_____

MAY 17

WORD FOR TODAY: PRAISE

I used to have a T shirt which read "Praise the Lard" right across the bust line. It was from a meat company and did generate some attention as people tried to figure out if "Lard" was misspelled.

I had another T shirt from my cousin's yogurt shop with "The Udder Delight" printed on the front but now I wear one from Dr. McDougall which simply states "It's The Food". It's an attention getter too.

We praise what benefits us. We recommend good documentaries, books and podcasts and extol the virtues of eating plant based food. We tell our friends about restaurants which are supportive and help us make healthy choices while eating out.

Last night we were invited to join family members at a Mexican restaurant. The actual menu warned us that they use lard. I let the moment override my good judgment. I had previewed the menu online, didn't see that and had decided to have a veggie burrito but in retrospect, I would have done better to have ordered a salad. I am still learning.

Praise requires scrutiny.

_____

_____

_____

MAY 18

WORD FOR TODAY: COMPLETION

Completion and beginning seem to be synonymous when it came to watching our granddaughter walk across the stage and receive her diploma from Claremont McKenna College today. Wasn't it just a few years ago that we babysat her in her early years and now she is ready to begin her career?

And so it is in life. We complete one phase and then begin another - over and over until we finally pass from this earth into the next realm where we start all over again or perhaps, just continue.

It is also true that who we are doesn't totally change, but as we complete a phase where we were once obese, we can emerge like a sculpture out of a piece of marble into a new creation.

This too happens over and over as we mentally make an adaption to a new lifestyle and create new beginnings upon the completion of previous stages. Be the new creation you want to be as you put a period to your last experience and open the door to new adventures.

FROM DONUTS...TO POTATOES

_____

_____

_____

_____

MAY 19

WORD FOR TODAY: BOX

Ever feel like you'd like to break out of your "box"? You know, the one where you feel like your life is so predictable? You get up in the morning, turn off the alarm, go to the bathroom, maybe you brush your teeth then you go to the kitchen to see what you might have for breakfast and then you get in your car, go to work the same way you go every day, get to work, put down your purse, sit at your desk and start that routine all over again.

Maybe you meet the same people for lunch every month and never explore any new ideas. Rehash.

Breaking out of the box is not always pretty. Yes there are some people who receive a gift and very carefully remove the scotch tape, un-wrap the box and save the paper. Then there are others who are energetic and just tear the wrapping off and open the box to quickly discover the gift inside.

We are not always gentle when we decide to make a radical change. After all we don't do "radical" very often.

Change is inevitable whether we embrace it or not. Some people resist change. They feel safe when everything stays the same. It gives them a chance to rely on predictability. But what about the butterfly, we ask? It has to emerge from the cocoon. What about the tadpole that turns into a frog?

As you change and evolve into your new body, mind and soul,

it will affect those around you as well. Be prepared and be patient, but keep alive your indomitable spirit and soar.

_____

_____

_____

_____

MAY 20

WORD FOR TODAY: CONTROL

Wow this is a biggie. We try to control so many things in our lives: Weight, blood pressure, diabetes, cholesterol, mental health, and depression and food addictions. But what if all of these issues could be cured instead of controlled?

Would the cure be advertised by the media? Would we embrace the cure as much as we embrace the medications which are advertised to control these conditions?

Perhaps one of the biggest things we are tempted to control is others.

Letting go of others and letting them find their own way is a big gift. Trusting that our family and friends are in their right place is love. It is allowing them to make their own choices, decide what works for them and learn - sometimes through trial and error what rings true for their lives.

When we find the cure or the answer to our own personal struggles, we must just live our lives, be congruent, be steadfast and if it inspires someone else to change, that is their decision. In the meantime, learning to control my tongue is a continual process.

FROM DONUTS...TO POTATOES

_____

_____

_____

_____

MAY 21

WORD FOR TODAY: BUTTON

Button, Button, Who's got The Button" is a game I remember playing as a child.

A button can be something that holds two things together. It can also be something that we "push" in another when we have a different point of view and likewise, other people can push our buttons when there is conflict and we strongly hold different opinions.

What happens when our buttons get pushed? Do we push back, try to reach an understanding and respect for each other or do we fight back defensively and try to prove our point?

Having our buttons pushed gives us an opportunity to step aside and view the world from another person's experience. It doesn't mean we must change our views but we can change our approach.

Love is the answer - no matter what the question, so when people ask me "Where do you get your protein if you're not eating animals", or "Where do you get your calcium if you no longer eat dairy products" or "How much more weight do you want to lose"? I can answer by saying something like I am doing an experiment and so far it seems to be working and my doctor is happy with my progress". That may de-escalate the perceived threat to a lower level.

And then there are times we want to be direct and cut right to the bone. We have a choice.

_____

_____

_____

_____

MAY 22

WORD FOR TODAY: TIMING

Some things happen in no time at all - like when your granddaughter moves to southern California. Some things take time, and even then, timing can be so important.

We learn when we are ready. Sometimes it takes crises before our ears open. How fortunate are those who learn before they have to hit rock bottom in order to make a life changing decision.

At Kaiser, yesterday, there just seemed to be good timing all around. We would not have had the time to get to know Johanna if her credit card machine had been working. It seemed like it took forever to boot up but what a blessing that extra time provided for us to get acquainted. Additionally, yesterday was her day off but she had responded to the call to come in on short notice.

And then when nurse Grace was telling us her story, we had extra time to listen to her because we had to wait for the surgeon to come and see us before discharge. I was out, having my lunch when the doctor probably came to the waiting area looking for me.

Hopefully, we learn to be in the flow - let go - and know everything is in divine order.

This morning, we had to return to the Emergency Room. We

went back, got a prime parking place at 6:00 a.m. and didn't have to wait at all to be seen and cared for.

Good timing.

___

MAY 23

WORD FOR TODAY: VISION

It has been said that without a vision, we "perish". Even if we don't die, we certainly do not stretch to reach out and extend ourselves to others until we see a better way to live and give of ourselves.

Without a vision, we stagnate, become slow moving robots and may not be able to aim for our highest good. Sometimes we feel like it is safer to stay in the dark, not think, grow or expand our consciousness.

But freedom comes when we set loose the bonds of the past, raise our sights and move in a healthy direction.

In the fall of 2016, I had been following The McDougall Program for Maximum Weight Loss for three months when I went to the ophthalmologist for a routine check up on the macular pucker in my right eye. He had been following its progress for quite some time and informed me that the condition was finally to the place where I could be referred to a surgeon.

I let him know that I had recently begun following a plant based diet which I believed would increase the health of my whole body including my eyes and that I would prefer to wait to see if in fact that was true. He agreed and each subsequent visit revealed the truth I was seeking - my eyes continued to improve over time. On December 10, 2018, I told him I hadn't been wearing my glasses for quite some time and wondered if I should wear them to protect my eyes from any deterioration. His response was "With your eyesight, you do not need to wear glasses".

Is my vision perfect? No. Do I still have cataracts? Yes. But I love the freedom of seeing without being dependent on glasses. I love the evidence that eating this way optimizes our potential for seeing into the future and becoming our best.

_____

_____

_____

MAY 24

WORD FOR TODAY: TOLERANCE

I don't think I needed to learn tolerance. Children are mostly tolerant. I think, over the years, I became intolerant by including biases, prejudices and self righteousness into my mindset.

As long as I am not tolerant, how do I expect to co-exist with people of differing views? If it is my way or the highway, I eliminate most people from being a part of my life.

Even in selecting a healthy eating plan, it is easy to adopt the same self righteous attitude in espousing my way over what has worked for other people.

Certainly I want to uphold healthy eating practices and denounce what I have come to believe to be unhealthy foods, but

FROM DONUTS...TO POTATOES

I must also remember that just a few months ago, I had an entirely different view on how to be healthy.

Being tolerant does not mean we must compromise. It means we accept people where they are and know that we are all on a journey. If we want to compete, we can do so with the person we were yesterday.

_____

_____

_____

_____

MAY 25

WORD FOR TODAY: ELIMINATION

Elimination is a key to life. If we physically do not have a good elimination system, we fail. Toxins must be eliminated from our bodies if we are to be restored to good health.

Likewise, we often engage in toxic thoughts, friends, relatives, practices, habits and environments...not to mention stuff that takes our energy and keeps us from living a simple life.

As I recognize negative thoughts, I can then decide to eliminate them and replace them with life-giving positive thoughts about how wondrous our bodies are made and how they yearn to be healthy.

How long we ignore the cry to eliminate what is hurting us determines the length of time it takes to get on the right path. We can take detours, vacations, and diddle doddle or we can set our sights on the future we want and take the appropriate and most expeditious course.

MAY 26

WORD FOR TODAY: REVIVE

How many times in life have you needed to be revived? Maybe it wasn't a dramatic heart attack or even a fainting spell, but it occurred when you retreated into old habits and you needed a jump start to get back on track again.

I am reminded of when I was knitting a baby blanket. I'd get several rows done without incident and then I would discover I had made a mistake. I'd rip out all of the stitches until I got back to the mistake. I did this so often that my white yarn had become gray.

A meaning for revive is to restore to life or consciousness. When we know better, we do better. We can go on. We don't have to punish ourselves by berating our willpower or any lack of determination.

We regain life each day. Being revived doesn't have to be an earth shaking event. It is simply an awareness that three steps forward and two steps backwards is better than no step forward at all.

Tap into your inner strength and move forward. You have what it takes to succeed.

FROM DONUTS...TO POTATOES

MAY 27

WORD FOR TODAY: FAMILY

Families come in all sorts of configurations. Some families come by birth, some through adoption, some through fostering and some through marriage. But families are also groups of people who live, work, play or worship together.

Yesterday when we arrived at the home where we will be staying for the next three days (Air B & B), we were greeted by the Chinese homeowners. We were invited into their home, offered slippers in exchange for our shoes and shared a few niceties.

Language was somewhat strained but after I noticed a wall decoration stating "Christ is the head of this home" I told the Mrs. that we were Christians too. She responded "Well, then, we're sisters" and we exchanged hugs.

Breakfast is provided so I explained that we are plant eaters and that we had brought our own food. They seemed impressed that we liked vegetables.

At 11:30 we will be meeting my nephew Brian and his wife for lunch in San Diego. I love all forms of family including the "family" that has become a part of my journey. Tonight will be an opportunity to welcome new family members.

MAY 28

WORD FOR TODAY: GLOW

Glow little glowworm or light a candle or set your light upon a hill, or brighten the corner where you are.

We all have a story and Facebook is a great platform to do just that. Some people write books, get them published and the manuscript may be saved for eons; however, many stories do not get told for various reasons.

My father had a great 80th birthday party but what made it special in addition to so many friends being able to attend was the fact that in part of the program, my oldest brother interviewed him on the platform and my nephew videotaped it. What a treasure it is to have him tell his life story (or at least the parts he wanted to talk about) recorded for all of us to review many years after his death.

Do your children know your story? My cousin recently said to me "You don't know what I have been through" and that is true. I need to listen and hear her story too.

This journey is my story. It is my almost step by step declaration of what I am learning - how a plant based diet has taken me into a new and exciting chapter of my life - and the end is nowhere in sight (at least as far as I know)!

FROM DONUTS...TO POTATOES

MAY 29

WORD FOR TODAY: LATE

Maybe this is not really late, but delayed from when I usually write my post.

We often say, "Better late than never" but in this case, it has just been a busy day.

I met a woman in the hot tub today who never comes to our gym - she goes to another location but work was being done there, so she came to "our" gym.

Her mother from Meridian, Idaho came with her and we had a nice chat. Get this: The daughter is a RN and an Advice Nurse at Kaiser, is plant based and eager to help people adopt this way of eating too.

There are no accidents - whether you are late or on time. Special times just occur as naturally as they are supposed to.

Be in the flow of things in your life and look for the unexpected events that may help you reach your goal in ways you would not have guessed.

All things work together for good.

ESTHER LEBECK LOVERIDGE

MAY 30

WORD FOR TODAY: PHRASE

By following a plant based diet, it is possible to delay death and disability.

Ah, that is quite a contrast to what someone said to me when I explained how I had lost weight and regained my health by eliminating animal and dairy products. The response I got was "Well, you might as well lie down and die". I quickly added "Well, I'm not lying down and I'm not dying".

Phrases stick in our minds. Sometimes they direct our paths. I like the phrase "What we think about, we bring about". Yes, it is what we give our attention to that we can then manifest in our lives.

I also like Dr. McDougall's phrase - "The fat we eat is the fat we wear". I like what Chef AJ says, too: "If it is in your house, it will be in your mouth".

My phrase is "There is no guilt, only learning". Need support and encouragement? Come join "Esther's Nutritional Journey" here on Facebook.

_____

_____

_____

FROM DONUTS...TO POTATOES

MAY 31

WORD FOR TODAY: NETWORK

Guess why I chose that word today, ha. Anyway, we all have networks in our lives. Some are alive and some are dormant. If our electrical networks are to be strong, the energy must have a pathway to express itself.

I have so much energy since I started eating a plant based diet and it is imperative to me to have an avenue of expression to let it out so I have room for more energy to come in.

When we withhold our gifts or our talents, they too can get stagnant. Fresh air and resources help to keep the energy flowing.

The old adage - give and it will be given back to you is a real principal. We cannot hide our candle for without air, it will be extinguished.

Every person who throws you a smile is inviting you to smile back and the connection and current is continued.

Thank you for staying connected here with me. I love sharing stories and becoming aware of how all of you is determined to be your best.

_____
_____
_____
_____

JUNE 1

WORD FOR TODAY: REVELATION

Revelations come to us in the night. When we are quiet and ready to listen, we have an opportunity to get to know ourselves at a deeper level.

What I have been learning lately is that there is no limit to what we can do once we set our minds to it. It is all mental. Without a dream, a goal, a purpose and a desire, we will be stagnant. Sometimes it feels safe to stay in our comfy zone. We know the rules, have friends who support us there and we don't really have to think.

Thinking gives us a chance to re-evaluate what rules we want to follow. We get to choose what is working for us and implement changes into our daily practice.

Today I received a revelation from a great great niece. Can you imagine how it feels to really be an elder in my family? Subsequent generations have not grown up with our restrictions and they are ready to grow and change the world.

What you need to know will be revealed to you. Trust your intuition. Test it. Try it out. Learn for yourself what works and then follow your dream.

_____

_____

_____

_____

FROM DONUTS...TO POTATOES

JUNE 2

WORD FOR TODAY: DANGEROUS

Have you ever been told you were dangerous? How did it make you feel? Did you feel like you needed to change, adapt a different behavior, soften your approach or did it make you feel empowered because what you were saying challenged the status quo?

What is danger to one may simply be an opportunity to reexamine our belief systems. Many of us do not want to think or even doubt what we have been taught. Who wants to "rock the boat"?

Nevertheless, it is important for all of us to be congruent in what we say we believe and what we do. It is in being in alignment with our body, mind and soul that we create an energy that can change our world.

When we are challenged, it is simply a chance to dig deeper into our roots, bring up what is true for us, add a little air (understanding) to it and continue to spread love to all.

Be strong. Be willing to listen. Re-evaluate often and then proceed with great vigor. When I use the word "vigor", I am reminded of President Kennedy.

The bottom line is to have support as you venture into new pathways.

_____

_____

_____

_____

JUNE 3

WORD FOR TODAY: APPROVAL

Life is often a give and take proposition. In giving, we receive but not always from the same source that we gave to. It can be a big circle as love circulates around the world.

But what do you give away in order to obtain approval? Do you give up a critical part of yourself in order to fit into your social, family, church, synagogue, mosque or neighborhood circle?

Who would you be if you didn't feel like you had to fit in? Would we all still be the same - that is congruent with whom we are? How much does membership in a particular organization require conformity to some issues you do not hold to be true? Do you pretend, keep quiet or dare to speak your truth?

Yes, getting approval from people who are important to us in our lives is important - it feels good, makes us feel like we are part of a community and that we are not the odd man/woman out.

But being aware of the internal cost it could be to our innermost being is something to consider. It is a real gift to find a place where you are accepted no matter what - where diversity is honored and respected and where you also accept others on their own journey.

FROM DONUTS...TO POTATOES

JUNE 4

WORD FOR TODAY: OUT

Have you ever had a coming out party? My guess is that when most people come out of their past, there is no party. What actually may happen is that the news just gets leaked out in a small way at first, to test the reaction of whoever is trusted most.

Once there is a sense of safety, our willingness to acknowledge our change gets expanded to an even wider audience. There may be some people with whom we never feel free to be totally ourselves. Perhaps that is okay. Why share the gems about us that are so precious with others who may not be in a place yet to receive it?

We get to be the judge of just how far we want to come out. Coming out in a nutritional way may mean explaining to others that you no longer eat the way you used to. It doesn't mean the end of relationships, but it does ask for respect and support. If that is not given, we have new information with which to evaluate the value of such non-supportive relationships. In the meantime, we need to make sure we are supportive of their life choices.

I remember playing hide and seek as a child, or was it Ollie Ollie Oxen Free when we would holler "Come out, come out, wherever you are" to end the game.

Whether you are in or out, you are a manifestation of something very special. Only you can contribute what is yours to give to the world. As my brother Leroy Lebeck recently preached "Stir up the gift that is within you". It is all there.

_____

_____

_____

_____

JUNE 5
WORD FOR TODAY: GAMEPLAN

I was going to name this post "Rules" but since I don't like rules, I changed the name.

What is important is that we have a need, define it, establish goals and write them down. When I started this journey, I used a sticky note on my computer to state that in one year, I wanted to lose 70 pounds, get off all of my medications, and even improve my eyesight. Why I thought of that, I don't remember but every time I sat at my computer, I could read my goals.

As I faced my crisis of having to lose 70 pounds before I could be referred to Orthopedics for possible knee replacements, I got serious. I like choices and at that point, I was stuck with the pain and loss of mobility.

You can go to YouTube to see "Esther Loveridge's Drastic Weight Loss Secret" if you want to be refreshed on my story.

I want to advise newcomers that I am just like most of you - I wanted to lose weight and getting healthy was not even my priority.

Health must come first if we are to make a lifetime commitment to eating to live because the weight will take care of itself to the extent that we are close followers of the plan. I followed "The McDougall Program for Maximum Weight Loss" book by Dr. John McDougall because I did not want to play around (plus, my friend gave me the book so it was free).

Esther's Nutritional Journey on Facebook is about my journey and my passion for helping others realize that they too can whip the food addictions that drive us crazy, keep us tied to poor habits and destructive thoughts.

Each day our commitments get reinforced with every step we take towards recovery and as I say quite often..."There is no guilt - only learning".

FROM DONUTS...TO POTATOES

_____

_____

_____

JUNE 6

WORD FOR TODAY: WAVES

Listening to waves was a nice experience last night. No, we did not have the windows open nor were we on the beach. There is a gizmo in this hotel room where one can listen to waves, thunder, white light, rain or "summer night" whatever that is.

In our lives, there are incidents which also cause waves. Waves can disturb us; make us feel insecure or uncertain. Waves crashing on the rocks at the beach are beautiful. Waves even serve in the U.S. Military.

We wave goodbye to our friends and loved ones as we depart from each other's company and sometimes even blow kisses as part of that waving.

So, how does all of this relate to my journey on Facebook? I just want to say how much I enjoy being here with you. In some groups, the waves come crashing down on each other as hairs are split, sometimes people major in minors and certain belief systems about food are held onto so tightly. I like the simplicity of Dr. McDougall's messages "It's the food" or "The fat you eat is the fat you wear" and also "People love to hear good news about their bad habits". Of course we do - it helps us to think we are not alone, that we have the "right" answer or that it is hard to accept that certain studies that support bad habits are often created by the industry that promotes poor health. It has been said, "Follow the money".

Follow your heart, learn all you can, treat yourself like the royalty you are and adapt as you go along with what works for you. This is your life. You get to choose which "sounds" you want to hear.

_____
_____
_____

JUNE 7

WORD FOR TODAY: LONGTERM

When traveling, we used to consider parking in the long-term parking lot in order to get cheaper parking rates but now we have a friend who is our personal UBER driver!

Seniors often stay in long-term living facilities - hoping that it will be a long-term experience.

What behaviors do we incorporate into our lives that will give us long-term results?

We are following a healthy eating plan for the long run. This is not a get quick weight loss scheme which we have all tried in the past. Sure, we lost weight but just as soon as we incorporated the food back into our diets which caused the weight gain in the first place, we gained it all back and usually more.

So, what is the answer to maintaining the weight loss we achieve by eating a plant based diet? The answer is forgiveness. We must forgive the small transgressions we make from time to time because when we average them out over the long run, they are nothing.

What has started a downward spiral in the past is magnifying the bad choice by saying things like "Well, I have already messed

FROM DONUTS...TO POTATOES

up this day so I might as well wait until. —— to start again" and that time lapse is easy to extend.

Someone once said, after you screw up, make the next bite compliant. I think it is healthier to change our thinking from "cheating" to non-compliant. So I say things like, just make your next bite a potato.

No guilt - only learning.

_____

_____

_____

_____

JUNE 8

WORD FOR TODAY: COST

What does it cost to eat a whole food plant based breakfast?

This morning I computed what I paid for a pound of beans, about $1.05 and .69 cents a pound for brown rice however, when I cooked 4 cups of beans and 2 cups of brown rice, the yield was a gallon of beans and rice "soup" at 13 cents a cup.

So my breakfast came out to 13 cents!

That sure leaves lots of room in the food budget for fresh fruit and vegetables. When we go to WINCO or Costco, I am amazed at the number of the aisles we do not even have to entertain. I walk past the meat department and tell the animals I am thinking of them. I pass the bakery departments and say, "Not my food". And then there are the large dairy cases filled with food which do not appeal to me at all.

My former doctor said "If I told people to eat like you, they would say it's not real food"... He went on to say, "Besides, there are no health food stores in this area" to which I replied "All you need is the produce department of any grocery store". End of relationship.

So, when we do a cost benefit analysis to the changes that we are making in our lives and the lives of others, remember that you have to have a vision of the "promised land" before you have a desire to cross over. The benefits of eating this way must outweigh (no pun intended) the cost to our health of doing otherwise.

Be a visionary.

_____

_____

_____

_____

JUNE 9

WORD FOR TODAY: POSSIBLE

What is possible in your life? Are there any limitations? If so, is that limitation talk coming from you or maybe others? If you are listening to any negative messages, I ask "Why"?

When I was a young girl, maybe about 8-10 years old, my parents, very devout Christians, took me to hear Oral Roberts who had come to Sacramento to conduct a tent revival. I wasn't sick, but I must have gotten into his healing line in order to have him autograph my Bible.

I still remember the song that was sung over and over as people moved through the line to be prayed for. The words of the song still resonate with me to this day - "Only believe, only believe, all things are possible, only believe".

FROM DONUTS...TO POTATOES

So what is holding us back from believing that we can achieve our optimal health and vitality from eating a plant based diet? Who contradicts the evidence? Who says it is not possible? Who says it is? We get to choose which voices to listen to and once we believe that which was always ours to have, we can manifest it in our lives.

Correction: I just went to look for Oral Robert's autograph and it was not there. I did see Billy Graham's autograph so maybe I just had Oral Roberts sign my autograph book. Now I'll have to look for that, ha.

___

___

___

___

JUNE 10

WORD FOR TODAY: COLORFUL

This word just came to me so I jumped out of bed to write before it disappeared into the air and space of non-remembering.

On a plant based diet, we are encouraged to eat the colors of the rainbow - red and yellow, dark and light and make a plate of oh so bright.

But what, I ask, about the color of my friends? Do they also reflect the colors of red and yellow, black and white?

How about the diversity of my political and religious friends? Is there a broad spectrum there too or am I preoccupied with only the colors that reflect me?

Am I sterile and boring or do I embrace the totality of humanity as it is afforded to me?

There is richness in participating in all of the colors of life. None are created to be ignored. We are all one yet variety is the spice of life.

As I create my plate, I want to be inclusive - honor all faiths, parties, nationalities and those with various sexual expressions. Everything may not agree with my palate at first, but I have learned that experimentation has led me to new delights and discoveries. I become what I consume.

_____

_____

_____

_____

JUNE 11

WORD FOR TODAY: SAFE

There is a direct correlation between the contents of your kitchen and your success in following a plant based diet.

Our success in eating healthy food rises exponentially according to what is available in our home.

When we create a safe environment, we will eat what is available. We are less likely to go out and find something off program if it takes just too much time and effort to get it.

It takes quite a bit of commitment and "seriousness" to just clean out the cupboards, refrigerator and freezer. To the extent that one makes that commitment, they are taking a big step. It will only hurt for a little while.

Most of us don't want to throw away food yet we will throw it

FROM DONUTS...TO POTATOES

into our bodies and think nothing of it. And if we truly believe it is not fit for human consumption, the garbage is the best place for it.

If we can see some food as toxic or poison and not fit for our bodies, we will have come a long way to putting action behind our goals.

When in doubt, toss it out. Be safe.

_____

_____

_____

JUNE 12

WORD FOR TODAY: ANNIVERSARY

Back in 1909, my mother came to this planet and blessed so many people. She was named Mary Beatrice Kearns and was here (on earth and then in this house until the day she made her transition at the age of 90. I remember her great hospitality - always having people stay with us and always willing to entertain visitors. She believed in 3 F's: Be Firm, Fair and Friendly. She told us kids "Just keep on keeping on".

Next month will be the third anniversary of starting Dr. McDougall's Maximum Weight Loss Program in 2016 and I am happy for every month I get under my belt. Still down 130 pounds.

Anniversaries help us remember our past and be happy about the progress we have made on our journey. It can be a way of measuring the way we have exercised the muscle of commitment and determination. Even momentary digressions are not valleys but simply a pot hole in the road. We feel the bump and go on.

ESTHER LEBECK LOVERIDGE

Life is a series of lessons to be learned. Anniversaries are like passing from one grade to the next. Recently, my youngest granddaughter passed the 6th grade. Today is the 64th anniversary of when I passed the 6th grade. It is fun to remember where we have been and be thankful for all we are learning.

_____

_____

_____

JUNE 13

WORD FOR TODAY: CLAY

Are you the clay or the potter or both? We are malleable. We are influenced by our parents, our peers our teachers and mentors. We respond to those we trust - sometimes, blindly.

But then there comes a time in our lives when we decide we are the potter. We are the ones who choose to think or not. We are the ones to engage our imagination as we forge ahead to our goals and dreams. We are the ones who get to step out of the box and try something new.

Yes, it is true, sometimes we try something on to see if it fits us and make decisions accordingly; however, even if thinking a certain way no longer fits us, we have the opportunity to change the direction of our sails and head in a different direction. As it turns out, so called "mistakes" were not the end of the world. We were just going in a direction which no longer served us.

After a lifetime of trying on the various diets, I never succeeded in maintaining any kind of permanent weight loss. Today marks 35 months I have been following The McDougall Maximum Weight Loss Program and I am sticking to it. It works, has worked and is still working and will continue to work for the rest of my life, but the even more incredible part is that I am no longer taking any medication, have reversed the need to have knee and eye surgery and have even eliminated the need to wear glasses at 75 years of age without having my cataracts removed!

Is it for you? Who knows? But the truth of Dr. McDougall's message resonates with me. If you don't like your story line, create a new one.

_____

_____

_____

JUNE 14

WORD FOR TODAY: TOUCH

When was the last time you were touched? Maybe a song touched your soul. Maybe it was a movie, a book, a telephone call, a special meal, or maybe just the smile from a stranger.

It is said that our biggest organ is the skin that covers our bodies and yet there are many people who go a long time without a personal touch.

I remember being with my Grandmother Lebeck just before she died and the best thing I could do for her was to just sit on the floor of that hospital room and reach up and hold her hand.

Many people are starving and just as many people are hungry

for the touch of someone - to know that they exist, that they are important, and that they are seen.

I got tired of creating stress in people's lives when I was a Revenue Officer for the I.R.S. and decided to make a 180 degree change in my life by becoming a Massage Therapist. It was a healthy transition for me.

The next time you think you are hungry, check your touch "thermometer". It may be that you are not yearning for food.

I remember my father, who was a Gideon, give a talk titled "Reach out and touch your world". Our world is where we live. Thank you, Dad.

JUNE 15

WORD FOR TODAY: LETTERS

As children, we learn our "letters". We sing songs about the ABCs. Then, as adults, we often educate ourselves to add letters to the end of our name. It is easy to evaluate the college experience of others by the kinds of letters that follow their name.

Letters of the past are held to be almost sacred. We can't go back and retrieve the messages in them if they have not been saved. Fortunately, my father saved the love letters between him and my mother written in the 1920's. He also saved letters between my mother and her parents who lived far away in South Dakota. They were smart enough back then to make a carbon copy of the letters

FROM DONUTS...TO POTATOES

mom wrote so we had both sides of the conversation. And yes, I have saved letters too.

Yesterday, I wrote a letter to Dr. McDougall:

..."Yes you are amazing to have held the course for decades knowing (not just believing) that you found the Starch Solution to health and obesity.

I promised early on that I was going to put your program to the test and that if it worked, I'd give you all of the credit.

Be well and know your efforts are affecting our whole planet. In less than two years over 1,100 people have asked to join my group and they represent countries all over the world.

With a thankful heart I remain your student."

Esther

_____

_____

_____

_____

JUNE 16

WORD FOR TODAY: FATHER

Albert J. Lebeck was my father. He lived from September 28, 1907 - March 13, 1996 but that little dash between his dates is what I want to speak about.

That dash is the period of time he spent here on earth, but he is not gone. You see, he had four children and we all have continued to manifest him in our lives in the time since his transition.

Every time I hear a train, I think of him. He was raised next to a railroad track and died at the Southern Pacific Train Depot while pulling himself up into the train for another ride.

I exhibit many of his traits - love of photos, family history, genealogy, travel and food.

Some people have never met their biological father and that is why fathers come from all kinds of sources. Maybe you never heard your father say "I love you". I'm not so sure I did. But his actions spoke loud enough for me to believe he did.

I don't recall ever taking a walk with my dad or sitting on his lap. (I do remember being laid over his lap for a spanking when I misbehaved in church), but one day, I went for what I wanted - a photo of me sitting on his lap. Sometimes we have to be creative and recognize what we need and go after it. I think he enjoyed it too.

What you want, wants you. Take action.

_____

_____

_____

_____

JUNE 17

WORD FOR TODAY: CREATE

All of my life, I have thought of God as the creator of the universe but recently I have come in touch with the idea that all of us have the power to create peace, harmony, love and health in our own lives.

If it is true that we are what we eat and we are the only ones putting food into our mouths, we now become the creators of the body we want to have. We also get to create a clean environment - one where healthy food dominates the scene thus making choices a lot easier.

We get to create the mood in our homes by what we listen to. I know when I put happy music on my computer, I just want to dance around the house and it helps me to want to get up and move and get chores done.

What we think about, we bring about so what we think about is critical to creating a healthy lifestyle. Do we glamorize the past foods we used to eat or do we focus on the benefits of eating whole, nutritious food?

Each day our thoughts lead us to creating a new world around us. When we are busy creating a positive world, we have less time to feel like a victim.

_____

_____

_____

_____

JUNE 18

WORD FOR TODAY: PREFER

What do you prefer? I prefer some foods over others. When it is cool, I prefer soups and lots of starches. When it is hot, I seem to prefer salads.

I prefer sweet potatoes over everything else. I find them to be as delicious as when I used to like pecan pie.

I prefer sweet onions so it is clear to me that I still have a desire to enjoy sweet foods - it's just that they are not as sweet as the ones I used to eat.

It is important to enjoy what you prefer from the four food groups: vegetables, fruit, grains and legumes/beans. Enjoy what you choose to eat. It is okay to be repetitious. It is even good to be boring. After all, it is just fuel, not a holiday.

The same idea applies to exercise. Do what you prefer to do. It doesn't have to be strenuous or hard. Just move your body.

Have a preference for a certain kind of music? Honor it and let it take you to new heights. Soar with the sounds. Feel the vibrations and shake off whatever binds you.

_____

_____

_____

_____

JUNE 19

WORD FOR TODAY: DIFFICULTY

When we face difficulty, what do we do? Do we choose to be a victim of our circumstances, choose to see it as a challenge, a lesson to learn or curl up in a corner and think it will pass?

Maybe we digress from finding a solution by engaging in eating. Surely that has been a momentary diversion in the past but did it ever solve a problem or did that just buy us more time to dwell in the misery or maybe process how we were going to proceed?

Difficulties come, and they will, it is part of life. I know when we have gone to the emergency room at Kaiser, we were always asked to identify the level of pain. "On a scale of one to ten, where would you say your pain level is?"

My guess is that often the pain level goes down once we are in the care of professionals and our fear has had a chance to subside. Help is on the way.

Perhaps what is really important is how we choose to think about the difficulty we face. Do we magnify the problem and give it a 10 or do we have faith in ourselves that we have the means and the intelligence to put it in its proper perspective as we tackle the issue one step at a time?

___

JUNE 20

WORD FOR TODAY: CONFORM

I wonder if conform means going along with the crowd, doing what is popular or maybe it can mean having a plan - that is adhering to structure or a prescribed way of achieving success?

When we feel good about ourselves, it is much easier to also accept a new path, one we haven't tried before just for the fun of it - to see if it fits us and is successful.

When I read "The McDougall Program for Maximum Weight Loss" book given to me by my close friend, it simply resonated with me. Yes, it was different. I no longer had to use portion control, count calories (although I did at first), nor did I have to weigh my food unless I wanted to demonstrate how much food I can eat and not gain weight.

I feel good; I love this way of life. I am so happy for my renewed health. Is this the healthiest diet on the planet? I think so. Test it for yourself. I haven't heard of other diets improving eyesight at the age of 75 while still having cataracts and no longer needing to wear glasses. That's pretty special not to mention being off all meds as well. I call it the miracle diet - it got rid of all of my pain and my need for knee replacements as well as eliminated the need for eye surgery. Weight loss is simply the bonus. Go for your health first. Your happy weight will follow.

___

___

___

JUNE 21

WORD FOR TODAY: ELEPHANT

I love elephants. Maybe it is because they just lumber along, minding their own business, loving each other and mourning when a member of their tribe dies.

But then, again, maybe I relate to them because they are baggy, wrinkled and have long eye lashes.

What I really want to talk about is the "elephant in the room" and that is, "Do we love ourselves"?

It is great to have goals, but how do we feel about ourselves today...just as we are? Are we thankful for a heart that keeps beating no matter what? Do we realize we are made of wonderful "stuff" that just keeps trying to heal regardless of how abusive we have been? We are made up of mind, body and soul and just because our weight has gotten out of control it doesn't mean all of us are off kilter.

FROM DONUTS...TO POTATOES

I remember as a kid never feeling like I "arrived". If I took two steps forward, it seemed like the "carrot" just got raised - now there was another level to achieve. But wait...we are the ones holding the carrot. We can love ourselves with our strengths and weaknesses as we realize we are okay, just the way we are.

Who we ARE, never changes.

_____

_____

_____

JUNE 22

WORD FOR TODAY: WILLINGNESS

Some of us are convinced, some are almost persuaded and some of us are willing.

It is important to identify what we are willing to do.

While it is true that jumping into this new lifestyle 99% creates the biggest change and greatest results, we need to consider what someone is willing to do. That gives them the power to decide for themselves the course they want to take.

For some, changing their lifestyle takes some thinking, planning and deciding to determine if they believe that the freedom and power they gain by being in charge of their own life will outweigh the perceived pleasure of staying static.

I want to be more patient with everyone around me. Yes, I wish everyone could jump on the bandwagon and experience life like I do but that is the joy of having individual thought and learning about one's purpose in life. It comes through careful thought.

Do we want to just live longer or do we want to enjoy all of our days? We get to decide how much we want to invest in this new lifestyle and that is exciting.

_____

_____

_____

_____

JUNE 23

WORD FOR TODAY: GATHER

We gather our thoughts as we organize our day.

This is a day many gather together - you know, where two or three are gathered together.

It is fun to gather around a fireplace - well, maybe not in the summer unless one is out camping.

Songs I like talk about gathering by a river but you know what? What is important is that we just gather. Community is important. We get energy from one another, new ideas, and support, love, encouragement and learning lessons. "No man is an island" and it is through mutual sharing that we realize there is a community of fellow believers out there who want us to be our best, which see the best in us and affirm that the best is yet to be.

Maybe some of us gather around the television and get sucked into what is going on in our "outer" world but I think what is really important is to go within, know ourselves, live up to our own goals and thereby be a light to those who might otherwise embrace fear.

Last night, we attended a gathering of beautiful people. Tony and Pete invited us to join in with Melissa and Carmen, Andrea and

FROM DONUTS...TO POTATOES

Jerry, Elisabeth and Gloria and Caren and Bruce - all connected through our mutual retirement.

Enjoy your support team.

_____

_____

_____

JUNE 24

WORD FOR TODAY: JOY

Joy comes in the morning. Joy comes in a cup of kava for some people. Joy comes when I hold a baby.

What is joy? Perhaps it is a feeling of fullness, satisfaction and even completeness.

I think it is important to be aware of what brings joy into our lives and one way to know when we are experiencing joy is when we smile. What is going on at that time? Is it being connected to someone else or perhaps an idea?

Sometimes I say, "Whatever rings your dinger" or I might ask "What turns you on"? It is in acknowledging those experiences that we can lead ourselves into more joy and maybe even into finding our purpose in life.

When it comes to making lifestyle changes, there is a hurdle. Until one makes the change, there is no way to know the joy that will follow. Sometimes we require a crisis but just maybe, we can love ourselves enough to take a step of faith and test it for ourselves.

The joy that follows is what makes following a plant based diet sustainable.

JUNE 25

WORD FOR TODAY: REAL

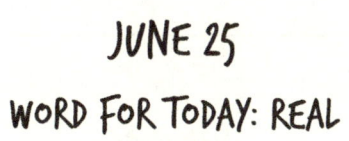

We used to sing the song about something being real and to have "Woman's World Magazine" put my story in their July 25th release of the August 5th, 2019 issue does validate the process.

When I chose to go on this journey, it was because I was in pain. Yes, switching to a whole food plant based diet has been a journey of perseverance, determination and dedication over the past three years, but the rewards have been more than I ever dreamed possible.

I still have a hard time getting my head around the fact that I am 76 years old and have NO pain in my body - anywhere. I am off all medications, have avoided knee and eye surgeries and don't even need glasses anymore in spite of the fact that I still have cataracts! If that isn't a testimony to what eating plants will do for any of us, I rest my case.

I can tell my story and inspire others, but how do we move beyond inspiration and motivation to teach others that joy awaits them on the other side of one of the biggest decisions they will ever make? I'm still looking for that answer.

I guess the real answer is that it takes a leap of faith to try something new before knowing that it is real. To convince someone to let go of the past and step out into a new life before they know

FROM DONUTS...TO POTATOES

how wonderful it is going to be is the real challenge. What have you got to lose? The side benefit for me was losing 130 pounds.

_____

_____

_____

JUNE 26

WORD FOR TODAY: WHOLE

I like to eat "whole" food.

So what is whole? It used to mean that when I ate Ben and Jerry's ice cream, I ate the whole pint. I shared it if I had to, but left to my own devices, I'd eat the entire pint in one setting.

Now, whole means eating food closer to its original form. I like to eat steel cut oatmeal which is less processed. I like to eat whole fruit. Yes, juice can be nourishing, but the whole fruit yields fiber and is more satisfying and filling.

I do take photos of what I eat and one can usually tell what I am eating simply by looking at the food which is visually identifiable.

I also want to be whole and that means balancing my life with healthy food, spiritual values, exercise, and the love of community and friends.

We can be whole. We can be made new. We can restore our bodies to the healthiness of our former days by eating a whole food plant based diet.

Everything we eat either contributes to our health or to our diseases. We get to choose.

ESTHER LEBECK LOVERIDGE

_____

_____

_____

_____

JUNE 27

WORD FOR TODAY: MODEL

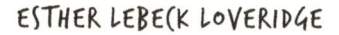

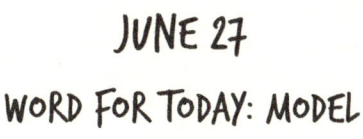

Guys are usually interested in the model of cars. Women are sometimes fascinated by fashion models and of course that statement does reek of stereotyping.

As it turns out, we are all models. Our children watch us. If one is a school teacher, their behaviors are often modeled. Sports heroes get mimicked as well.

Yesterday I got to experience what it must feel like to be a model for a short period of time. Well, actually, the photo shoot for the Woman's World Magazine took a total of three hours - one hour for the make-up and then two hours for the photo shoot.

During the makeup session, I felt like my face was a canvas as the artist applied the "paint". Grandma Kearns used to say "Women wear paint to make them what they ain't".

I had no idea of the precision of the four photographers' work. The setting had to be just right, the lighting was important and then there were the strong winds we had which required a lot of patience for the outdoor photos. And then, I had to learn how to stand and pose like all of our granddaughters do on Facebook.

Equipment is so technical now. They had a computer set up which showed the photos taken by the long lens camera and even the magazine's photo editor in New Jersey was able to see the work as it developed from a live feed.

FROM DONUTS...TO POTATOES

It will be interesting to see how the photos turn out. I learned yesterday that the magazine cost $2.50 and is published weekly. The issue date will be August 5th with a release date of July 25, 2019.

This was an exciting day and a happy way to spread the good results of following a plant-based diet. Model what you believe.

_____

_____

_____

_____

JUNE 28

WORD FOR TODAY: PROMPTING

Have you ever been tempted to do something and then your thought process was interrupted by a small inner voice telling you to do otherwise?

Maybe it is like being in a play where the actor forgets his/her lines and someone on the sideline whispers words to help them continue.

I think the small inner voice that comes to us may be a warning or it could be prompting us to push ahead in our plans but the important thing is to take time to listen and evaluate for ourselves.

Some call these promptings "red flags". I remember I was out for dinner with a friend years ago and he told me how much money he owed the IRS. Yes, that was kind of like a red flag - at least something to pay attention to.

Even as we choose the best foods for our body, we find ourselves in situations where one little voice tells us to go easy but another voice says "One bite won't hurt". We know which voice has our best interest in mind and ultimately that is the voice we want to nourish. The best advice may be to step away from the situation and delay a decision until we are sure which action we want to take.

I want to listen to my own prompts. They are my guiding lights as I navigate my journey.

_____

_____

_____

JUNE 29

WORD FOR TODAY: ASPIRE

There were so many words floating around in my head this morning but I liked the image that came to my mind when I thought of the word aspire. You know – a-spire?

When we have aspirations, it is kind of like establishing goals. I remember Grandma Kearns asking me "What is your gift?" As a young girl, I had no idea. Back then, it seemed like the choices were limited. As girls, we aspired to be a teacher, a mother, a typist etc. I remember in the 7th grade, my aptitude test revealed I would do well in clerical work. I wonder how many categories were even identified back then. Would any girl have been told her test results identified her as a future President of the United States?

I also remember feeling less than my contemporaries when we were assigned to "groups" X, Y or Z as we moved on to high school. You knew if you were an X you were college material. I was assigned to the Y group and I guess that was kind of like being in the middle of something and students that were identified as belonging to the

FROM DONUTS...TO POTATOES

Z group may have felt that some kind of manual work would be their forte. (What would we do without the workers in our world?) And furthermore, how often did those classifications limit what we dreamed we could do?

Spires are pointed objects often gracing tall buildings. They get narrow as they extend to their highest point and they always draw our attention as we focus on the tip of its slender beauty. We gaze upwards and wonder just how high we can go? The sky is the limit... or is it?

_____

_____

_____

JUNE 30

WORD FOR TODAY: HAVE

We hear about the "haves" and the "have-nots" and place value accordingly. But what do we really have?

We think we have owned so much. We who are fortunate, have a roof over our heads, we may even have a car to get us around. We are thankful to have someone to love and it is a blessing to have food on the table.

But who are we without the things we have accumulated and maybe even had to put in storage? Are we more than all of our collective goods?

I've been thinking about Dr. McDougall and his family. They lost what most of us would call "everything" in the Santa Rosa fire in 2018. They were awakened in the middle of the night and told to "get out". Yes, a swimming pool remains but all else, even their beloved cat Einstein who lost his life is gone.

So who is Dr. McDougall now? Is he a man who had a nice comfortable home and all of his material possessions or is he a man who survived and continues to tell his story, get back on YouTube and help all of us find our way? We know the answer. He is about more than seeking fame or material wealth. He is teaching what he has learned in his 50 years of being a medical doctor. He has not hung up his shingle. He is still himself, revealing his truth and hoping to persuade the rest of us to know how we too can have good health.

Thank you, Dr. McDougall for saving my life through your book "The McDougall Program for Maximum Weight Loss".

JULY 1
WORD FOR TODAY: JEALOUSY

This morning, Ben and I had an early morning discussion about how easy it is to withhold love and support from a friend or family member if the relationship is tinged with jealousy.

Jealousy can raise its ugly head when we are not feeling very good about ourselves. Maybe we resent how smoothly someone else's life is going. Maybe we still get caught up in the game of one-upmanship where we can't rejoice in the good news from another until we reach that point in ourselves where we feel good.

So, how do we feel better about ourselves? I think we start by acknowledging our gifts, our talents, our kindness to others and any unselfish deed we can accomplish. Be your own cheerleader. I find that when I focus on what is on my own plate, meaning, how well I accomplish the tasks that are right before me, I feel better. It is safer to compete with who I was yesterday than to look to someone I greatly admire and wonder why I am not like them.

One of the best ways to feel better about myself is to be in control of what I put in my mouth. It is also a way to put myself down when I make less than best choices. That's where forgiveness comes in. It is not good or bad. It is simply a choice with consequences.

No guilt-only learning.

_____
_____
_____
_____

FROM DONUTS...TO POTATOES

JULY 2
WORD FOR TODAY: DICTATE

I grew up working in my parents' business "Lebeck's Business Equipment Company" and one of the worst jobs I had was listening to my father dictate instructions to me on the Stenocord Dictating Machine. He would dictate letters etc. but the problem was it was hard to understand him. His diction was not clear and I'd have to repeatedly hit the foot pedal to go back and listen to him over and over until I finally understood what he was saying.

Dr. McDougall reminds me a lot of my father even though he is younger than me. He has written over 13 books, has a free website where one can search for answers to any questions and has appeared on many webinars telling us that starch is the solution.

We often think we know better or that we can take short cuts or that just maybe another doctor who tells us good news about our bad habits is worth listening to. It is as though we, in this modern age, still choose to "wander in the dessert" because we choose not to listen.

Sometimes I wish I could be a dictator. I'd love to save people years of wandering, years of being in poor health, years of yo-yo dieting and years of illness - both physical and mental. Since I have reached the "promised land" - the place where all of the puzzle pieces fall into place, where health is restored, where the solution has been found, it takes so much patience to remember that in July of 2016, I was in the same place.

Now I listen to Dr. McDougall over and over and his diction is clear. It is to the point. It is stark reality. He knows what he is talking about. I do not have to question what he is trying to say.

Today, I am putting on my dictator hat and telling everyone who is open to follow the success I have had to listen to his presentations.

If I were a teacher, it would be required "listening". If you don't have his book, don't worry. Everything is in his presentations.

We live in a democracy. The choice is yours.

_____

_____

_____

JULY 3

WORD FOR TODAY: CONNECTION

I have an old computer. I have a relatively new printer and neither of that matters if I don't have a connection.

Often we are required to not only make the connection but to have a password.

So, what is the password that keeps us connected to others?

Is it love, need, dependency, support or something else? Does it matter? The point is that being connected is a good thing. It is through sharing the ups and downs of life that we get encouragement from each other and learn that we are not alone. The battle is not just ours. It is a collective battle to learn and exercise the truth we receive that will led us to good health.

It may only take one person to give us the support that will lead us forward. It may be a relative, a friend or maybe even a good doctor who we follow on You Tube.

Yes, for some, connections are made through the internet and I give thanks for the connections I have made with my friends and my new friends who have joined Esther's Nutritional Journey.

FROM DONUTS...TO POTATOES

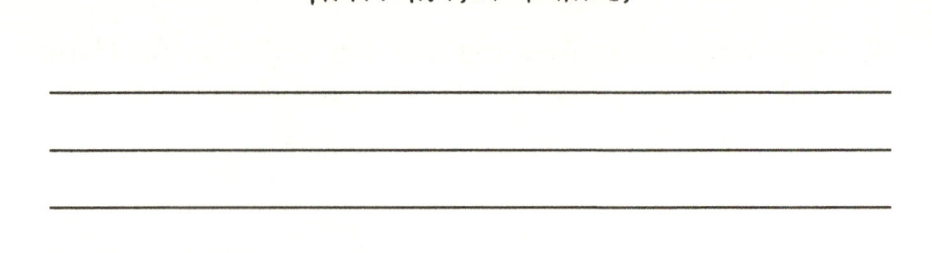

JULY 4

WORD FOR TODAY: FREEDOM

In the United States, the Fourth of July is celebrated in many ways. There are often BBQs, parties, parades, and of course fireworks.

As a kid, I loved fireworks. I'd gaze into the sky and marvel at their beauty as they exploded into the air. There would be one wow after another until finally there would be a big explosion at the end.

Now we stay at home and watch celebrations on TV with great musical presentations along with televised fireworks.

Meanwhile, families gather all the way down our street and create their own firework shows well into the night.

These days, I mostly think about the freedom I have from food addictions. It's hard to explain that while we need food to survive, there are many of us who are food addicts and find it difficult to be moderate in our choices. I feel as free from my old "haunts" as if I have been freed from drugs and it is a big joy in my life to celebrate that freedom today and every day.

Free at last. Thank God, I am now free.

JULY 5
WORD FOR TODAY: CARE

Care seems to be a word that implies action. We can care about someone or something without doing anything about it but when action accompanies our heart's desires, we have better results.

Everyone cares about their health. All of us want to be healthy but to everything there is a cost. There may or may not be a financial expense, but certainly there is a cost in terms of how much energy we want to expend to get the desired outcome.

There is no doubt about it. When we make life style changes, we must invest a lot of energy in order to change old habits and create our strategy for developing new ones.

Sometimes we get scared into making choices. We may be faced with a life threatening disease at which time, we usually do seriously look at all of our options for improving our health.

But just maybe, all we want is to simply look better. I had wanted to look better for years and in an effort to do so, I tried every fad diet that came down the pipeline. Yes, I did feel like I cared about my body and I certainly thought I was adding a lot of effort to the cause but no matter what I did, it was not sustainable. Did I really want to eat that way for the rest of my life and if so, were any of those fad diets really healthy for my body?

The tipping point finally came in the form of pain. Looking good was no longer the goal. Now I had to face my health issues. Thank goodness I woke up and discovered how to care for my body, heal

FROM DONUTS...TO POTATOES

food borne diseases, eliminate the need for surgery and discover energy and a clear mind. Yes, plants were the answer.

_____

_____

_____

JULY 6

WORD FOR TODAY: SMELL

Smell is an interesting sense that I don't think about very often, but this morning, I awoke at 5:45 to the smell that emanated from the kitchen. I could smell the onions that Ben was sautéing while he chopped vegetables for his veggie soup.

As I lay there in bed, thinking about the word smell, I went back to my childhood when I'd take an afternoon nap on my father's bed. I could smell his essence on his pillow and found that to be comforting.

Mom never had a smell. She didn't splurge on fancy name brand cologne so when we were taking care of her the last three and a half years of her life, I bought her a bottle of RED cologne. That became her "signature" smell. She made her transition 20 years ago and I still sprits some on me when I want to feel her close.

We all know the aroma of coffee, bacon on a campfire, bread baking and now, it's Ben's soup. I have heard it said that we eat with our nose but when we have a stuffy nose, food just isn't as appealing.

Now my favorite smell is what escapes from the oven when I

roast sweet potatoes. I don't really need to set a timer because the fragrance lets me know when they are ready.

_____

_____

_____

_____

JULY 7

WORD FOR TODAY: FEAR

What am I afraid of?

When I do have fearful thoughts, what do I do? I go back to clichés I learned as a child - "What you fear has come upon you". But, on the other hand, I think of "Fear not"...or more recently "What we think about, we bring about".

The encouraging thing is that we get to choose our thoughts. My Grandma Kearns used to say "You can't keep the birds from flying overhead, but you can keep them from building a nest in your hair".

So, when I feel afraid, I try to sit there for awhile - wonder what I am afraid of and just feel it. Then I move into the space where I can ignore it or perhaps get more information about the issue.

Today I was concerned about the liquid oozing from my healing wound from the biopsy that was done a week ago. I could have drummed up all kinds of scenarios about why that process was going on and I did. Then I turned to Google to get more information about the process and learned that it was normal and my fears subsided.

Information can dispel fears, and choosing what we focus on gives us the power to move forward.

FROM DONUTS...TO POTATOES

___

___

___

JULY 8
WORD FOR TODAY: BE

It is not who we have been, it is not what we used to believe; it is all about what we want to be.

We tell our young people that they can be whatever they want, but what about us?

As adults, do we believe the same for ourselves or do we operate under the concept that we are already all we can be? Is change and growth possible? Of course it is.

What we think about, we bring about and there is no limit to what we can determine to be.

It all starts in our minds. If we can imagine it, we can manifest it. Limitations exist to the extent that we look to our past and think we have already been defined.

Want to be more loving, giving, understanding and supporting? When I was a kid, cleaning up my room was a big job. My mom would say "Just start in a corner". That advice helps me to this day.

Start in the corner of your mind and clean out the cobwebs which hold you back. Be free to enjoy all you can be.

___

___

JULY 9

WORD FOR TODAY: FLOW

We all experience "bumps" in the road - times when the unexpected happens and the question is "How do we respond to those bumps?"

Yesterday I had one of those times. I fell. Yes, I was in a lot of pain after my head hit a big rock next to the sidewalk leading up to our house. I wondered if I was going to be able to get up by myself. I did and once I was inside and Ben came to me, I cried.

My face had quite a cut. He got me cleaned up and we applied ice. We went through the process of what to do next? Did I need treatment? We decided it would be best to get me checked out.

As the doctor was getting ready to put the 5 stitches in my face, I was busy telling him and his nurse about my journey. She took one of my cards as she complained that it would be hard to get her husband to go along. As the doctor worked on me, I told her that sometimes "you just have to be the example".

It's not easy to go alone. It's not easy to be the one who stands out in the crowd. It is not easy to eat differently than others when you join them for a meal. The benefits of having a healthy body are great when you need to heal.

The CT scan of my facial bones and head turned out good. No broken bones, no injury to my eye, and just think - I'll get to see my plant-based doctor again when I have my stitches removed next week.

I admit that I actually thought about having a treat last night and so I did - a nice cold banana.

FROM DONUTS...TO POTATOES

Go with the flow and always give thanks. There is always a silver lining.

_____

_____

_____

JULY 10

WORD FOR TODAY: SMILE

Smile...you're on Candid Camera...whether you realize it or not.

All around us, there are cameras. They are embedded in the eyes of everyone we see. Some have not seen a smile for awhile and our smile may just be the turning point in making this a great day for someone else.

A smile conveys hope. It helps people relax. It reminds us that no matter what is going on in the outer world, the inner world is at peace.

A smile connects us immediately with strangers. It is kind of like a nod of the head - letting someone know you have seen them but it seems to go a bit deeper, letting them know you have invited them inside.

Combine a smile with eye contact and your intention to connect with someone in a meaningful way is relayed.

A smile is a frown turned upside down. Having a good day? Smile. Having a rough day? Smile. What an antidote. Try it on for size. It doesn't hurt.

ESTHER LEBECK LOVERIDGE

_____

_____

_____

JULY 11

WORD FOR TODAY: KNOW

I often say "I know…" but is that true? There are some things I have come to know through experience but on the other hand, I have often just thought I knew something because someone else told me it was so.

So, how do we know what is true and what is simply tribal rule? Perhaps it is easy to play it safe and just believe what we have been told so that we don't have to think about what is true for each of us.

Some old sayings come to my mind such as "Children should be seen and not heard", "Spare the rod and spoil the child" or "Wives must be submissive to their husbands" or maybe it is just that "Obesity runs in our family" and then there is the idea that "You can't teach an old dog new tricks".

What makes life fun for me is questioning everything. Why not? What is there to lose by determining for each of us what works or is true for us?

Now I wonder what I know. I am still in process. I am still learning. I am still evaluating. I am open to learn what is true for me today. Tomorrow I may have new information.

One thing I know for sure is that I do not need to eat animals in order to have a healthy body. I am a starchivore.

FROM DONUTS...TO POTATOES

_____

_____

_____

_____

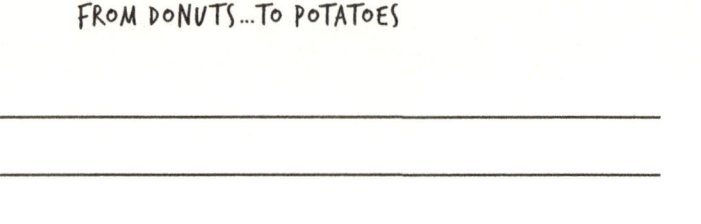

JULY 12

WORD FOR TODAY: PAUSE

When children act in ways that are not pleasing to the adults in their lives (it doesn't necessarily mean they are "misbehaving" they may just be exercising their own will), they are often given a "Pause" or a "Time Out":

I was at Starbucks on Wednesday with my friend for an afternoon chat which means we also felt like we had to buy something to pay for our "seat". As I was enjoying my Majesty herbal tea, an employee passed by our table and offered us a free sample of a concoction. All we heard was that it had coconut milk and perhaps a fruit.

I think there was a slight pause before we declined. Now, why did I decline? If you know me, you know I like "free". Well, all it took was a pause for me to remember I do not drink calories so at that point, it did not matter what it was. It was not on my agenda.

Taking time to pause, gives us a chance to really decide what we want in life rather than act on an impulse.

There used to be a commercial declaring that a certain beverage was the "Pause that refreshes". Now we know better. If we don't pause and think, we just may be repeating old outdated habits.

Take time to pause. That is what is refreshing. It allows us to hit the re-set button and begin again.

_____

_____

_____

_____

JULY 13
WORD FOR TODAY: IDENTIFY

Early on, in my nutritional journey, I identified the goals I wanted to achieve within the first year. I still have the list on an electronic sticky note on my desktop:

7/13/16 I want to:

Eat plant based foods,
Lose 70 pounds,
Lower Cholesterol,
Refrain from pain and sleeping pills,
Increase joint flexibility
Lower blood pressure and
Improve my eye sight before July, 13, 2017

Two year later – 7/9/17, I got there. Got there! I was down 82 pounds from 257 to 175."

If I had not identified what I wanted, I would not have had a measurement with which to chart my progress.

How do we get anywhere without mapping out what we want in life?

Name it and claim it. I also identified food that I could live without – forever. For me, abstinence is my friend. I don't have to

FROM DONUTS...TO POTATOES

decide at every event "should I or should I not". Not is the answer and that struggle is over. I realized no animal would have to die so I could live.

It's a done deal.

What is your done deal?

_____

_____

_____

JULY 14

WORD FOR TODAY: VIBRATION

This morning, I am thinking about what and with whom I vibrate.

Is there an internal system of vibration which actually reflects back to us when we are in the company of like-minded people?

I'm beginning to think so. We are all energy fields. We always find comfort when we are gathered together with people who are "in one accord".

It is so exciting to have my energy level increase when I am around people who "get it", who realize they control their own destiny, that they are not victims of past expectations but know they can rise to the occasion, pay attention and listen to their own bodies.

Two of my brothers had great minds when it came to mechanical issues. Robert was an airplane mechanic in the Air Force. He became a pilot, was later able to convert a brand new car into a convertible and still makes sure his boat is "running smoothly".

My youngest brother was a genius when it came to repairing

those big printing presses. It has been said that when Campbell Soup Company had a problem with their printing press, they could call Paul and often all he had to do was have them put the phone near the printer and just by listening, he could diagnose the problem.

And then there are our bodies. Are we in tune? Do we pay attention to whether or not our "machines" are humming? I vibrate with whole food. It keeps me running smoothly.

_____

_____

_____

_____

JULY 15

WORD FOR TODAY: ATTEST

There are a few things in life that I can attest to and this is one of them.

I can attest to the fact that for the past 3 years (3rd anniversary was 7-13-19) I have been following "The McDougall Program for Maximum Weight Loss" written by Dr. McDougall. I decided, you know, "committed" to following the program to see if it would really work for me. No other program has ever been sustainable for me. This was going to be my own personal experiment and I was the guinea pig.

I vowed early on that if this program worked for me, I would give Dr. McDougall the credit.

Well, my story has been like a miracle. I never dreamed that I could not only lose weight, but get healthy in the process. I do not want to go back. I do not want to reintroduce toxic food into this

FROM DONUTS...TO POTATOES

body of mine. I do not want to eat food that even tastes like the food I have left behind. I do not want substitutes. I want real, whole, unadulterated food. I eat simply.

Has this transformation been easy? No, because now that I have found the answer for me, I tend to think it is the answer for everyone but 37 months ago, I would not have listened either. Timing, pain, desire and determination come to each of us on a different time frame...or not.

I created this Facebook page to tell my story, to post what I eat each day (even an occasional "slip up") and to encourage others who struggle with food addictions. This is not a group to complain or magnify any errors in judgment. If you have a success story to tell, please post it in one of the McDougall groups where you can inspire others to be their best or maybe even start your own FB page. We need to spread the good news to those with an open mind.

Life is exciting for me now and how you use the positive reinforcement here is up to you.

I can tell you about the plan I followed, what I eat and offer a few recipes but I am not a chef, a doctor, or a psychiatrist. I am a 75 year old woman who has discovered the "Fountain of Youth" and I never thought it would be in the form of whole food. Dr. McDougall was right when he said "It's the Food".

Some people seem to want to see how close they can get to their addictions without falling off the cliff but I say it is better to be on solid ground. This is not the place to argue about minute differences or split hairs. This is where I tell my story and if you find it helpful, I will say "Mission Accomplished".

_____

_____

_____

ESTHER LEBECK LOVERIDGE
JULY 16
WORD FOR TODAY: ILLUMINATE

Ah, sometimes we just don't want to be illuminated. Staying in the dark can be comforting. It can give our eyes a rest. It can maybe even make us feel like we are back in the comfort of the womb where we are taken care of and don't seem to have any responsibilities. We don't have to think or even plan any action.

But then someone or something turns on the light and if we have not been warned, it can be startling and invasive. We want to cover our eyes and see less...at least for awhile.

So what illuminated my journey? What made me wake up and realize I no longer wanted to live in pain? What woke me up to the fact that at 257 pounds I was actually uncomfortable? When I'd try to get up off the ground, I had a visual of what my awkward attempts must have looked like from someone observing me. And how about the embarrassment of having to ask for a seat belt extender on a flight, I ask? Or maybe because Ben and I were both fat, we looked like a matched pair and felt comfort in that? If we were both in the dark, did it really matter?

Once the light comes on, it is kind of like the song about how can you be happy back on the farm once you have seen gay Paris?

We can deny the truth of our enlightenment and push it to the back of our minds, but it will always be there - waiting for someone to nourish and water the new truth until it can flourish. For me, my "light" was reading "The McDougall Program for Maximum Weight Loss" and realizing that I needed to try a new path. My way has been made clear and I don't even have to wear my glasses anymore!

FROM DONUTS...TO POTATOES

JULY 17
WORD FOR TODAY: SONG

I think I have as many songs in my head as I have jokes. What a wonderful computer we have as part of our brain.

It doesn't matter if we can carry a tune or not. We may not even remember all of the words, but whether we sing, hum, whistle or internally chant the song; the vibrations of those songs can bring healing.

Songs just seem to resonate with our spirit someway. They are kind of like s musical prayer but at a higher level.

What is interesting to me is how songs of the past take on new meaning as I listen to the words I once memorized but now, with a new awareness, they come alive in a new dimension.

Sometimes the songs of the past seem ridiculous - perhaps because I am not tuned into the experience of the writer. The words of some songs are no longer true for me. They reinforce an emotion of the past.

I like JOY songs. They lift me up and raise my sights to new goals. They make me want to get up and dance. Feeling down or weighted down by obligations? Don't be afraid to sing or whistle a happy tune.

JULY 18
WORD FOR TODAY: GUILT

I often say, "There is no guilt, only learning" and that is pretty straightforward when it comes to deviating from an eating plan because it is only about me and my food.

But what do I say when I lose my cool and strike out at friends? It takes more than just me learning and going on. It is going to take some love and some repair work whether or not my friends were offended by my off the cuff remark.

I can blame it on many things...but there really is no excuse for retaliation. In this time of polarized views, tit for tat just doesn't work. We must rise above emotionally charged issues. Setting the standard for our behavior has nothing to do with anyone else. It is us who sets the bar for our behavior and when we duck beneath that bar to get in a jab or a sharp retort, we are the ones who suffer from "what to do next".

I know what to do and will find the time to apologize and recognize that my remark was uncalled for.

Do I feel guilty? Well, it sure sounds like it but maybe taking the time to talk with those I perceive I may have offended will open the door to talk about our differences in a civil manner.

Yes...I'm still learning.

FROM DONUTS...TO POTATOES

JULY 19

WORD FOR TODAY: WITS' END

You might think I have a sick mind and you might be right because I recently got excited when someone told me she was at her wits' end regarding her weight.

Wow. What a possibly great place to be! To have come to the end of herself just may mean she has come to a place of new beginnings and is ready to listen, learn and be open to a radical change in her life.

I remember when my brother reached the end of the bottle. It ran dry. It was no longer fun to drink. He had lost what seemed like everything -family, health and income. Having fun paled when compared to what it had cost him and he made the decision to give it up. He became radicalized you might say. When eating out at a fancy restaurant, I remember he didn't even want to eat the soup if there was a chance it contained any wine. I was so happy he enjoyed living an alcohol free life before he died in 2004.

For us food addicts, we too, often face a crisis before we recognize how our poor health is in direct proportion to the toxic food we have eaten over decades. The process is much the same as what others have gone through but the roadmap is not clear... we still have to eat. We stay in the same arena but have to learn how to dodge the "bull" of calorie dense food. We can't quit eating altogether.

Why is it that we don't get serious about our health until we are at our wits'-end? I don't know how it is for you, but when pain crept into the equation and threatened my freedom to travel, I had had enough.

Even though I had many chronic conditions listed on my Kaiser Office Visit Report, I didn't think I was sick. Obviously the report indicated I was "morbidly obese" but that hadn't slowed me down.

I had pre-diabetes and pre-high blood pressure so I hadn't really gotten sick yet, I thought. After all, I was on statins but isn't everyone at a certain age?

The answer has often been vague. Some of us have been reluctant to seek medical help because the prescription is always "You need to lose weight" but the how to do it and have it be sustainable for life was something I had not learned until I was almost 73.

This information had never crept into my mind before. I had taken a nutrition class at Consumes River College years ago and that gave me a false sense of knowing without knowing.

The prescribed "balanced plate" approach still included food which I now recognize as toxic or more clearly stated as "food poisoning" - animal and dairy products and the greatly touted oils including extra virgin olive oil. How clever was that ad campaign?

To anyone suffering from any disease - even depression or fatigue, I challenge you to love yourself enough to go on a fast from those toxic foods for 21 days and put it to the test for yourself. Are you not worth a three week trial where you still get to eat until you are full and never be hungry?

You are not stupid. You are among the millions who have been sucked into following the sad American diet and taught to believe that moderation is the key.

When our "god" is our belly, it is amazing what we will do to satisfy its cravings and demands. It is like a whining child making cries for what he/she wants until as parents we give in just to get the kid to shut up.

The quiet only lasts a short time until the next demand raises its ugly head and the cycle begins all over again.

Abstinence is the answer. It takes awhile to get rid of our former desires and develop a new tongue...one that recognizes what good food tastes like, but believe me, it does happen.

This is the road less traveled but aren't you sick of traffic?

Check out some of the documentaries if you need more information such as "What the Health", "Forks over Knives" and the new one - "Game Changers" or maybe you will want to read "The McDougall Program for Maximum Weight Loss" that set me on my path to freedom.

There's a new game in town. Get on the team. We're all here to help.

_____
_____
_____
_____

JULY 20

WORD FOR TODAY: CHANGE

Change your oil. Change your tires but if we change, pressure to be who we were is often increased.

Some of us have a hard time with change. As a matter of fact, my parents moved into this house 60 years ago and guess what? The sectional that mom bought when they moved here is still in the same place.

Does that mean I don't like change? Not necessarily. Our children grow and develop and sometimes we have a hard time letting go of their "cuteness" and maybe even their dependence on us. But if they were not growing and maturing, we'd have something else to worry about.

When I made my recent transition to a whole food plant based lifestyle, I met with some resistance. One of my brothers even said "It seems like Esther has found a new religion". Well, that would take a lot of explaining but you know, at first I defended myself. I said, "No, I still believe." but what he may have really been saying is

"Esther has a new passion and has become a food evangelist" and if so, then he was right.

This way of eating has not only saved my life and delivered me from every possible disease in my body; it has also strengthened my spiritual values and opened my mind to many possibilities. I have given myself permission to challenge everything - question things I would never have thought about and see that there is no limit to what we can become.

What we think about, we bring about. The sky may not even be the limit.

_____

_____

_____

_____

JULY 21

WORD FOR TODAY: DECEPTION

Some deceptions are intentional and some are passive and some may even be unconscious.

I have been thinking about the photo shoot for the upcoming Woman's World Magazine to be released on July 25th for the August 5th issue. It was a learning experience for sure. Yes, it was fun having 4 photographers here setting the "stage" and the makeup artist painting on the canvas of my face for an hour in preparation for the event.

But what about the before picture that I presume will be included in the article? I submitted several, as I recall, but do not know which one will be used. What I do know is that the before shot will not be "photo shopped" or touched up in any way so is it fair to compare the two photos and think there is a real or authentic transformation between the two photos?

Yes, I agree, there has been a miraculous transformation as I have continued to eat a whole food plant based diet but I also see now where the difference will be magnified somewhat by the artistry of the beautician who applied her trade to my face. Is that deception? Well, I think so, when we don't compare "apples to apples".

After reflecting on this experience and realizing how young girls compare themselves to models in magazines and wish they could look like them, I think it is important to be honest. When we have a natural make over in our lives, I think it is best to have natural photos taken - just like we did in our before pictures. I am not putting down the "magazine experience". I am thankful that we can spread the word but I just think the transformation is wonderful and doesn't have to be exaggerated.

_____

_____

_____

_____

JULY 22

WORD FOR TODAY: MAKE-UP

When I was in school and we missed an exam, we were lucky if there was a make-up test available.

If someone is short of funds, they might get to make up the difference some way.

But when it comes to women, make up means something entirely different. I am wondering what we'd do without it. But my real question this morning is what has the need for makeup done TO us?

I don't know of any man who wears it. When they get up in the morning, they are who they are. It is not as though they have to do a makeover before they can be seen.

Make up is what it is - I don't really want to make a big deal of it but I am becoming aware of how we have been sold a bill of goods - one that could make us feel that we are not good enough as is. That is what I am concerned about. We are who we are. We are okay. We can be natural or made up, it is a choice, but let's not let it go any deeper into letting it be WHO we think we are. We are strong. We are women. We are able to do wondrous things - whether made up or not.

My grandmothers (born in 1880 and 1884) never wore make up and they were beautiful women. Neither dyed their hair. Neither wore slacks. It was a different generation and I am glad I got to observe it.

_____

_____

_____

_____

JULY 23

WORD FOR TODAY: OPEN

Signs often flash in the windows of businesses to let us know when they are open.

FROM DONUTS...TO POTATOES

We know when schools are open when we see groups of children playing in the school yard but what about us?

How do we know when we are open? Open to new ideas? Open to change? Open to growing?

Our openness may become evident when we start asking questions. It may come when we explore reading, researching and looking for answers in new venues.

Watching movies have often opened the minds of people to consider alternatives to the way they have seen the world, their families and their associates. Watching "Forks over Knives", a documentary on Netflix, has been repeatedly reported to have opened the minds of many to a new way of thinking about how we view food.

And then there are times when we are faced with a crisis and the avenues of relief that we once sought no longer seem to work. Getting at the end of one's rope does create an opportunity to think differently and sometimes, in desperation, we ask for help.

Ah, asking for help. How dare we need anyone or anything outside of ourselves? Are we not sufficient to handle all of life's daily problems?

_____

_____

_____

_____

JULY 24

WORD FOR TODAY: QUOTE

Quotes help me remember snippets in time.

My mom always talked about the 3 F's - 'Be Firm, Fair and

Friendly" Her mother said "Pretty is as pretty does". Her brother, Uncle Clarence joked "Do you know the best way to eliminate temptation? The shocking answer was 'yield'."

At church we hear "The Best is yet to be", "What we think about, we bring about" and I have heard others say that what you want, wants you.

Chef AJ has helped me with her quote speaking of food "If it is in your house, it will be in your mouth".

Dr. McDougall says "It's the food", "The fat we eat is the fat we wear" and "People love to hear good news about their bad habits".

I say, "No guilt-only learning". I also like to say that when we know better, we do better and of course the Golden Rule is something to always keep in mind.

Quotes are short cuts to important concepts. Use the ones that are helpful.

_____

_____

_____

JULY 25

WORD FOR TODAY: CHRISTMAS

As a kid, and maybe sometimes as an adult, I have counted the days to Christmas.

Christmas elicits so many different responses with many of us. The point here is that it is a time of looking forward, anticipation, longing and perhaps even surprises.

FROM DONUTS...TO POTATOES

I haven't counted the days to any events in quite awhile. In fact, I can't remember the last time I had a countdown.

Then, something out of the blue came into my life. Something I would never have dreamed would happen to this 75 year old woman.

In McDougall Friends, a support group on Facebook, another member of the group said "Esther is an inspiration" and I looked to see what she was referring to: A nation-wide magazine was wanting to do a story on plant based eating and was looking for someone over 70 who had lost over 70 pounds, got rid of disease and was on a plant based diet. I realized I fit the criteria and responded.

I was then connected with one of the editors of Woman's World Magazine and in less than a week, the photographers and makeup artist were at my house for the photo shoot. What a whirlwind - submitting photos, conducting a 40 minute phone interview, and editing some of my comments, determining I had no solid colored tops to wear, having to go shopping and having our place scoped out a day early for possible photo locations.

So, this date, July 25, 2019 is supposed to be the release date of the August 5th issue. The countdown is complete, I think. I'll stop by a store and see if it really is today.

_____

_____

_____

_____

ESTHER LEBECK LOVERIDGE

JULY 26

WORD FOR TODAY: SUCCESS

. What does success feel like? Who is successful? What is the measure of success?

I attended a very small high school and in a class of only 36, I was voted "The Girl Most Likely to Succeed". Now what did that mean to a 17 year old? Maybe it was a little flattery? Maybe there was some hope that I would amount to something someday or maybe it was pressure to live up to someone else's expectation?

So did I ever become successful? Did I have a fancy house, a new car, a big salary or rise to the top in any of my many jobs? No. Did I complete a Master's Degree? No.

Was I a "housewife" who raised two wonderful sons? Did I participate in their activities? Yes. Did I contribute to the well being of Ben's family when we got married? Yes but doesn't everyone do that? What would have to happen in my life to make me feel like I was successful? What would it take to make me feel strong, like a conqueror and an over comer?

Who would have guessed that it would be standing up against the biggest demon in my life - my battle of the bulge? It was a fight that most people deal with. Dieting had been a part of my life since high school. It was my almost constant companion. Why could I be so successful in taking off the weight but not in keeping it off?

It was because I did not have a good road map. All of the directions led to a dead end...almost literally. But when the solution came (when the student needs to learn, the teacher will appear), I was ready. I took the new wheel of my life and put the plan to the test. I was now a chemical engineer protecting my life with health-giving nutrients...and it worked.

The best part of this story is that success is not a respecter of persons. Enjoying the McDougall Program for Maximum Weight

FROM DONUTS...TO POTATOES

Loss is not dependent on one's station in life, income, education or status. It is free and able to release one from past demons as well. Can you imagine how good I feel being "drug free"? Yes, food can be used just like a drug and deliverance from it is just as exhilarating.

I love the feeling of success that is available to all.

_____
_____
_____
_____

JULY 27

WORD FOR TODAY: REAL

It is exciting in life to determine what is real and what is not. Just because something resonates with us does not mean it is real. Dr. McDougall says "People like to hear good news about their bad habits" and that was true for me.

I loved hearing about the weight loss benefits of eating a high fat diet because I loved my fats. I won't give them space here or focus on what they were because "what we think about, we bring about" and I do not want to glorify them anymore.

How many times have we made a purchase that turned out to be useless, yet we still extolled the benefits of it just because we did not want to admit we were swayed by a fast talking salesperson.

I remember as a newlywed being talked into buying a set of encyclopedias. After all, we would want our future children to be educated, right? I didn't know about the upcoming explosion in the information age.

When we grow up, we get to acknowledge when our decisions

came from a sound mind or perhaps from the influence of eager peddlers. I think my garage is full of those!

So, yes, we have all followed fad diets. If they worked, we would not be searching for the latest fad diet - we'd simply defer to what worked for us in the past except obviously they did not work or we wouldn't be in the market for the next magic solution.

What is real is what stands up to the test of time. This is real - three years and counting.

_____

_____

_____

_____

JULY 28

WORD FOR TODAY: VALIDATION

Validation is a recognition or affirmation that a person or their feelings or opinions are valid or worthwhile.

Getting to be a part of the story of Dr. Neal Barnard's work (as published in Woman's World Magazine of 8-5-2019) and having the link to dr.mcdougall.com included in the article gave me a great sense of validation.

When we learn the truth about what our bodies need and put it to the test and it works, we can then say we know the way. The question or challenge remains - how can we encourage others to try this lifestyle BEFORE they have had a chance to experience the relief from addiction or increased energy and a feeling of well being? Must they step out in faith? Are they able to commit to a big lifestyle change on hearsay alone?

FROM DONUTS...TO POTATOES

I say it takes education. All changes must first occur in the mind. Sometimes we get curious when hearing success stories. We might ask, "Is this transformation really available to me?" But something has to click in our brain. Or, maybe, out of uncertainty, the evidence looks pretty compelling and we decide to do an experiment ourselves. Or just maybe, we are facing a crisis.

There are always those who have not experienced this transformation who will challenge it. They are happy, feel healthy and like me, 37 months ago, did not view themselves as unhealthy. After all, are not aches and pains a part of the "Golden Years"?

Setting an example certainly brings awareness to others. One cannot discount the changes I have made. But getting one's story published has added a new level of validation and it feels a lot better than free parking from a validated ticket.

_____

_____

_____

JULY 29

WORD FOR TODAY: NUMB

I could recently, literally, be called a "numb skull".

On July 18, 2019, I had some skin cancer removed from my forehead and ever since then, almost my entire skull has been numb. It feels really weird to brush my hair and not have any feeling. The 40 topical stitches (8 more underneath) were removed a week later and it is amazing how quickly our bodies want to heal and be well...but the numbness will continue for awhile until the nerve endings find each other once again.

This too will pass, as we often say, but what about the years I numbed myself with food? That numbness was a choice. It was a way I used food to numb any unpleasant feelings or even thoughts I did not want to think about.

It is so easy to become numb to the negative changes in our bodies as we slowly disregard the importance of good fuel to run these wonderful machines we call our body.

It is time to wake up. It is time to take action. It is wonderful that we have time to engage in a whole food eating program. It is never too late.

It can be a radical change or it may be one where a person just dips a toe into the water to see how it feels. That is a choice. We all have the option of entering the water at our own pace.

___

JULY 30

WORD FOR TODAY: BAR

Today I am referring to a definition of bar that may have something to do with drinking...but then again, my mind may be working on an entirely different level.

I am thinking about how high we set the bar for our own performance. If we set it low enough, certainly the probability of failure is reduced. If we aim too high, discouragement may set in and thwart additional efforts to push ahead.

So, where did I set the bar? As I have mentioned, when my friend gave me "The McDougall Program for Maximum Weight Loss" book, I set the bar high. I wanted to put this book to the test and how could I do a valid experiment if I set the bar at just following his program 5 days a week? How could I tell if this was my answer to a lifetime of yo-yo dieting if I said, "Well, I think I'll digress on holidays...or birthdays...or weekends? No. I set the bar high and committed to following it even though at the time, I did not realize that it would evolve from being a way to lose the maximum weight to becoming a lifestyle I would embrace for the rest of my life for my health. Has every day in the past 36 months been perfect? No, but I have learned that as a food addict, I reject the myth of moderation.

Interesting how an initial goal of weight loss turned into realizing I had found my answer for optimal health. I mean - what other diet ever healed me completely? No meds, no knee replacement, no eye surgery and now, no glasses. It is amazing.

How high we set our bar predicts what we can expect to achieve.

_____

_____

_____

_____

JULY 31

WORD FOR TODAY: FOLLOW

We follow many people, ideas, trends, thoughts, directions and examples.

ESTHER LEBECK LOVERIDGE

Sometimes, we risk being led astray, but that is just part of the process of evaluating and discovering what rings true for each of us.

When we take a turn which seems to lead to a dead end, we can use our internal guidance system to make a correction. It is not the end of the world. It is just a learning experience.

I have been led down the path of destruction, if you will, by following so many fad diets, diets which did work for awhile and led me to believe I had found my answer. But fortunately, time has been my friend and allowed me the joy of finding what has worked for me. I have become like an evangelist - thinking my answer is the best one for everybody and I continually need to remind myself that we all find our way in our own time.

Yes, the side effects of following The McDougall Maximum Weight Loss Program (or The Starch Solution) have all been positive (except for getting colder in the winter, ha). I love my new life. I love helping people take the chance of following a plant based diet while it leads them to improved health and a good weight.

AUGUST 1
WORD FOR TODAY: FIRE

70 years ago, I was on fire as a result of watching my brother play with matches. We had our photo on the front page of The Sacramento Union newspaper.

Today, I am also on fire but in a different connotation. We can be "on fire", or maybe "ignited" or in a more subtle way - "aglow" and the energy that is emitted from our fire can be positive or negative. Just ask Dr. John McDougall - No, don't, he doesn't have to be reminded of the effects of the Santa Rosa fire in October, 2017. They thought they lost "everything", but the fire that is still within them continues to embolden all of us.

What lights our fire? What rings our dinger? What makes my face light up with a smile? What consumes me? It is a new life, revolutionized by finding the "The Healthiest Diet on the Planet".

Hopefully, the embers or sparks from the fire that burns within me reaches others who are willing to sit around the campfire of wholeness, energy, health and vitality and listen to the multitude of success stories from other "Camp Fire Girls".

I just remembered that as a child, I was member of the Camp Fire Girls after having moved up from the "Bluebirds". Good memories.

Anyway, fires have a tendency to burn out, but candles lit from the fire can be used to pass the light to others and that is what breathes new life into me.

70 years after "The Fire", my photo is on the cover of Woman's World Magazine and I have the opportunity to spread the good news which is so much better than evoking sympathy for two kids who suffered as a result of playing with matches. Perhaps that lesson needed to be taught too.

FROM DONUTS...TO POTATOES

_____

_____

_____

_____

AUGUST 2

WORD FOR TODAY: INADEQUATE

"Our deepest fear is not that we are inadequate, our deepest fear is that we are powerful beyond measure" from "A Return to Love" by Marianne Williamson.

Feeling inadequate can certainly keep us from performing at our highest level. I am thinking of the book by Eric Berne - "Games People Play" and one of the games, as I recall, was called Broken Leg. After all, as it goes, if I have a broken leg, how in the world would you expect me to ____?

Whenever we are sick, there can be secondary benefits. Maybe we get to have a pedicure since we cannot reach our toes. I remember Gerry Cooley, our tour guide in Dublin taking care of me - making sure I had a place to rest in between stops on our tour. (Actually, there was a benefit to that too because we got better acquainted and our friendship has continued).

But if we aspire to be our best, is living up to and maintaining that level of performance scary? Will we be able to continue or would life be easier if we just stayed in our comfort zone?

Growing, learning and loving all have risks as well as benefits and expanding the idea of what we can become comes in baby steps.

ESTHER LEBECK LOVERIDGE

_____

_____

_____

_____

AUGUST 3

WORD FOR TODAY: HONOR (YOUR PARENTS)

⋈

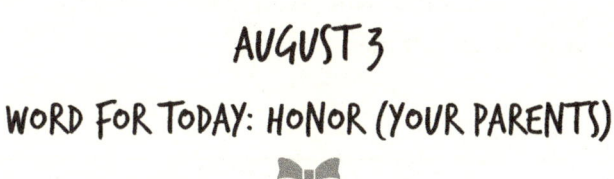

110 years ago, in 1909, my mother was born. 90 years ago today, my parents got married. 8-3-29

Times were hard during the stock market crash (not that they had any investments).

Dad loved photography but for some reason, they did not have any wedding photos. They got married in a tent. The church was having a "revival" and mom was so practical that she saw no reason to move the chairs back into the sanctuary for their wedding ceremony.

After being pronounced "Man and Wife" they both sat on the "platform" and dad told the guests about their future plans. They were going to take a "honeymoon" with two other women who had a car and they would conduct some meetings together.

Soon, they settled in Colorado for a few years. One church was in Holly and the second place was Ft. Morgan, I think. They returned to California and took a church in Hollister where they had their first two sons. Mom was also an ordained minister so when dad went to the church in Hollister, mom went to another small meeting in San Juan Bautista and of course had to minister while simultaneously wearing high heels and attending to the needs of her first baby. Yes, she was a strong woman.

Dad used to read the neighbor's newspaper after he was done

FROM DONUTS...TO POTATOES

with it and they went to a parishioner's house once a week for a chicken dinner and to do their laundry. It is hard to imagine life 90 years ago.

By the time the next two children came along (my brother Paul and me), dad was in business in Sacramento. That's just a bit of family history for my kin.

Dad continued spreading his good news by being very active in the Gideon organization so whenever I stay in a hotel, I think of him.

Honor your history. It made you.

_____

_____

_____

AUGUST 4

WORD FOR TODAY: COMPROMISE

Give and receive. You scratch my back and I'll scratch yours. What blesses you, blesses me. Your bliss is my bliss

But the time comes when we choose not to compromise.

I remember going out to celebrate the anniversary of a relative. I was new to this way of eating and it was even newer to them. I was asked, "Well, you can have zucchini, can't you" when we looked over the menu.

"Yes, that would be fine", I replied. But when the appetizer came, it was heavily coated, deep fried and presented with a dip so I passed. Then came the words we hear so often..."Well, a little bite won't hurt you".

Eat just a little bite? Is there such a thing for a person self described as a "food addict". Not for this addict. One little bite of zucchini, could become one little sip of a concoction and then one little bite of chocolate cake.

For me, abstinence is so much easier than sampling what I used to eat or drink. Those yearnings are now a thing of my past - a place I don't want to return to. It is over. The battle has been won and my taste buds look forward to what has become my food.

We can keep the past alive or we can let it die and move on.

AUGUST 5
WORD FOR TODAY: PAY

Long ago, I was working with a doctor who delivered my second son Steve. His wife was an RN and they had a group they called "The Center for Family Process". I had a volunteer position there and really enjoyed conducting group sessions to help new couples make the transition from being a couple to becoming parents. The classes were free.

Dr. John McDougall came into my life and all of his information is free too. We can go to his website and search any topic freely. While it is true that guests must pay to attend his "retreats", going to those seminars is not necessary to get the facts. It is all on-line.

It is his model that I strive for. Initially, I did not even have to buy his book. It was given to me. Later, I was still quite thrifty when I

FROM DONUTS...TO POTATOES

wanted to share the information in his book with others and bought used books, on eBay, to give away.

But the time came when I knew I wanted to pay back so I did take his Starch Solution Certification Course and even went to his 3-day program last September and the payoff for me was getting to thank him in person for saving my life.

Paying it forward or backwards is fun and as we give, our capacity to receive increases.

_____

_____

_____

AUGUST 6

WORD FOR TODAY: WAY

There is "No way". "This is the way". "Find your way" and "Can't find your way out"?

So, where is the way and is there a toll booth on it? Speaking of toll booths, one time our GPS directed us to go home from San Francisco and we couldn't figure out why it directed us to go clear across town and take the Golden Gate Bridge when we were already close to the Bay Bridge.

We later determined that we received those directions because the device had been previously programmed to "avoid toll booths"!

Are you set to avoid toll booths? Is something or someone pre-programming you to live a certain way, behave a certain way or are you a free agent who gets to decide what is the best way for you?

Do you give away your power in order to "get along"? Do

you compromise more than what is common courtesy in healthy relationships? What is really fun about life is learning that we are the commanders of our own "spaceship". Yes, we listen to logic and reason and understand the wisdom of others, but ultimately, we are the ones who create our future. We are the ones who put the food on our forks. We are the ones who do our own research to determine what is best. And we are the ones who get to adjust our "sails" to the winds that blow and often change over time.

As you find your way, hold it close. It is yours. It is your starting point. It is what is true for you at the moment as you test its efficacy for your life.

_____

_____

_____

_____

AUGUST 7

WORD FOR TODAY: TOXINS

Getting rid of toxins in our bodies, environment and even in our work place is popular these days.

Some people go to extreme efforts to remove toxins. At least detoxifying our bodies is something individually we might choose to do and have control over.

The question remains, once a body is detoxified (by whatever means), what happens when one returns to ingesting the very toxins they wanted to rid themselves of in the first place?

Wouldn't it make sense to continue eating a plant based diet and just forget about the need to detoxify?

FROM DONUTS...TO POTATOES

We get our teeth cleaned every 6 months, but maintenance on our part will increase the likelihood of better oral hygiene.

The alcohol industry would never want to be known as producing toxins for our bodies but the other day I got to thinking about what we say of someone who has had too much to drink. We say they were in-toxic-ated. Interesting?

Our bodies want to be well. It is amazing how quickly a burn will heal, a cut will close and how we get over food poisoning in spite of how often we require it to do so.

_____

_____

_____

_____

AUGUST 8

WORD FOR TODAY: RE-UNION

This weekend, I have reunited with the "kids" I met 60 years ago when we all left home to go to Canyonville, Oregon to attend Canyonville Bible Academy. But why did we do that? Why do we continue to re-unite each year and what brought us together in the first place?

That is another book I would like to write. There were as many different reasons why we all chose to attend CBA (a 4 year boarding school) as there were students at the school. The total enrollment was 150 for the high school and our class of 36 was a special unit. We bonded like family. (Perhaps that is what some of us needed in the first place). We lived together, slept together, ate together, played and attended church together. And now, most of us at age

75+ are retired. Yes, Shirley is still a surgical nurse and Les is a floor installer and Dave is still working as a sales rep.

But what I am thinking about this morning as we gather for another meal and time of sharing is how many of us get stuck in our past. Is it our past that still represents who we are? Or have we evolved into our better selves by moving on with healthy thoughts, life patterns and ideas that propel us into a future of greater awareness? Are we limited by our past or "at our age" is there still room for growth and enlightenment?

We come together in love, to support each other, learn from each other, sometimes compete with one another and like family, may have some jealousies and resentments mixed in as well.

Reunions happen in our thought life too. We often gather thoughts that keep us in the dark and don't let "newcomers" join in. But it is the light, the fresh water, the new knowledge that feeds our soul and mind into expansion. This is a time to both reflect and to give thanks for having found "The Starch Solution". What a life changer.

_____

_____

_____

_____

AUGUST 9

WORD FOR TODAY: SING

Sing a joyful noise. Sing to the top of your lungs. Sing in the shower, in the car, while taking a walk and sing while you work.

FROM DONUTS...TO POTATOES

Singing creates a great vibration in our bodies (and our bodies don't even know if we are in tune or not)!

Pick a song that you like. The words will be like a prayer that vibrates and raises you to new heights.

It's hard to be depressed and sing at the same time. Well, maybe if one sings country songs, ha.

Ben sang to me this morning as, today, we celebrate our 30th wedding anniversary. I love it when he sings some of our old favorite songs. His head is full of them.

Lift your voice. Be heard. Spread your good news and be alive.

_____

_____

_____

_____

AUGUST 10

WORD FOR TODAY: REFLECTION

Years ago, people didn't even have mirrors. They would not have had those dreaded mirrors in dressing rooms and probably when they walked down the street, they did not see their reflections in store front windows. So were they all living by the water where they could see themselves reflected in the water?

What matters is what the mirrors are telling us today since they abound and we have so many opportunities to see and judge our own appearance and we are often our own worst enemy.

But then there is a different kind of reflection - the times when we sit back after a wonderful event and recall the special moments of a day or experience.

ESTHER LEBECK LOVERIDGE

Today, I am reflecting on yesterday where we received so many good wishes for continued happiness as we celebrated our 30th wedding anniversary. Thank you.

In addition, we had a "signing" party at Zest Kitchen in Rocklin for the publication of Woman's World Magazine which documented my weight loss while eating plants.

We were happy to have Nora come with us. We were joined by Peggy and her husband Larry. Peggy had interviewed me on her radio show in Nevada City and that is when we discovered that Ben and Larry played music together over 50 years ago. Anita Faye came too as well as Jim and Margie, Tom and Tami and Sue, my friend since 7th grade. Most of them are members of "Esther's Nutritional Journey".

Good conversation, support and sharing stories are important as we reflect on the joys of finding renewed health.

_____

_____

_____

_____

AUGUST 11

WORD FOR TODAY: CONSTIPATION

Ah, such a "dirty" word to discuss, or is it?

In the distant past (up until 3 years ago when I changed to eating plants), I suffered from constipation. Yes, there were "remedies" such as drinking more water, eating more fruit and of course the usual increasing of bottled fiber, Miralax, and suppositories for hemorrhoids etc.

FROM DONUTS...TO POTATOES

But what if this chronic condition could be CURED by changing one's diet? Think of the pain free days one could have. Think of the money one would save from not having to buy all of the "remedies" which didn't permanently cure the condition anyway?

So you don't have constipation? That is wonderful. But there is another kind of constipation we can suffer from which keeps us stuck in old patterns of thinking.

We can get stuck into thinking we need a certain number of meals a day. We can believe that diet drinks are better than alternatives. We can still believe that we need animal products for protein - forgetting about the way people have eaten for centuries... on starch. We can focus on looking for a magic pill.

Sometimes we think the way we are living our life is a healthy one and after all, we are overdosing on exercise without realizing that weight loss is 80% nutrition and only 20% exercise.

Getting "unstuck" is possible. It is easy. It is forever. It saves money and it frees our minds to advance and learn better and better ways of respecting our bodies.

Love yourself enough to set yourself free.

_____

_____

_____

_____

AUGUST 12

WORD FOR TODAY: EASY

We often say, "Take it easy" but do we really mean that?

I remember one of my uncles telling me a "joke". He asked me

"Do you know the easiest way to get rid of temptation?" Of course I didn't know the answer so I took his bait. "No, I replied" to which he responded with just one word - "Yield".

This morning I heard from someone who said she was sick and tired of being sick. I replied: "Making a change in our lives is much easier when we get to the point where we are tired of feeling sick and depressed. If you have Dr. McDougall's MWL book, be sure to read the section on depression. It is all connected. Yes, making a clean break takes a commitment and payday is sweet.

So, is converting to another lifestyle easy? The Wall Street Journal reported on Friday "Going vegetarian is actually quite difficult. One large U.S. survey from 2014 found 84% of would-be vegetarians abandon the diet in less than a year." If you are one of those who have changed and maintained your new lifestyle, know that you are in a league of your own.

This is not easy in the beginning. It takes really believing that this is "The Healthiest Diet on the Planet" and that you are worth the effort.

Educate yourself. Surround yourself with support, love and even meditate as you continue your journey. The road less traveled is beautiful.

_____

_____

_____

_____

FROM DONUTS...TO POTATOES

AUGUST 13

WORD FOR TODAY: REFORM

I have often heard, "We are made in the image of God" and if so, why don't we leave each other alone?

If an artist is happy with his/her sculpture, it is not necessary to throw the finished work back onto the spinning wheel in an attempt to re-form it.

I have been guilty all my life of trying to re-form myself as well as my friends into becoming what I believe are a better "form".

One time, a very wise nurse told me "Esther, your happiness is dependent upon your ability to change blah, blah, blah". Wow - no words have stuck with me like those. I wish I could find her and let her know how much her words woke me up.

But I'm still not fully awake. Often I think I know best for other people but what I want to do is change my thinking. I am reflecting on "Mr. Roger's Neighborhood". I think I learned more from him than the thousands of sermons I have heard over my lifetime. He taught love. He taught acceptance. He listened and let people be who they were. He wanted to be their friend - not to reshape them but to enjoy their presence.

Viva la difference. Just as I would not want all fruit to taste the same or every flower to resemble the others in the bouquet, I want to treasure each of you, get to know you, and appreciate how your life story has made you the strong person you are.

Growth and development are open to all of us as we decide what, if anything, in us needs to be re-created or reformed.

_____

_____

AUGUST 14

WORD FOR TODAY: FEAR

Fear not, I bring you tidings of good joy. But wait, you say, Christmas is over 4 months away. Are you getting into the Christmas spirit already?

Christmas does not have exclusive rights to new birth. We receive the opportunity to accept new ideas on a daily basis.

So, whatever we fear can be released. Fear keeps us functioning in our past. I used to fear starting a new diet because I was judging my future by my past performance. So many failures seemed to teach me that the possibilities of a new start were thus diminished.

However, there is good news. Today has not been lived yet. Today we set new goals. Today we have new tools in our handbag to guide us along the way. We have learned the lessons of preparedness, community, support, nutrition vs. dieting and we are more knowledgeable than ever.

We are setting a new direction for our lives. Today is uncharted territory and we get to create new experiences by making new decisions, doing something we have never done before, breaking out of the box of repeating only what we have known in the past.

Fear not and look for what brings a smile to your face.

FROM DONUTS...TO POTATOES

AUGUST 15

WORD FOR TODAY: MIND

Mind your manners, mind your parents, and mind your teacher but what we often forget is that we need to mind our thoughts.

It is our own thinking that gets us into trouble. We listen to those voices in our heads that tell us "You can't start over", "You always fail", "You will always be fat", "You never learn", "You never change", "You came from a fat family", "You have slow metabolism" or the worst "____", you fill in the blank.

We know those voices. We have been friends for years. They resonate like they are real and we never seem to have the courage to tell them "You are just a habitual way of thinking and I am going to let you go".

We change our tires, we change our hair and nail color, we change our clothes, we even have changed families and we can change our minds.

Start by telling yourself I AM statements. I am strong. I am determined. I am able to take one day at a time. I am capable of making better choices. I am able to handle stress better than I did yesterday. I am love. I am kind. I am considerate. I am smart. I am going to win this "battle of the bulge".

Weed your mind (and I don't mean "pot", ha) of negative thoughts. One by one tell each of those "speakers" that they are no longer welcome in your mind and you are doing the weeding today.

Refuse to gain attention by enumerating all of your imagined ills.

Put positive action behind your new life-giving thoughts. Add some good nutrition and feel the "Miracle Grow".

_____

_____

_____

AUGUST 16

Word for today: MASTER

I remember Dr. Nicholas A. Bond, one of my college professors writing just one word on the blackboard - "MASTER".

He went on to say it is not enough to read the material, attend lectures and take the tests. He said it was important to master the subject.

And so it is when we change our lifestyle. It is not enough to just read the book or even join a group. If we want to totally change the course of our life, we must work at it.

It takes a lot of energy to plan our food and make up our mind that this is the way we want to live. We have to be willing to stand firm in the face of opposing family members and friends. It is not easy to stand alone, but neither is it easy to suffer from the ills that beset us when we continue to eat the standard American diet.

Once we make up our minds and apply the tools i.e. reading material, listening to podcasts and reading the material again, we get immersed and little by little, this becomes a way of life for ourselves.

Eventually, it can become second nature and the joy of being free from what once dominated our thoughts and actions passes and we are free to explore new adventures while enjoying our health.

Enjoy the freedom from food addictions.

FROM DONUTS...TO POTATOES

_____

_____

_____

_____

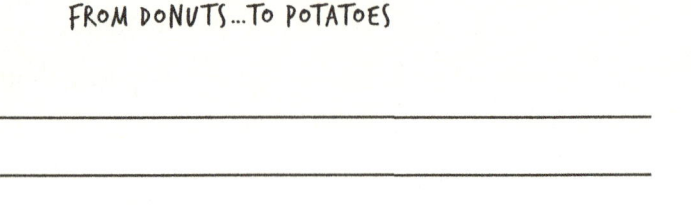

AUGUST 17

WORD FOR TODAY: ALIGNMENT

When my car is out of alignment, it still runs. It gets me to where I am going. The air conditioner still works and after yesterday's "Miracle" (that's another story), I can still listen to my favorite CDs.

But, just because all of these elements work, is that good enough? What about the wear and tear on our tires as we attempt to steer the car and keep it from drifting to the side of the road?

So, the same is true in our bodies. We can be out of alignment and still function. Yes, life becomes more difficult but since our bodies are such fabulous "machines", it always amazes me how much abuse it can take before it yells, "That's enough...I won't take any more".

Next we evaluate what or with whom we desire to be in alignment. We can align ourselves to any idea which helps us be our best. We sometimes align ourselves with a certain political idea, a spiritual truth, a lifestyle or even resonating with our social circle.

The truth is that when we decide what we are going to follow or align ourselves with, the trip becomes so much easier and the wear and tear on ourselves is reduced.

We can reduce the stress in our lives by determining our goals and then adding reinforcement and support to help us stay on track. Being your best need not be a lonely experience.

AUGUST 18
WORD FOR TODAY: ORDER

Getting organized is a big order. Mom taught me how to get started when I have a big task before me i.e. cleaning a room. She would say, "Just start in a corner". I think the key is to just get started.

Putting my life in order seems overwhelming yet I can look back on the past 25 months and see that I have been able to make some progress in my kitchen by eliminating all animal and dairy products and even vegetable oils. More recently, I got rid of the alcohol which we didn't need.

The order of the day for me is baby steps. I want to clean up a corner and establish order which leads to peace of mind.

FROM DONUTS...TO POTATOES

AUGUST 19

WORD FOR TODAY: WORD

Word is an interesting "word". We say, "I give you my "word". Does that mean we no longer have it? Where do our words go when we give them away? Do some stay with us so we only give part of a word away?

Oh, there is so much to ponder. Where do I start?

Words convey so much - our feeling nature, our desires, our condition, our hopes and dreams and even, sometimes, ideas we don't believe. We might say what we think is socially acceptable.

When asked how he was feeling, my dad used to say, "Do you want the short version or the long version"? We say, "I am fine" when that may only be part of how we are at that moment but we don't trust that the inquiring mind wants to really know the whole story.

The words we choose to identify ourselves are so important. Remember when women used to say "I'm JUST a housewife"? Oh, how that wonderful position in life was diminished.

We sometimes describe ourselves as overweight, old, lazy, depressed, or even useless. Oh, my, those parts of us certainly do not make up the "whole" of us. We have billions of cells yet it is tempting to put ourselves down and pick out the worst genes to describe ourselves. What are we afraid of? Why are we afraid to claim who we are? We are magnificently made. Our body continually tries to repair any damage we may have unconsciously caused it. Over and over again it forgives us and gives us a fresh start.

Today is a new day. What words are you going to claim to describe your world, your life, your emotional state, your goals your dreams and aspirations and of course, don't forget who you are - a very special person in this neighborhood of new friends. Just think - we are scattered all over the world to plant the seeds of kindness and grow the idea of health with all we meet. Yes, some will not listen and that is okay. They are where we once were. There is hope. Timing is important. As we unite in groups like this, we know we have found our answer - for the moment - and will continue to evolve into our best selves as we choose our words carefully.

_____

_____

_____

_____

AUGUST 20

WORD FOR TODAY: STILL

Stimulation abounds. Noise is everywhere. TVs are blaring. Ear buds prevent discussions and the list goes on.

It is in those precious early morning hours that I relish the quiet. What if everything we needed to know in life was already within us and all we had to do was take time to listen?

Do we already know what we need? Do we already have the answers to life but maybe, just maybe, we don't want to believe it or accept it?

If the search outside of us is over, then we get to put into practice what we already know.

Then there is no excuse for looking outside. There is no magic recipe, book, speech or pill. We do know the truth. Searching may just delay the process by which we act on what we already know.

Maybe you don't think you know everything. Well, believe me; you don't have to because applying what we already know is a full time job. We are only required to live up to what we know to be true and when we need to know more, it will be ours to embrace as well.

We can change "I know, but..." to "I know... and will act".

_____

_____

_____

_____

AUGUST 21

WORD FOR TODAY: IT

You may recall the phrase from "Forrest Gump" "- - t happens". Well, I have just discovered that "It Happens" too.

You see, in my evangelistic fever to spread the news about how to get healthy by eating plants I wrote to Oprah. (Do I need to add a last name?). I wanted to explain to her how she could elevate the Weight Watcher's Diet by teaching people that trading out healthy food for addictive food doesn't address the issue of food addiction or help people be their healthiest. Sure, one could trade a nice potato for a high calorie/fat dense food and stay within the WW point system, but what about one's health?

I wrote to her because I thought she was "it", you know, the one with a big megaphone who could help so many reverse disease and regain their health. I elevated her to that position in my mind.

Then, the light went on and I realized that the whole planet is made up of people who have already received the news and are now the new "it" - capable of touching lives and spreading the news in their own world.

We are the "IT"
Hush. Don't keep the secret.

_____

_____

_____

AUGUST 22

WORD FOR TODAY: FOCUS

This morning, I am thinking about all of us who have an excess of 100 pounds to lose. That number looms so large in our minds everyday and I am concerned that we loathe that part of ourselves.

But what do we do about the parts of us for which we give thanks. Maybe we have a nice pleasant smile that we can share with others. Maybe we have the gift of helps (that is how I answered my grandmother when she used to ask "What is your gift"?

Maybe we hold a child in our arms and offer comfort. Being 100 pounds overweight is not the end of the world, but focusing on that keeps us from appreciating the gifts we do have to share.

The body we now have is what we have to work with. It may never meet society's expectations or even our own so how are we going to achieve happiness if it is dependent upon what the scale reveals to us each day?

It is time to shift our focus from losing something (weight) to gaining something (health). We need to love our bodies as they are right now. We need to tell them thank you for all of the chores they accomplish for us each day. We need to promise to give thanks by

FROM DONUTS...TO POTATOES

taking care of it and making sure we help it by offering the healthiest food available.

Take care of your body - regardless of its size. Pretend it is your very own baby and that from now on, you are going to make sure it gets the best food. Punishment is not the answer.

AUGUST 23

WORD FOR TODAY: FALL

We often say, "I fell off the wagon". "I fell for that line" and some even say "I fell from grace".

Whatever was your experience, it was not the end of the world. What is important is the emotion or judgment we place on it or ourselves which can magnify the shame.

Think of the toddlers. How many times must they fall before they have a steady gait? Do they ever condemn themselves and say "Why can't I walk like my older brother...I'm a failure...I'll never learn to walk...or I think I'll just sit here because I am tired of failing?"

No, of course they would not do that. They pop up without a second thought.

As we get older, we are cautioned to be careful...don't fall. Well, I have fallen 3 times in the past three years - one time I missed a step, one time I fell at the gym and hit my head on the corner of a metal chair requiring 3 stitches and in July I fell on our walkway and that required 5 stitches but am I still sitting out there on the walk?

No. What did I learn? Steps in the dark are hard to see...that I shouldn't stay in the hot tub so long that I get lightheaded and on the walkway, I don't know what I learned. Perhaps just be more mindful.

Correct self talk. Remember...there is no guilt...only learning. Get up, quit berating yourself, think about what the experience taught you and self correct. You are in charge.

___

AUGUST 24

WORD FOR TODAY: FILL

Fill is another important four letter word.

We fill our cars with what we think is the best fuel (or maybe the cheapest). We fill our plates to overflowing with eye appealing food. We fill our homes with collectibles, souvenirs and our closets with clothes we may never wear again.

But my issue today is "With what do we fill our minds"? What do we do with negative thoughts that creep into the soil of our mind? Do we take out the weeds and say "be gone" or do we add fuel to the fire and rehearse them over and over?

I have heard it said that depression is the state we are in when we feel like we have experienced failure. Some people even think they ARE a failure - not that there have only been times that their attempts to do something worked out differently than planned.

As dieters, we have all experimented with what we thought was

FROM DONUTS...TO POTATOES

the best plan at the moment. I remember thinking The Dr. Aitkin's diet was the best - I could eat all the fat I wanted until I almost died from Pancreatitis and Gall Bladder disease.

When we fill our minds with positive affirmations and prayers or mantras it moves us towards a direction of hope. We finish the sentence "I am ___." with statements that create a new vision of ourselves.

I am making better choices. I am capable of having healthy food available. I am learning to appreciate oil free food. I am satisfied when I fill my tummy with whole, starch based food. I am happy to have found my answer to a lifetime of yo-yo dieting. I am experiencing a clearer mind. I am on my way to total health. I am worthy. I am filling my cup to overflowing with new, fresh ideas of what I want to do with my life.

_____

_____

_____

_____

AUGUST 25

WORD FOR TODAY: WANT

This morning, I came to write but was distracted by the TV so I decided to do something I could do. I made the bed, spotted some gum off a jacket I want to wear today and now the room is quiet and I can write.

What do you want? I have heard it said "What you want, wants you". I'm still pondering the ways that will be manifested in my life.

We typically spend so much time and energy in our past. In

fact, I am learning that everything in our brain is about our past. It is through our past that we most easily make decisions and reinforce our thinking but what if we took time to be quiet and envision what we want?

As of this moment, we are identified by our past even if that past was just yesterday but as we create what we want in our lives, we set new thought patterns into motion and let go of who we have been to grow into who we want to be.

Our past has brought us to this point in time and we can give thanks for everything that has led us up to this point. The question remains, do I want to repeat the past or do I want to wake up and be all I can be?

_____

_____

_____

_____

AUGUST 26

WORD FOR TODAY: EXERCISE

We balance our checkbooks, we balance our energy and we balance our lives with whole food, exercise, meditation and love.

Exercise is one of the four ingredients that Dr. McDougall addresses but it is not the only answer to healthy living. To quote him, "It's the food"!

This morning I weighed 127.5 (my goal is to stay under 130) and I have not done any exercise from July 8 to last Friday almost 7 weeks. (I fell, had stitches and also had some skin cancer removed which turned out to be a bigger issue for swimming than expected).

FROM DONUTS...TO POTATOES

Yes, I could have done some walking or got on a treadmill but my mind didn't go there because my exercise is to swim.

I have heard it said that our food is 80% and exercise is only 20%. Having said that, do I think exercise is good for us? Of course it is. We were made to move, bend, stretch and keep active. It can clear our brain, energize us and tone our body. We just cannot out exercise our fork.

So, take heart if you are not a gym geek. Do what you are willing to do, capable of doing and do it with a smile on your face. If you have to grimace, you just might be working too hard.

_____

_____

_____

_____

AUGUST 27

WORD FOR TODAY: STRESS

Back in the 80's, I worked for the I.R.S. (Guess you know where I am going with this).

It was the first full time professional job I had. I had just graduated from college as an "older" adult and was in the top 10% of my graduating class which was a requirement to be in a newly formed group of Revenue Officers. We were brought in from the outside, meaning we didn't rise from within the organization.

It felt good to put my college degree to work in something besides clerical. Maybe this was still "clerical" but the pay was better. As a "field" revenue officer, it was my job to contact tax payers directly in their place of business or at home.

Yes, it was stressful - given the task at hand. I tried to approach people with the information I had and asked for their input on the situation to resolve the question at hand.

After a few years, I got tired of creating stress in the lives of others and decided to switch gears - I went to the Integrative School of Massage Therapy and became a Massage Therapist.

That was just another evolution in my life but it demonstrated that it is possible to recognize stress in our lives and do something about it.

We can all evaluate how much stress contributes to our emotional eating...and over-eating never solves the problem. It just delays taking the proper action that will make a difference.

_____

_____

_____

_____

AUGUST 28

WORD FOR TODAY: RISK

We take many risks in life. We learn to get up after we fall down. We learn a new skill and then discover that we have to practice it if we want to remember how it is done.

I took piano lessons for about 5 or 6 years, but it didn't seem to take me. I took a typing class. Now that took. I have used that skill most of my life in many clerical jobs.

We take a risk when we get on the freeway. We take a risk when we fall in love and we take a big risk when we decide to start what seems like just another attempt to lose weight by starting a new "diet".

But just as in learning any other skill, it takes practice. Sure we screw up from time to time, but if we take time to think about it, there is always a learning opportunity in what we may have thought of as another failure.

How were you feeling when you "lost it"? Were you hoping that somehow by eating non-compliant food it would magically improve your life? Is standing up for your own health a weak point when surrounded by "others"? Sure. We all want to fit in - to belong - not stand out but as we take the risk to be true to ourselves, we strengthen that "muscle" every time we practice.

What was hard at first will become second nature.

_____

_____

_____

_____

AUGUST 29

WORD FOR TODAY: TEMPTATION

Someone asked "How are you able to maintain the lifestyle in the face of so many of life's daily temptations".

Maybe it's like monogamy! You make a decision and then live it each day. Practice, practice, and practice. Maybe sometimes you stay out of harm's way by not putting yourself in compromising positions until you are stronger. You have the power to have a clean house. And then, when faced with it, you make sure you are never hungry. Be prepared and full of starch.

Ads on TV only make suggestions. Others we live with may not comply and we can engage in a blaming game or we can put on our big girl pants and be our own boss. We are the ones who talk ourselves into eating "food poison". We are the ones who say we deserve it. We are the ones who put decadent (notice decay in that word) foods on a pedestal and think we deserve to be rewarded. We are the ones who focus on the temptation instead of the cure.

Focus on what you want in life and determine if you want that more than the alternative. Life is a choice. Be honest with yourself. Are you desperate enough to pay the price of putting energy and thought into this way of living?

This way of life is not an easy road. How does your belief system reinforce your commitment? Do you actually believe that this is the best way to regain your health with weight loss being a "side effect" or do you just want to take off the weight "the easy way"?

And as you gain the strength to resist temptations, be kind to yourself as you learn. No corporal punishment allowed. Learn and grow. No guilt - only learning. It is a lifetime process.

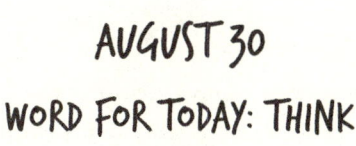

_____
_____
_____
_____

AUGUST 30

WORD FOR TODAY: THINK

We think, most of the time, but are we conscious of what we are thinking about?

Are we aware of the thoughts that we focus on? Do we realize

FROM DONUTS...TO POTATOES

how many times a day we just pop food in our mouth and don't even remember eating it...it was just there and it was easier to eat it than discard it or save it for another time.

Taking time to think before we make a decision is certainly a good step in the right direction.

Sometimes I pick up something that needs to be put away, but then I just set it back down until I talk to myself and say, "Now, just go and put it away right now".

Taking time to think is a pause that can give us clearer direction and an opportunity to choose what we want - not just act out of a knee jerk reaction.

Choose what you want in your life today. Imagine it, and then think about the joy that that decision will bring to you and smile, knowing that the best is yet to be.

_____

_____

_____

AUGUST 31

WORD FOR TODAY: MINIMIZE

There is a lot of talk these days about how to minimize. We are encouraged to re-cycle, donate and even dump what is no longer serving us.

All of these suggestions speak to me because I have a hard time getting rid of things I no longer need. My Grandmother Lebeck had a neat barn in which she was able to store things and I remember how much fun it was to explore what she kept on shelves.

ESTHER LEBECK LOVERIDGE

I guess those who came through the Great Depression learned about the benefits of saving "things" for a rainy day. My Aunt Christel lived in the mountains and she saved plastic bags. She also saved old newspapers because she had a wood burning stove in her kitchen and could use the papers to kindle a fire.

I think the easiest thing for me to minimize has been the non-compliant food in my kitchen. Well, it wasn't easy, but I was able to finally do it when I identified food I was no longer going to eat and when I asked Ben if he was going to use it and he said "No", I was able to toss it out.

When I need a pat on the back, I remind myself that it was just a year ago that we had a dumping party and poured all of the liquor down the drain. Some of it was gifts and some was stuff we had for over 30 years! It was so cathartic to open the bottles and just dump it. And the good part is that some of it had filled the cupboard over our refrigerator and I have kept that cupboard empty ever since. That is about as good as my bragging rights get when it comes to minimizing.

_____

_____

_____

_____

SEPTEMBER 1

WORD FOR TODAY: CAN

The little Choo Choo Train, it is said, thought he could and he did.

Sometimes I think about what I can do and it often conjures up ideas about growing into a healthier body, spreading the news, maybe writing a book and maybe helping others in new ways.

But this morning, I had a new awakening. Thinking about what I can do isn't limited to accomplishing great tasks. It isn't about increasing my prosperity (although that is a given since being a positive person is being prosperous).

This "I can" idea took on new a new dimension for me today. It centers on the mundane, the routine, the thankless chores and the functional part of life.

Since I have been thinking about de-cluttering, I am changing my thoughts from "I have a hard time releasing things I no longer need" to "I can release them". "I can experience release from being held captive from small tasks or things". "I can work through piles of paper that clutter my desk". "I can eliminate files I no longer need". "I can clean out a cupboard."

I just never considered making the "I can" work for tedious jobs as well as accomplishing great and uplifting aspirations.

And if I worry about what will I do without____. I can remember the lesson I learned from Rev. Cherie Larkin. "Whatever we have manifested once in our life, we can manifest again". If you don't believe her, just empty your junk drawer and see how quickly it fills up again.

_____
_____
_____
_____

FROM DONUTS...TO POTATOES

SEPTEMBER 2

WORD FOR TODAY: FLOCK

With whom do you flock?

We gather together for many reasons - to be with family, to congregate at places of worship, to assemble for community affairs and of course, to eat.

Some of us gather together to drink and celebrate life. Some play sports together and so it is...we gather to share in mutually enjoyed events.

But what happens when the focus of flocking changes? What happens to the person who can no longer tolerate alcohol? Does he/she exclude themselves from the gatherings or is that person able to switch to a non-alcoholic drink and still enjoy his or her buddies?

Does that person's change affect the others or do they even care?

There is no one answer. We all walk our path and find our comfort zone but I think there is a degree of "ease" by being with people of a similar mind. Birds of a feather flock together.

So, if you feel alienated after changing any of the reasons why you used to flock, know that life is constantly changing, you are evolving. I remember a poem about the duration of time that some people stay in our lives. Some connection last for a brief spell while others seem to last a lifetime.

_____

_____

_____

_____

ESTHER LEBECK LOVERIDGE

SEPTEMBER 3

WORD FOR TODAY: RID

Advertisements bombard us on how to get rid of pimples, wrinkles, saggy eyes, fat bellies and of course, weight while they never teach us how to reverse disease - only how to manage it for the rest of our lives on medication.

What I really want to talk about is the necessity for us to get rid of the idea of going on a diet. Yes, it is a common word in our vocabulary and does define a plan of eating - even when it describes a healthy eating pattern. It is interesting that the book I followed does not use the word "diet" in the title "The McDougall Program for Maximum Weight Loss".

Often, a diet is viewed as something we do for a given period of time to get certain results. But what happens when that time expires and we DO get all that was promised to us?

I can tell you. We have this false sensation or belief that we have arrived. We have reached our goal. We are successful. Wow. But then, (I can attest to having done this dozens of times), we feel the relief of having achieved our goals and go back to our old eating habits.

So, what is the answer? I have come to believe that education is the beginning. When we learn about how we are causing disease in our bodies by what we eat, we are then in a better position to make an intelligent choice.

Yes, it is pretty radical to give up animal and dairy products and then when we learn that processed oil has no legitimate place in our lives, we are often shocked. How could that be?

Don't take my word for it. Test it for yourself. Be your own lab. Try getting rid of the toxic food for one week and see how your body responds. It's miraculous.

SEPTEMBER 4
WORD FOR TODAY: AROUSED

This morning, Ben wondered if I was awake and I said "I am aroused". Is arousing any different from awakening?

We slumber and then we come out from that state of being into the present.

Sometimes, our brain is dulled and we walk around like we are in a coma, not conscious of what we are doing or even why.

Once we are aroused, we can become alert as to who we are, what we want and how we are going to aim towards fulfilling our goals.

New thoughts stimulate our brain into thinking differently. The old paths are familiar but not necessarily better. They are simply paths that have brought us to this point.

What arouses me is realizing that it is never too late nor are we ever too old to take on new experiences and pleasures. Certainly our bodies show signs of wear and tear but our minds can be fresh and eager to explore, learn, grow and expand into new heights.

SEPTEMBER 5

WORD FOR TODAY: PATIENCE

Is patience a virtue or an acquired skill? Is it a gift or something we think we lack?

How do we get patience? Oh, yes, we say "Rome wasn't built in a day" or we are just told to have it.

Patience comes to me when I can put things in perspective. As I take time to breathe and inhale positive energy and then release any negative emotions I might have as I exhale, I find stress leaving my body. I become more relaxed. I consider what I can control and what I cannot and trust that events will occur in their own timing.

It helps to have realistic expectations while still leaving room for adjustments. It means not always seeking my will. It means I don't have to understand everything at once. It means loving me, being kind to me and exercising trust that all is well.

Keeping an open mind to alternative outcomes helps me too. Sometimes accepting the fact that what I think is best is just how my mind is thinking at the moment.

How easy it would be if we still viewed life through the lens of that old TV show "Father Knows Best" but struggle is a part of getting to acceptance and patience requires practice.

FROM DONUTS...TO POTATOES

SEPTEMBER 6
WORD FOR TODAY: BAIT

I've never really gone fishing and had to bait the hook (put a worm on it) but I do realize that in order to catch a fish, there has to be an attraction, a seduction, or a lure in order to get the fish to bite.

In life, we are often attracted to things by its aroma, sight, or sometimes we are drawn to something because of the memory we attach to it.

Our minds then make the connection and a desire to succumb may surface. But what we do with that attraction is up to us. We can relish, glamorize or idolize the bait. We can spend time remembering previous experiences with it. Some attractions are very strong and we may even call them addictions and feel helpless in the presence of them.

So, what's a mother to do? When I am tempted, I try to reframe how I look at it. Often I refer to bakery items as poison but when we were in Croatia and the tour guide treated everyone in the group to an ice cream cone that was difficult. Ben and I just stepped away from the group while they did their licking. More than not eating the free ice cream cone, the difficult part was feeling estranged from the group. I felt isolated. I did not want to be excluded so I finally went to the guide and asked if we could have a bottle of water instead. Yes, of course.

Substitutes help and whenever temptation arises, there is always a way to escape. At home, our success at staying compliant is much easier when we control our environment.

ESTHER LEBECK LOVERIDGE

_____

_____

_____

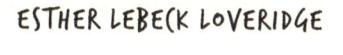

SEPTEMBER 7

WORD FOR TODAY: TURNOVER

When you read the title of today's word, what popped into your head? Was it a pastry? I'm just wondering. When Ben had his donut shop (yes, good things like him do come from a donut shop) he also made apple turnovers.

But I am thinking about how we can turnover things in our life. Surrender is a big part of moving into a healthier place. We can think of giving things up or if that makes us feel like we have less, we could simply think of it as releasing the old and making room for what nourishes us.

Yesterday, we went through "stuff" in our storage room. I would hold some items in my hands and turn them over as I made the decision on what to do next...Garbage, Goodwill, or Give to a friend...or, delay the decision?

To whom or to what do you want to turnover your desires? Like stuff we no longer need or use, we make room for new healthy thoughts as we turnover past ways of thinking and embrace life giving ones - you know, learning the value of eating whole food.

Like Lot's wife in the old story, we can look back and yearn for what we are leaving behind and become rigid - not knowing how to go forward and knowing we cannot go back. Or, we can let go of the past, turn over a new leaf in our journey and go forward into a new life of health and vitality.

FROM DONUTS...TO POTATOES

_____

_____

_____

_____

SEPTEMBER 8
WORD FOR TODAY: GLORIFY

Glorify - that is a nice "Sunday" word. What do I glorify? What things do I put on a pedestal and elevate above all others? What are my idols?

Well, there are many, I am sure. I elevate gifts that have been given to me. I attach emotion to them and see them as a reflection of feelings between us. They then hold memories for me and I treasure them. But do these "gifts", once they have served their purpose, eventually become a burden, take up space just for the sake of glorifying their meaning in my life?

In the past, I had my favorite meals, restaurants, ice cream and candy shops that I could actually salivate over if I thought of them for awhile. To me, there was no better candy than See's and no better ice cream than Ben and Jerry's - the richer the better.

About a year and a half ago, I bought a pound of See's for a friend in Virginia and ended up with 3 samples which I brought home. Chef AJ says "If it is in your house, it will be in your mouth". Well, I had reached that smug stage after following The McDougall Program for Maximum Weight Loss for awhile and thought I'd put her to the test. I kept that candy hid under the sink in the bathroom for a whole year...but one day, I went for it even though it was stale. I had put it on such a pedestal that I would not let myself throw it away.

The secret is that we have all we need - yes I am still working towards accepting that. What we have glorified or manifested in our past we can recreate if we want. So why do we have the attachment? Why the fear of letting go? Do I need physical evidence to feel like I am loved? Sometimes I do. I'm still growing.

_____

_____

_____

_____

SEPTEMBER 9

WORD FOR TODAY: STOP

Do people in your neighborhood still stop at the red stop sign or is that sign just a suggestion to stop or to cruise on through?

Stop signs have a specific purpose in our lives. They give us the opportunity to take a mandatory pause.

Sometimes we don't stop a specific behavior until we reach a tipping point. Maybe we get sick, a relationship becomes stressed, we run out of steam or we just put on too much weight.

Stopping helps re-evaluate what we are doing to ourselves. If gives us time to think and choose a different option as we move ahead.

Many of us have ignored stop signs. We are sure we know best. We are sure there won't be a price to pay because we have gotten away with that behavior for a long time. But eventually, our body says "Stop, I can't take it anymore".

The stop sign is not a nagging parent. It is not mean. It is only an opportunity to rethink a situation. We are still in the driver's seat and we are the ones with our foot on the brake.

Stop. Then go enjoy yourself as you incorporate the best life has to offer in your journey.

___

SEPTEMBER 10

WORD FOR TODAY: MISSING

What is missing in my life today? What has been missing for 15 years yet what is still with me even at this moment? It was my childhood side kick. It was the older yet youngest of my 3 brothers. It was Paul.

Yes, I could feel sad. I could feel regret that when I told him I had some glucosamine for him that he'd have to come out and get it - I wasn't going to take it to him. (Was I practicing tough love?)

I can counter those feelings with "I'm so glad he didn't get old and have to live alone in a nursing home". "I am glad he is no longer suffering with chronic pain." "I am glad he died suddenly".

There are blessings even in death. But, at times like today, the 15th anniversary of his passing, he feels close to me. I have one of his watches here on my desk.

What is missing isn't really missing from our lives. The form may change, but the energy that kept us together for 61 years still surrounds me. He reminds me to question. He reminds me that sometimes life is hard for one of us yet seems easy for another.

The place he held in my life will remain his. It is a special place to come to on days like this.

Enjoy your health, your life and your family.

_____

_____

_____

SEPTEMBER 11

WORD FOR TODAY: LIMITS

Sometimes I say the sky is the limit as to what I can accomplish. Most of us have no idea of what is possible in our lives. We subconsciously may have been thinking that includes what is easily possible but not necessarily what is actually achievable.

So, what do we do with the gap that exists between what is easily accomplished and what tempts us to reach beyond where we have ever been?

Many times, I have just rationalized my position in life by telling myself that this is where I belong, this is my comfort zone, this is where I have less stress in my life but then...some idea creeps into my mind that maybe I can have more. Not more like in things, but more in terms of what I can actually do. Sure, I may fail as I try on new habits, or experiences, but on the other hand, I just might be getting a glimpse into what is possible.

When we get a taste of that joy, that idea that we can stretch ourselves and be kinder, more loving, more giving, more understanding, more compassionate and more whatever, we cannot easily go back. The river rushes forward as we learn new and improved ways of being.

It has been said, and may be true, that what we fear most is what we are capable of doing.

_____

_____

_____

_____

SEPTEMBER 12

WORD FOR TODAY: ENJOY

To enjoy, is to be "in-joy". Sometimes we struggle in our journey through life. There are ups and downs but are we able to find nuggets of pleasure in the in-between times?

It is helpful to focus on our goals. It is good to imagine a better future and we can create what we want in our lives but it is important to incorporate joy, thankfulness, and gratitude and hope as we go along. It is easy to get so focused on one aspect of our lives that we forget to breathe and inhale the joys that are right under our feet.

Taking time to notice the little moments along the way that cause our lips to turn up into a smile is good. Notice what those events are and treasure them. Embrace them.

When we eat, it is helpful to take time to be thankful and be mindful of what we are eating. Where did the food come from, how was it made, how does it taste and feel in our mouths? Are we taking time to chew our food with awareness or are we washing it down with our favorite beverage? Pause and enjoy each bite.

What we think about we bring about. Where do you put an

exclamation point in your life? Is it centered on lack, need and illness or can we choose to focus on the fact that we have all we need and that step by step we are moving forward?

_____

_____

_____

_____

SEPTEMBER 13

WORD FOR TODAY: FLOW

Here we are, sitting on a plane transporting us from China to India and we are just that, passengers traveling at the mercy of those in charge. It is indeed a time when we let go and allow the crew to do their thing.

But we had to do our part. We had to get ourselves from one gate to another when we arrived in Guangzhou, China from San Francisco. The process went quite smoothly when we went through another security check and were then advised of the number of our departure gate. The officer was helpful and even wrote the gate number on our boarding pass -165.

It was quite a walk but we got there with a few minutes to spare. There was only one problem - no one else was in the waiting area and it was an eerie feeling that something was amiss. Ben found someone to double check on the gate number for us and instead of it being 165, it was 145! We high tailed it back the long path to gate 145 where the crowd was already boarding the plane. There was no time to sit so actually, it worked out real well. We got to have a nice quick walk instead of sitting again.

FROM DONUTS...TO POTATOES

It is easy to get anxious in unfamiliar settings but if we can just go with the flow, it is amazing how often events turn out in our favor.

It's easy to say that since we made it to the gate before the plane took off.

We are very comfortable on China Southern Airlines - there is plenty of leg room and the vegan food we requested was delicious. Shelly, who sat next to me on the first leg of this trip did not preorder her food and had a hard time accepting the fact that she couldn't get a vegan meal upon request.

Rule #1: Plan and prepare.

I have no idea of what time or day it is but I know we are headed to New Delhi and sometime in the near future, we will be at our first hotel.

_____
_____
_____
_____

SEPTEMBER 14

WORD FOR TODAY: HELPERS

I loved watching Mr. Roger's Neighborhood on TV with my kids (and can't wait for the new movie to come out with Tom Hanks playing Mr. Fred Rogers).

One of the things he would tell us was that when there is a problem, we should look for the helpers. They are always there when we need them.

I can certainly say that the helpers in the airports were always gracious in answering any questions we had even though they probably get asked those questions multiple times. At the hotel, we had trouble accessing Jude's floor with our room key so the clerk at the hotel counter left his post to show us how it works and then ended up adding the 5th floor to our card so we could get there in the elevator from our 4th floor. Good security.

When we went to the mall to look for something to eat, we were continually guided by local helpers. One man even helped us order and showed us where to sit and the food was brought to us. Kindness abounds. Another helper walked us around to several eating establishments until we found a vegetarian place.

We are here to help one another. Seeing how helpful strangers have been to us motivates me to be open to strangers at home who may feel our country is just as foreign to them.

It is fortunate that most people speak English. After arriving at the airport and retrieving our luggage, we found the representative from Gate 1 Travel and he walked us to the parking lot where a driver was waiting in his air conditioned Toyota to take us to our hotel. His English was very good but some things were hard to communicate. When I asked about the cows along the side of the road, he said they roam freely but when I asked "What do they eat?" He thought I was wondering if they were eaten!

He was a very skilled driver and knew how to negotiate between the cars, the little Tuks, motor bikes and anything else on the road. Lots of horn honking in this busy city.

The weather tonight was a little balmy with a nice breeze and walking to the mall was an interesting experience. The sidewalks were quite broken up and the streets very busy but inside the huge mall, every top name store was there along with IHOP, Burger King and KFC and we could have just as easily felt like we were in New York. (There was a security screening to enter the mall).

It was a long flight getting to India plus we lost 12 1/2 hours so we practically missed all of Friday the 13th

FROM DONUTS...TO POTATOES

_____

_____

_____

_____

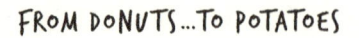

SEPTEMBER 15
WORD FOR TODAY: GROUP

There is a group of us on this tour of India -14 to be exact and a small group makes it possible to not only get acquainted, but to get in and out of the bus easily and actually have a chance to learn what brought us all together from Florida, Texas, Virginia, Ohio, California and New Zealand.

Groups form for various reasons and this group is no exception. We are all retired and enjoy learning about faraway places as well as our neighbors next door.

Today at the mosque, it was tricky walking around barefoot because of the slippery marble floors. They are beautiful to look at but when wet, create a risky situation. We did see people who had fallen - including three from our group.

The mosque was very impressive but then so were all of the stops along the way. I especially enjoyed looking at the children and they seemed interested in us as well. I'm sure we stand out as "others" and they must be curious too.

We had a tuk ride, a ride in a bicycle driven "rickshaw", enjoyed the museum, an Indian restaurant for lunch and two meals at the hotel. We also got to spend time at Gandhi's home and learn more about his life.

Although we did wear name tags all day, tonight's welcoming dinner gave us a better chance to learn more about each other

We spent most of our time in New Delhi, but also got to see Old Delhi. The traffic was very busy in spite of this being Sunday. I guess tomorrow, the traffic will be even heavier.

This little "groupie" is going to bed. It has been a very big day.

_____

_____

_____

_____

SEPTEMBER 16

WORD FOR TODAY: ONUS

Now where did that word come from? I guess the onus is on me to explain.

In life, we have the privilege of having so many choices. Along with getting to make decisions around those options, we also have to accept the consequences of our actions.

That leads me to the next step of relating this to how we eat. We can blame our ancestors for the genes we have, we can blame our spouse/partner for not wanting to go along with a WFPB eating plan, we can blame our social life and our friends and we can blame ourselves by saying we just lack the willpower to stick to a healthy eating plan.

We get to choose what results are important to us...important enough to make a commitment even before we have experienced the joys of sustained health. Each step we take leads us closer to achieving our goals.

By blaming outside circumstances or people, we think we can

FROM DONUTS...TO POTATOES

fool ourselves into not taking responsibility for ourselves. But in the end...the onus is on us.

_____

_____

_____

SEPTEMBER 17

WORD FOR TODAY: WITNESS

We witness life in so many special ways. There are our experiences, our personal events to which we testify. What is interesting to me is how we all have the capacity to see what we see through the lens of our own experience. It is often what we bring to a situation that defines how we interpret a happening.

I remember seeing a movie years ago in college and never forgot it. It was called something like "In the Eye of the Beholder" and how every person's reaction to an event put it in the context of their own life. We certainly do that to each other when we try to explain why someone does what they do.

But there comes a time when we own an experience. Yes, motivation can be interpreted in many ways, but when we experience a life changing event, all of that goes out the window when the evidence supports what we have personally witnessed.

I am a witness or an expression of what occurred in my life as a result of following The McDougall Program for Maximum Weight Loss. I followed the book. I did not have any other instructor, mentor or guru leading me. I put the book to the test and said from the beginning that if it worked, I'd give Dr. McDougall the credit. It was a test. The results are in and although I have been supported by my husband and close friend who gave me the book as well as having my intentions supported by watching the whole food plant based documentaries and the stories of others, it is my personal story and I bear witness that it has saved my life from a path that was leading to my own destruction - a path I freely chose until I learned.

Even when we see the evidence of what can change our lives it is insufficient for many people. We have our excuses, our "yes, but" retorts. Not all of us want the same thing - at least that "want" is not strong enough to sustain the surrender required for long term success. We are human. We are normal. We love pleasure. We want our cake and eat it too. We love our lifestyle and for some, it just isn't worth what is seen as a "sacrifice". And if that is true, I say be honest. If you are not "there" yet, then be real but be aware if you still complain about the results you get from the behavior you choose.

We have freedom of choice, freedom from disease and freedom to learn at one's own pace or freedom to maintain what is comfortable. Isn't life grand? We get to create the story of our own life. If we see food as our life-giving source, we are the ones who get to raise our forks to our mouths and put it in. We are in charge and we are a witness to the consequences of our choices.

_____

_____

_____

_____

FROM DONUTS...TO POTATOES

SEPTEMBER 18

WORD FOR TODAY: QUESTIONS

Question everything. That is how we learn and make choices of our own. When we wonder whether or not something is right for us, it means we are thinking, re-evaluating for ourselves and coming to our own conclusions. Then we can "own" it until it is time to re-think it again. We are constantly growing, learning, adapting and moving forward.

I notice when people ask questions about whether or not a certain food is "allowable" or "compliant", it most often is not. I keep it very simple. If it looks like whole food, there is very little to think about. I have found for myself that when I even think about the substitutes that are out there that could replicate the food I used to eat; it keeps me "attached" to my old way of thinking and desiring.

I want to be free of the old attractions. I do not want to entertain, in my mind, about how much I miss them. So many of the substitutes are fat laden and we know what fat does to our body - it clings like glue.

For those who do use some of the alternative foods as a bridge to get to where they want to go, that is a choice. Minimizing the use of animal products is a step forward.

I think abstinence far exceeds moderation in terms of becoming healthy and successful in losing weight especially for people like me who classify themselves as food addicts. Yes, we can play with our temptations but trying to figure out when is something enough takes a lot of thought and energy.

Know the truth for you. It sets us free. Dabbling is a choice when we give power to something outside of ourselves. Go within. Ask yourself "What do I really want? What is important to me? What do I want in this present life time experience? I heard Dr. Dean Ornish ask during an interview what we are WILLING to do. That is what will lead you to making positive choices in your life whether it includes your food choices, exercise, meditation and prayer and of course surrounding yourself with love and support. This is your life. Go for it.

_____

_____

_____

_____

SEPTEMBER 19

WORD FOR TODAY: INTERACTION

While it is fun to learn the history of a country or geographical region, the real joy for me comes in the interactions we get to have with the local people.

India is a great place to do just that. Hospitality reigns and so does a willingness to engage, to talk and to laugh together.

Yesterday, we stopped at a beautiful gem shop where Ben spotted a pair of gem-laden earrings. Yes, he does have good taste and often selects something to show me which is over the top. They would have cost $8,000. In silver, a smaller pair was only $150 but it didn't matter how much they cost. I am trying not to buy more "stuff". I have all I need...but when we got to a sari shop, I did find 3 tunics and of course buying clothes is a lot more fun now even if I am a size 1X here. The shop was clean, had a nice dressing room with a mirror and the price was right - $14. That would be easy to believe if I had bought them on the street, but I sure was surprised to find something at that price in this lovely shop.

Back on the street, I noticed a young local man wearing a very

FROM DONUTS...TO POTATOES

interesting hairdo and asked him if I could take a photo. He said "No" but then I pursued it like the bangle selling chaps who don't like to take no for an answer. We had so much fun playing together and of course this brought him a lot of attention as the other young men enjoyed the "game". He finally gave in but the photo did not do justice to the unusual hair do.

Last night at dinner here at our new hotel in Jaipur, the staff was notified that we were vegan and the soup, salad, pasta and banana dessert were delicious. I can certainly remember when I used to feel "cheated" if I didn't take advantage of included items but when given a choice of beer, wine or a soft drink, I am very comfortable in taking water.

The interactions we are having with the other travelers in our group are so easy with only 14 of us. There are 6 couples and two single women and we get to spread out all over our big air conditioned bus. It's unfortunate that the bus driver and his assistant are closed off from us and their section is not air conditioned.

Today is our last full day with Seema our tour director. She has been so helpful and educational with her stories as we travel down the road. We will be getting a new tour director when we get to Nepal and await new interactions there.

_____

_____

_____

_____

ESTHER LEBECK LOVERIDGE

SEPTEMBER 20

WORD FOR TODAY: HEALING

In the midst of our daily life, there is a need to come away from the crowd and the hustle and bustle of activities. In India, there are lots of sounds to hear, unusual photos to take and certainly an abundance of visual stimuli as we just watch life going on all around us.

And so it was this morning at 5:30 we had a before breakfast departure to go on a Safari. While it is true that the big hope was to get to see a leopard, it was actually very healing to me to just be in nature. I don't remember when I have taken time to just listen to the birds, see trees stretched out with limbs which looked like they had been dancing and then got frozen in time.

The monkeys were out playing and the antelope were teaching their one day old babies to fend for themselves already. Some were Bambi's - spotted antelope and many of the females traveled in harems.

It was interesting to hear the peacocks screech as they are the alarm signals to danger since they have such good eyesight. We even heard their mating calls and got to observe a male spread his "glory" with a female nearby.

As we traveled down the rocky roads in our Jeep, we stopped long enough to observe the tracks of a leopard and its cub.

The sun was hidden from plain view and there was a slight breeze before the dawning of what most likely will be a hot afternoon.

Just to be in nature and even smell some mint was refreshing. My soul needed that - time to reflect and meditate on the wonder of life in all of its forms.

After spending about 3 hours in the forest our jeeps took us back to our bus and as we returned to the hotel for breakfast, we passed what is referred to as the "slums", yet people are just doing what comes naturally- gathering food, living in small rooms and having time to chat as the day progresses. The cows, dogs and pigs do their own thing in the middle of life here at Jaipur.

Healing comes as we release fear, give thanks for the gifts we are given and breathe in the wonderful life-giving force.

_____
_____
_____
_____

SEPTEMBER 21

WORD FOR TODAY: UNTOUCHABLE

When I heard that there is a classification of people in India called "Untouchables", I was intrigued. What would it feel like to have that as one's identification?

We met a group of women who were sweeping the sidewalks and we were told that they were untouchables. What would the world be like without these people who take care of some of the necessary cleaning jobs? The three women were related by marriage (married to her two brothers) to the lady in the center. All three of them had not attended school but all of their children are in school today.

We took photos of their foot jewelry and even though they are paid for their work, they do get additional tips from tourists who choose to have their photos taken with them.

What in my life is untouchable? Are there people I choose not to associate with? What about food? Yes, I can say I'd prefer to stick with my plant-based diet. It has served me well and decisions are made more easily when food I used to eat is now classified as "untouchable".

As I learned as a child, "some things are legal, but not expedient" and so we all have choices we get to make - none being better than another - just different. People have argued over the centuries about the benefits of eating a certain way and so it is that we get to define that for ourselves.

I'm not sure what the folks on the street eat (I think most Hindus are vegetarian) but obesity definitely is not an issue here. Some of the women have fuller bellies as evidence by their saris not covering their mid drift but the men are quite slender.

We are leaving India and will fly to Kathmandu, Nepal after an early breakfast at our hotel. More adventures await us as we continue this wonderful journey.

_____

_____

_____

_____

SEPTEMBER 22

WORD FOR TODAY: SUSPEND

Sometimes some accused people have their sentence suspended. But what have I to suspend?

What I must suspend as a world traveler is the expectation that all things are predictable. Each day offers an opportunity to learn about the people and the culture and the realization that we are here to learn. Each day is our teacher. Each experience teaches us that we are all one.

FROM DONUTS...TO POTATOES

   I remember a funny incident (at least funny to onlookers) when a passenger ahead of me had to remove so many things before he could pass through the metal detector at an airport in New Jersey. First came the coins, then the belt and when he still beeped, it was determined that it might be his suspenders. Yep, that was the key. His suspenders, once removed, allowed him to pass through the metal detector but alas, he was also asked to raise his arms over his head as the security guard waved the wand over his body. It was at that precise moment when his trousers fell to the ground! Embarrassing moments happen to all of us to remind us we are human.

   So what holds me up? It is the belief that I am in my right place wherever I am. It knows that I am loved. I am a child of the universe and I am here to learn. I realize how fortunate I am to be able to explore the world and that happiness is always within me wherever I am.

   I want to continue to suspend my judgments of how others choose to live their life. I want to suspend the idea that my thinking is right for everyone.

   I love my journey and am thankful that others are taking it with us.

_____

_____

_____

_____

ESTHER LEBECK LOVERIDGE

SEPTEMBER 23

WORD FOR TODAY: CUP

Songs from long ago often come to my mind in the early morning hours. A song came up this morning about filling my cup and having my thirst quenched and becoming whole.

That is what I want - to be whole...in my body, mind and soul. We are spiritual beings in a physical body and of course it is easy to focus on what is visible - our bodies; however, there is a deeper longing that I have that food cannot fill.

It is the desire to be full of joy, peace, love and faith. I want faith that I can be my best by nurturing my body with good food. I have faith that following Dr. McDougall's Program has been my guiding light for health. I want joy in being freed from past addictions. Peace of mind comes when we are honest with ourselves and identify what is important to us.

What fills your cup? Is it loving your family, caring for an animal, feeding the poor, sharing your talents with others, donating to a good cause or something else?

When we empty our "cup" of foods which have filled us up in the past, I believe we need to find new sources of joy to give us that sense of being of value. Maybe it will be taking a walk. It could be practicing a new language. Maybe solving puzzles or making phone calls to people who may be lonely. As you empty your cup today, enjoy new ways to keep it full and overflowing.

_____

_____

_____

_____

FROM DONUTS...TO POTATOES

SEPTEMBER 24
WORD FOR TODAY: TRY

⋈

If at first you don't succeed, try again. Yesterday we had an excursion planned to fly to see Mt. Everest. We all boarded the plane but the pilot was notified that visibility was not good and we all elected to get off the plane. I don't know if all tours are this honest - where they don't just take your money and fly knowing that you are not going to see anything and then say, "Well, you know, you can't predict nature" or whatever.

We had a second chance to try again this morning. We knew the "drill" by this time and navigating through the small airport in Kathmandu was less stressful. We boarded the plane, got strapped in and took off. It was a lovely drive out to the runway where we sat for quite awhile before not taking off. Again, visibility was reported to not be good and so we had a nice plane ride back to the terminal.

Our guide hoped we were not disappointed. We have experienced so much in life and even things we think we want and don't get are minimal.

Ben asked Sanjay on the way back to our hotel "Is there a high rate of suicide in Nepal". He said, "No." He continued to expand by telling us that the temples here serve as cheap psychiatrists – which he sometimes goes to the temple to argue with God when things are not going as planned. They are a great place to meditate and listen to the inner voice help them reach peace. He said, "If you try, and something doesn't work out, you have done your part and it is out of your hands".

I do believe all things work together for good and that our own dreams and expectations do not always serve us well. Letting go is so important if we want to go with the flow in life and reduce unnecessary stress by holding onto what we think is best for us.

And so it is that our second try did not work out...but we did get a free plane ride - we just didn't make it off the ground. We will have two opportunities to see Mt. Everest when we fly from Nepal to Bhutan and also when we return to New Delhi from Bhutan.

The good thing about life is that sometimes we try to do something and then there are times when we choose to DO something. We all get that choice in matters we control. I am so glad I chose to follow Dr. McDougall's Program. It was in my hands.

SEPTEMBER 25

WORD FOR TODAY: DASH

What makes up the dash between the year I was born and the year I will die? It is a period of time we call life. How we choose to spend that dash, is up to us.

Today we witnessed the cremation of three people in Nepal with the body of a fourth person being prepared for cremation. We don't often talk about death in the U.S. at least not so blatantly and openly about how natural a part of the life cycle it is.

How did I experience watching this custom? Yes, I did think about a lot of things like how different it is to have a loved one die and then have them cremated within 24 hours. It seems so sudden and quick yet that's just what I think because it has not been the custom in my family.

On the other hand, it seems so simple and direct. It just is what happens here.

FROM DONUTS...TO POTATOES

Yes, it is stark and not sugar coated but in some ways, it seems so healthy.

And so it is that travel and experiences add more dimensions to our own lives. We get to learn from others about the importance of their rituals, beliefs and customs. We learn that it is not weird but truly a valuable alternative - one to respect and honor.

We acknowledge the miracle of birth and the span of time we refer to as the dash or time we call life.

I am reminded that our dash may be short or long yet meaningful. We get to write our own story and being healthy certainly increases the odds of extending the dash.

_____

_____

_____

SEPTEMBER 26

WORD FOR TODAY: IDENTITY

We hear stories about identify theft and I guess at some level, that has happened where an imposter has acquired enough information about a person to convince others that that is him or her.

However, can one's true identity be stolen? We heard an interesting story from Sangay our tour director. This is paraphrased but I want to remember the gist of what he said. He told us about a man who wanted to study under a great master and he was told where to go and what door to knock on. He presented himself at the identified door, knocked, and a voice from within said "Who is it?" Sangay used his name in the story and replied "It is Sangay". The master replied, "I don't think you are ready yet."

The next day, Sangay appeared at the door again and decided the master probably needed more background information so when the master asked "Who is it?" Sangay said "It is Sangay Nepal," and named his father. The master still responded "Hmmm, you're still not ready to learn".

On Sangay's third day, the master asked "Who is it?" and Sangay replied, "That is what I want to know". The master then said, "Now you are ready".

Perhaps that is the cry of many of us. Who are we? Why are we here? What is our purpose and mission? Once we get in touch with that, we will know who we are and that identity cannot be stolen. It is in our very fiber and being.

_____
_____
_____
_____

SEPTEMBER 27

WORD FOR TODAY: CLIMB

Climb every mountain; ford every stream...until you find your dream.

This morning, we got up with our 4:30 wakeup call and met our group in the lobby for our bus trip at 5:00 a.m. We boarded a small bus which took us up the mountain to the beginning of the 420 steps climb up to the summit. If we didn't have the smaller bus, a large bus would have not made it up that far because it would have had to park at a much lower elevation which would have meant

FROM DONUTS...TO POTATOES

that we'd have an additional 45 minute walk just to get to the stairs. Thank you, Sangay for arranging a small bus. It was just one more good reason to be traveling with a small group of 14 people.

Sangay, our tour director warned us that if it was raining, we wouldn't be able to go. There was only a slight mist, no umbrellas needed and so we headed out.

I didn't know how my knees or legs, for that matter, would hold up and decided it was worth it to try and see how far I could go. To think that just 3 years ago, I started "The McDougall Program for Maximum Weight Loss" in an attempt to lose 70 pounds in order for me to be referred to orthopedics for possible knee replacements and here I am in Nepal at almost 76, ready to try to make it to the summit of 420 cement steps.

Were the views grand at the top? Did I care? Not really. My dream was to navigate the steps the best I could and we all made it.

I used to think we should just do things. Not just try but now I see the advantage of giving something our best shot. As Sangay said, "When we try, it is in our own hands".

We used to sing a song about climbing up a mountain where heavenly breezes blow and I must say there is a special feeling from letting our bodies show us what we are capable of doing.

_____

_____

_____

ESTHER LEBECK LOVERIDGE

SEPTEMBER 28

WORD FOR TODAY: PEOPLE

Some singers have sung a song telling about people who love people are the luckiest people in the world and I certainly relate to people more than buildings, cars or even temples.

Yesterday, we went on two safaris on our last full day in the Tiger Jungle National Park. We could really observe how people in the villages work together especially when our Jeep got stuck in the water-filled muddy ruts.

The "Naturalist", the driver and the guys from the second Jeep all hopped off the Jeep to work together to get us out of there. Some carried rocks to fill the holes and one used a shovel, some tried to push the Jeep but what was interesting was to see them all turn into civil engineers who knew what to do.

One of my favorite experiences yesterday was watching the elephant trainer clean off the back of the elephant while it was lying down. This elephant is 44 years old and after his back had been cleaned, I was wondering how the trainer was going to ride him. He simply walked up the elephant's leg like it was a ramp and onto the back and off they went, out into the grasslands so the elephant could feed.

There is a military presence here in the park and it has been effective in preventing poachers from killing the rhinos.

As we passed through the villages, it was as though the residents were just waiting for us to pass, much like we would watch a parade at home. As I waved at the little children, their eyes would light up and they would very excitedly wave back - it felt like a happy reaction to being seen, noticed and valued.

The 14 of us (plus Sangay, our tour director) are the only visitors in the park. On our safari yesterday we were treated to a picnic lunch at the river's edge. The benches from our earlier boat ride

FROM DONUTS...TO POTATOES

served as benches with cushions for our picnic and a bounty of food was there waiting for us.

After finishing our picnic, the benches were loaded back onto the two boats which carried us down the river on a nice ride. We sang every river song we could thing of from Row Your Boat to Moon River, Old Man River and a few others that Ben came up with.

We didn't see any rhinos or tigers but did spot a crocodile, spotted deer and many identifiable birds. Most of all, it was quiet and authentic as we splashed through the rutted roads nearly hidden by the tall swaying grasslands. Oh yes, we did get to see a leech on the hand of our guide. I had seen one on an earlier safari and thought it was an inch worm.

Last night, after another well prepared meal including bananas and pomegranate seeds with a sweet dressing for dessert, we were treated to village dancers entertaining us.

Yesterday (and again today) we received an unusual wake up call. There was a knock on the door and two people were standing there with cookies and coffee or tea. I usually have hot water which they provided as well.

At night, when we return to our "suite", geckos - about 6 of them greet us above our door. I guess they are the ones who keep mosquitoes at bay. (I haven't seen a single mosquito on this whole trip). What I do hear singing quite loudly is the cicada. This place gives a whole new meaning to the word "quiet". There are no TVs in the rooms nor is there any internet. Usually, there is an internet connection in the Dining Hall, but service has been interrupted due to a recent storm.

After breakfast this morning, we will have another plane ride to another city in Nepal. This flight will only take 15 minutes. It is easier to fly than to travel the roads.

The people have been so hospitable here. They help us oldsters get in and out of the jeeps, up and down the usually wet stairs to the dining hall and have even plugged in my iPhone during a meal so I could have my battery charged.

There was a special moment yesterday when we stopped for

some to use a restroom. I saw a group of young men standing off to the right and asked our guide if I could go say "hello". He said I could so I walked over to where they were, struck up a conversation about age (they were in their early 20s) and they laughed when I told them I was 75. They, in broken English, wanted to know where I lived and of course we also talked about the fact that they rarely see white haired westerners. I got to shake the hand of each of them and they agreed to let me take their photo.

These are the times that people lovers get their reward.

SEPTEMBER 29

WORD FOR TODAY: NAMASTE

II woke up this morning thinking about this wonderful word. I don't claim to know the history of it, but what I do know is how I feel when I am greeted over and over again each day with someone holding their hands together, in front of their chest as they say "Namaste" to me.

There is a special connection at these times. It feels like there is one soul touching the soul of another. It feels genuine and a greeting which doesn't require a made up response like when we in the west say "How are you"?

I remember my father joking about our custom of asking someone "How are you" and he would chuckle and say, "Do you want the short version or the long version?"

FROM DONUTS...TO POTATOES

Do we really take the time to listen to the response we would get if we paused long enough to listen or are we just performing an obligatory greeting?

Every time we enter a hotel, a restaurant, a sidewalk shop or even pass a toddler on the street, we get this special greeting. To me, it says, "I see you, we are in this space together and I recognize your presence." These are moments when eye contact is made and we realize that we are one.

In Unity, it is said that we want to behold the Christ spirit in another. Is there not goodness in everyone? What if we suspended all judgments and just recognized the value in every one who crosses our path instead of looking for differences which separate us and keep us feeling isolated and alone?

Imagine. Namaste.

_____

_____

_____

_____

SEPTEMBER 30

WORD FOR TODAY: TENACITY

It's in the middle of the night and we are both awake and excited about the connection I made with Corinne Nijjer in Melbourne, Australia who wanted to hear my "story".

This technology is amazing. Here we are in different hemispheres and we can talk on the iPad freely using Skype. It was like she lived down the street.

Ben was energized too. He's not a preacher like me, but in his own way, wished it could be easier for people to switch to a plant based diet to restore one's health.

We chat on and on about the various ways eating this way has changed our lives. We recall the difference it has made for each of us. He wonders what difference it has made in his life other than losing a lot of weight. He never was on meds for the usual things that affect people our age. Then we recall the days when he had sleep apnea. My goodness, he could fall asleep anywhere - even in Disneyland, in a restaurant, on a park bench. Oh yes, and then there was the pain in his knee from an old football injury- gone. Bursitis in his shoulder was gone. Needing to shop in Big and Tall stores was gone. Now with a waist size of 36 instead of 52, he can shop anywhere.

Aches and pains creep up on us over time and like the frog in a pot of water that comes to a boil, we forget we can jump out of old environments and save ourselves.

So why did I choose the word "tenacity" this morning? Well, it was because when he ended our conversation, he said, "I love you little girl". Then I added, "What is it you love about me?" He said your "tenacity".

_____

_____

_____

_____

OCTOBER 1
WORD FOR TODAY: GRANTED

There are so many things we take for granted and we forget to be thankful for them. I know there are many people who are not interested in being on Face book for a number of reasons and that is fine. But... if you are like me and spend a lot of time using Face book as a means of communication with friends and groups, not having easy access certainly points out how important the connection is to many of us.

When we flew from Kathmandu to Bhutan, Ben and I had seats B and C which meant that we did not have the window seat. James, a gentle 27 year old man from China had that seat and boy did he gain "good karma" today by taking some photos of the Himalayas for us and a number of other people who were on the other side of the plane and had no access at all. He had studied in the UK and his English was excellent.

We talked about his life in China and how they still do not have Face book or Google nor can they easily travel to the U.S. He was thrilled to get to go to Bhutan.

Sometimes we get impatient when we have to obtain VISAS to some countries, but the point is we GET to go! We get to have freedom of religion which is not true for everyone.

Bhutan probably has the most beautiful airport I have ever seen. What a nice welcome. Our new Tour Manager, interesting that his name is also Sangay, met us and got us all through immigration and customs and onto the bus for our 1 1/2 hour bus ride to our beautiful hotel. The scenery along the way was delightful and there was no traffic. They did not even have a highway until 1961 and up until 1974, "others" could not even enter this closed country. People cannot move here to live unless they marry a local. The internet is limited and pretty new here so I am not sure how many photos I will be able to include, but I'll save them and send as I can.

FROM DONUTS...TO POTATOES

The men wear skirts with long socks with their knees showing (yes they do wear underwear per our guide) and the women wear long skirts. The students wear uniforms and I would say the residents have more of an Asian appearance than those we saw in India and Nepal. No more "Namaste" and I do miss that, however, they are friendly and helpful.

The mountains remind me of Lake Tahoe and it is a bit cooler. We had time to explore the downtown area and go through some of the shops. This definitely has a resort feeling and there are no sidewalk "vendors" trying to sell us trinkets.

We had lunch and dinner at our hotel today and their food is a bit spicy - meaning more hot than spice. I enjoy it but they tamed it down a bit for dinner tonight.

Our guide said they will be having eggs for breakfast and asked what we would like to have. I requested boiled potatoes and appreciate all they do to accommodate us.

One of our travelers was taking a photo of a dog and the dog bit her. She went to a hospital to get her rabies shot just to be safe. Dogs are plentiful and since they do not want to eliminate any of them, there is an effort to get them neutered to keep their population down. I hear they howl at night so I'll let you know. We did see cows on the road to the hotel as well, but not as plentiful as previously seen.

The most popular religion here is Buddhism and colorful monks were seen as we walked downtown. This may be the only capital of a country without a single traffic light. A policeman stands in the town square gazebo and directs traffic. Many of the 6 story buildings have no elevators. Our room in the hotel is more like an apartment. It is huge.

Be aware of the parts of your life that you take for granted.

_____

_____

OCTOBER 2

WORD FOR TODAY: BEAUTY

Beauty may be in the eye of the beholder and for me, I have enjoyed looking into the faces of the older women of Bhutan. They appear to be older looking even though I have not asked to learn their ages.

They enjoy accepting my extended hand and instead of shaking hands, we just seem to hold each other in that moment in time. I am not sure what they are thinking but for me, it is a moment when time stops and it would be easy to want more.

Bhutan is a beautiful place. It is clean, the architecture is lovely and it does have a feeling of a resort area. The country costume abounds and it is interesting to see it being so consistently worn by the young students to those in their senior years.

The mountains surrounding this area are pretty as well and we are so fortunate to visit this tiny country nestled in between India and China. How they have managed to keep their own identity is admirable.

Dogs love it here too. They are seen lying around; sleeping during the day but at night they come to life and bark quite a bit. (Makes me feel right at home with the sounds of our neighbor's dog)!

I am glad we have a third night at this hotel with a suite as large as an apartment.

There is a sense of preserving the environment here and also an emphasis on workers' rights. I saw a sign that read "I want happiness". If we remove the "I" and then remove the "want", we will be left with happiness.

FROM DONUTS...TO POTATOES

_____

_____

_____

_____

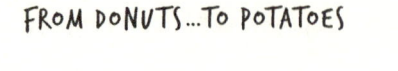

OCTOBER 3

WORD FOR TODAY: RE-ENACTMENT

When Ben and I worked back east, we had the opportunity to view a Civil War Re-enactment. It was amazing to us how much energy was involved in dressing up in period clothes, sleeping in tents and showing off priceless, saved memorabilia.

Yesterday, we attended an event where we got to re-connect with some of our friends. An interesting interaction occurred when one of them told me I should not lose any more weight. This is the second time someone has told me that and this time, I did not hold back. I told her that if she didn't take the opportunity to "warn" me in the past that I was putting on too much weight, she did not have the right to tell me that I should not lose any more weight. I mean, who was she to decide what my perfect weight would be? I advised her that my doctor was over the top happy with my success and asked her to drop it - the conversation, that is.

Anyway, there was another moment when she suggested that following the McDougall Plan wasn't the best and when I asserted that it had certainly been what I think is best for me; she answered "That is your OPINION".

I nearly hit the sky (we were outside) and we decided to end the conversation.

When we change the direction of our lives, we may face many in the "peanut gallery" who want to direct our lives and put us back in the cage from which we have escaped. Arguing doesn't solve the conflict. People are vested in their own ideas and may not be open to even acknowledging how much the change has benefitted you. Getting angry did not make the evening go any smoother, but I chose to stand my ground.

Now I realize that we have a choice. We do not have to keep re-enacting the past of personal conflicts or even competitive relationships.

By the way, we got to meet our granddaughter Danika and her boyfriend before going to the concert for one of her delicious, long hugs. The concert was wonderful and we were invited to a reception afterwards where we met wonderful, warm people, one of whom wanted to get my contact information for her overweight daughter.

This "road" isn't without bumps and potholes but we are riding on the backs of so many people who have blazed this trail of eating and promoting a plant based diet before us. The road will be smoother because of them.

_____
_____
_____
_____

OCTOBER 4

WORD FOR TODAY: BIRTHDAY

I have been asked if I ever cheat. What about birthdays, weddings, family dinners, Easter, Christmas, Thanksgiving? The list of opportunities goes on and on and when exceptions are made, it

FROM DONUTS...TO POTATOES

simply weakens our resolve to stick to a plan...there are simply too many opportunities to make celebrations an excuse.

When we were in Bhutan, our guide went to extraordinary means to honor me on my birthday. We were staying in a remote resort and in order to have a cake for me; it required traveling down a rut filled road to get to the bakery where he had arranged to have a personalized cake made.

At the conclusion of our dinner, the guide brought out the cake, all lit up as our group sang to me. Jude, our friend from New Zealand asked me if I was going to eat the piece they sliced for me. I was torn. It was not an easy decision. We finally agreed to share a piece and fortunately there was no opportunity to go overboard and go on a binge.

Dr. Doug Lisle, in a lecture, suggests we need to seek excellence, not perfection. This is a long journey. That is not to endorse making exceptions. It is just what I chose to do.

_____

_____

_____

_____

OCTOBER 5

WORD FOR TODAY: CONCLUSION

I have come to the conclusion that animal and dairy products are toxic to my body.

I want to create a new healthy body and nothing toxic belongs there.

I have concluded that I am the only one who can choose what I ingest.

I am not on a diet that will end at goal weight. Following Dr. McDougall is what I do. It is how I give my body fuel. I accept the scientific basis for it and don't want to argue.

I believe Chef AJ when she says, "If it is in your house, it WILL BE in your mouth.

I believe Dr. Doug Lisle (The Pleasure Trap) when he says it is normal to be drawn to the most calorie dense food in our environment. Remedy - don't have it in your house. Realizing that it is normal, takes the guilt away and makes sense to me and removing the offending food makes even more sense. It is not a lack of willpower. It is what we normally do - go to the richest food in our environment in order to survive.

I have concluded that I am worth buying, preparing and eating the best, most nutritious food available.

I am human and have slipped up. The key is to make our next bite a healthy one. We must minimize any gaps in healthy eating. Forgive yourself and learn something more about you, your personality, and what set you off.

Slip ups can be brief and no longer need to turn into a binge. You know...the old thinking that says, "Well, I have already screwed up so I might as well eat everything I have been denying myself". No, with extended time under our belt, getting back on target with the next bite is easier. We are creating good habits.

_____

_____

_____

_____

FROM DONUTS...TO POTATOES

OCTOBER 6

WORD FOR TODAY: BROTHER

Yeah, I guess that really is more of a relationship type word but today, it works for me.

I want to tell you about my oldest brother. Yes, he was very happy the day I was born - he was getting a sister who could do the dishes and release him of that chore. Little did he realize that by the time I could reach the kitchen sink, he would be well on his way out of the house.

All through my life, he has been there to support me...not the other way around. I joked at his 60th Wedding Anniversary Party that he was the only one to attend all three of my weddings. He would take me on camping trips, took me to my first real movie in a theater, taught me how to water ski, invited me and a date to join him when they celebrated their wedding anniversaries on New Years' Eve and even has been there for my significant birthdays.

When I turned 40, he let me take the "steering wheel" of his plane as we flew to the Nut Tree for dinner. When I was 50, his daughter Valerie Stewart gave me a birthday party and I used the $50 he gave me to buy a 14K gold charm for my bracelet. He came to my 60th birthday party here at our home, my 70th birthday party at the Grand Island Mansion down the river and on his 86th birthday, came to my 75th birthday party here.

When I had my first child, he brought his daughter Ruth Paz out to my house to meet Tim. When I was in the hospital, he came to visit me. When he was serving in the U.S. Air Force in Okinawa, he answered my scribbled letters and when I was in-between jobs, he even hired me as his secretary in his insurance agency.

What is the point of all of this? It is an example of how love lasts, even though political differences and slight changes in religion occur and now we are learning how to navigate differences in food preferences.

I think the desire to serve lives strongest in my brother. Thank you, Robert. You helped me navigate this life. Happy Birthday Eve to you.

_____

_____

_____

_____

OCTOBER 7

WORD FOR TODAY: REJOICE

Rejoice is kind of like being thankful but maybe with a bit of celebration thrown in! Yesterday afternoon, we welcomed our group of 10 people who made it to the top of the Tiger's Nest in Bhutan and back as they returned, tired but excited for their big accomplishment.

This group was comprised of 4 couples and two single women and I believe their ages spanned 53 to 76. Several of them were still contending with drawn out colds and coughs but being the strong travelers they are, they were determined to at least try to make the trip and make it they did.

Last night at our pre-dinner gathering, we got to hear their stories of being brave, tired and exhilarated but most of all, rejoicing in the way they all pulled together and helped each other along the rough terrain. What a bonding experience to take to this path with those who were strangers just 26 days ago and are now cemented

FROM DONUTS...TO POTATOES

in this wonderful experience...something none of them want to do again but neither do they regret having done it.

We took turns reflecting on our time together and our appreciation for being able to be in this part of the world where happiness does seem to reign and the people are as friendly and as helpful as can be. Hopefully we will take this experience home with us to encourage us to be friendly with everyone who crosses our path and be just as willing to be helpful to others as these wonderful people have been to us.

We are all so thankful to the Gate 1 team who literally held our hands and guided us along on this wonderful trip. Our driver navigated the tightest turns in the road and made it through traffic, our bags always got to our hotel rooms before we did, our guides told us great stories and inspired us with their version of Buddhism and certainly lived out the love in their heart and comforted me in so many ways. They made sure I had a wonderful birthday celebration and I could not have asked for a better trip.

This morning, we are up at 3:30 for a 4:30 departure for the airport here in Paro, Bhutan where we will fly back to Kathmandu for our final full day together. We will have one last chance to view the Himalayas and maybe see Mt. Everest.

Rejoice in every good thing...and there are so many.

_____
_____
_____
_____

ESTHER LEBECK LOVERIDGE
OCTOBER 8
WORD FOR TODAY: CYCLES

Endings and beginnings and all kinds of changes in between exist as we cycle through life and accept the idea that all thinks change, there is no permanence and flowing with the comings and goings of life are continually with us.

Our group is continuing to change. All fourteen of us flew from Bhutan back to Kathmandu yesterday and a Gate 1 representative escorted us from the airport back to the Yak & Yeti Hotel. What a difference 9 days make! When we left Kathmandu, we were told that their holiday had begun and that when we returned, we would find that Kathmandu was deserted. They were right!

The streets were so quiet, no traffic, and it was as though the city had been evacuated. There was a ghostly feeling with stores all closed with rarely a person in sight. When they have this 10 day holiday, the people go back to their villages to be with family. We have times in America where people travel in groves, but not by leaving any area deserted. It is more a time of leaving and arriving than a one-way exodus.

Just as was done each time we changed hotels, our bags preceded us and were waiting for us in our assigned room. Now, as a group, we were on our own. The representative, who escorted us to the hotel, was also going to go see his family and there was no longer a need to have a representative with us.

This turned out to be a very quiet day, a day to rest and to take a stroll through the deserted streets to see if we could find a place to get something to eat. Some of our group wanted Pizza and found a Pizza Hut. We found a nice bakery which had "Veggie Burger" on the menu and we ordered that. Ben found a shirt he liked and we had fun looking for a non-existent NAMASTE sign.

We had agreed to meet our group in the lobby at 6 pm and

FROM DONUTS...TO POTATOES

share our last supper together. We had a private area to share this dinner and of course I had to tell them about the time we were selling plaques of the Last Supper to Christian Book Stores in our territory. When the product started being reproduced in China, it was funny that the description on the box read "Final Dinner" instead of "Last Supper". Something was lost in translation.

Our group was now down to 12 as we ordered off the menu. Ben and I selected a vegetarian soup with some sides: steamed spinach, potato wedges and grilled vegetables. Sides are a great way to find something to eat on an otherwise overwhelming menu. Of course, we had to take more photos.

Today, we will all be taking different flights back home. Some go by way of NYC and one couple even has to have an overnight in Istanbul before getting back to the east coast. Our flight will take us through China, Los Angeles and San Francisco where our dear friend Charlie Cassell will meet us and drive us back to Sacramento.

Our breakfast with Jude, Jeff and Key concluded our included meals and Jude will be taking the transfer to the airport with us at 9:00 a.m. for her return to New Zealand. We got all of our belongings packed into the two carry on pieces of luggage which we will check through with only a small carry on piece to tote with us on our trip home. (We did buy another bag for the extras we picked up along the way, but got that packed too!)

It is time to disperse as we go our separate ways but there will be changes in each of us after having spent this time together. We now begin a new cycle in our lives.

_____
_____
_____
_____

ESTHER LEBECK LOVERIDGE

OCTOBER 9

WORD FOR TODAY: HOME

Home is where my heart is...but when the world becomes our home, does it really matter where we land?

Yes, it does matter, because home is where our safe environment is. Home is where we maintain a "kosher" kitchen, so to speak = where one can eat anything there because it is all compliant with a whole food plant based way of eating.

It is relief spelled with a capital "R". No more special requests for food that is animal and dairy free. No more knowing that I did not have the nerve or respect for myself to also request food with no oil. It just seemed like it was over the top to ask and expect that so I tolerated and worked around it as best as I could.

In India, they use a lot of ghee - clarified butter and once we learned about that, we did have that eliminated but there were still the roasted potatoes, grilled vegetables, and we noticed some oil in other dishes.

All of the fresh fruit was appreciated but now I am home and after about 75 meals of eating out, it will be a joy to return to my simple cooking of whole food, no oil, no added salt and plenty of fresh water.

Home, home on the range and in the Instant Pot!

_____
_____
_____
_____

FROM DONUTS...TO POTATOES

OCTOBER 10

WORD FOR TODAY: MONOTONY

Why would I glorify monotony? I mean, isn't that just ordinary? Who wants to be mundane? Or, certainly, when it has been suggested that variety is the spice of life, why in the world would I even comment about being bland?

Well, let me tell you. Plain can be our friend. All we have to do is reframe how we see things in order to use them to our advantage.

I had two of you ask me if I had weighed since getting home and I answered, "Yes, of course." It is what I do to be informed about my machine/body. I weighed 127.3 on September 12th when we left for our 26 day trip and yesterday, upon returning and eating out about 75 meals, I weighed 136.1.

Was I scared? No, I know that eating out includes lots of salt and even though we did walk a lot, sitting on a plane for long periods of time doesn't help. So, what did I do? I made dump soup and ate 9 cups of it yesterday. This morning, I weighed 130.3. Now you can see that I can view eating only dump soup all day as monotony or as a cleansing. It's all in how we frame our food - fuel or ecstasy.

If I embraced variety, I would have eaten much more, I will keep it simple again today and keep you posted on how long it takes me to get under 130 and back to 127.

Know your "friends". Let your experiences add interest and excitement to your life and try keeping your plate monotonous to break bad habits or get back on plan.

ESTHER LEBECK LOVERIDGE
OCTOBER 11
WORD FOR TODAY: WEIGHT

Yesterday, I enjoyed lunch at BJ's with friends from the pool. What did I want to order? A baked potato with guacamole but what did I order? I ate the fresh salad with no dressing because I really wanted to keep my food intake light.

We make choices every day. Sometimes we are strong and sometimes we give in to what psychologically rings our dinger. What I knew was that I'd be happier with my choice. I am reducing the salt and oil that I ate while on our trip. What I really want above something tasting special is to get back to my goal weight of under 130 which I did today (128.9) and will soon be back to 127.

But is weight all that important? We discussed this around our table and I shared that I wish we, as a culture, and specifically how we as women often focus on the number on the scale. It can send us into a dither or it can make us feel successful. But what it can do is have our self esteem measured by something OUTSIDE of us.

What I want to help people see is that as long as we focus on something outside of us, we will be a victim to it. We often play games with the scale and learn how to make decisions based on it instead of making healthy choices. What I want us to be aware of is that as we select the healthiest food for ourselves, we will be building a healthy life over the long run and we are only cheating ourselves to do otherwise. Let your choices be life giving.

FROM DONUTS...TO POTATOES

OCTOBER 12

WORD FOR TODAY: MOTIVE

When we read about someone performing an abominable act, we often want to know "What is their motive".

It is not as though knowing what motivated them would change the outcome or really give us any understanding as to why they did what they did. Does the why matter? If it does, then what we need to think about is why we do what we do. What is our motive for changing our lifestyle so radically that we get set apart from our friends and family? What makes us really commit (if we do) to a whole food plant based way of eating when the odds are against sustaining such a life changing decision with our present lifestyles?

Many members of "Esther's Nutritional Journey" state that they want to join in order to get support and motivation. I am suggesting that the motive must come from within. I think it has something to do with our belief system because to sustain a change, the desire and belief that it will work must be paramount. Commitment and surrender to another way of life is enhanced to the degree that it coincides with one's belief system.

My passion for eating this way has been reinforced with every step of success that I have achieved in regaining my health, getting off all medications, eliminating the need for surgery and then the bonus of losing 130 pounds. That is such convincing evidence that I have no desire to go back to eating the sad American diet.

My motive for creating this group was to share my story...a story which has worked for the past 3 years and one I believe can change the lives of any who are ready to listen with an open mind and accept the truth in it. Truth sets us free.

ESTHER LEBECK LOVERIDGE

_____

_____

_____

OCTOBER 13
WORD FOR TODAY: SUPPORTERS

Supporters come in all shapes and sizes and even functions but what I am thinking about are the people who are in our lives and choose to recognize what we are doing (getting healthy) and choose to support us and not sabotage us especially in our early attempts to change the way we eat.

It felt so loving to be with my cousin Charley Kearns and his partner Frank Ching this weekend. First of all, they invited us to a very special event and pre-ordered our vegan meal for us. Wow. During the cocktail portion of the evening, sparkling cider was offered as well as water laced with slices of lime.

The dinner salad and entree were delicious and the appetizers were mushrooms and hummus on crackers. There was a dessert that I tasted. Not sure what it was. It tasted like a poached pear to me but I'm not sure.

For breakfast, I had a ball trying about 6 different spices on my steel cut oatmeal that they made for us. It was like a wine tasting party trying on cinnamon, fresh ground nutmeg, cardamom, pumpkin spice and turmeric. See, we can have fun experimenting too.

For Sunday dinner, they suggested we go to Sweet Tomatoes - a great salad and soup buffet where I filled 2 plates with veggies and poured some of the vegan soup over a potato. The second potato I took and ate on the way home as my dinner.

FROM DONUTS...TO POTATOES

Now that is love in action that we can all learn from...Thank you so much for taking the worry out of the equation of being together and staying compliant.

Before returning home, we visited Charley's sister who is in a care facility (diabetes and Alzheimer's) and we had fun singing together as a lady in the group room played her ukulele. Life is good in loving families. Be the support you want others to be.

Love you guys.

_____

_____

_____

_____

OCTOBER 14

WORD FOR TODAY: WANT

Sometimes I struggle with the word want because what usually comes to my mind are material things and knowing I have all I need, I am tempted to denounce that word.

However, want is also like desire and it is admirable to want to be our best, feel our best, eat the best food available and strive to have the healthy body we were intended to have.

But how do we materialize what we want in our lives when there is a cost involved? The cost could be financial, but usually it has to do with exchanging one thing for something else that we want even more. For instance, the other day, I wanted a potato instead of a salad but I made the choice for a salad based on my short term goal of getting back to my goal weight.

Dr. Doug Lisle talks about "cost-benefit analysis" in his podcasts on YouTube which is something to consider when we make decisions. This is a good lecture to watch. He explains that cost is often the amount of energy, planning, thought and preparation it will take to make different choices.

The path of least resistance is to follow old habits but when we want to chart a new path, it takes energy. Are we willing to pay the price?

Getting honest with ourselves is a key to accepting new challenges. Do we really want to improve our health, and if so, what price are we willing to pay? Are we willing to go the distance or do we just want to play at it and pretend we can have our cake and eat it too?

What do we really want? If you are having a crisis, it can be your friend. Embrace it. Let it teach you what you need to learn.

_____

_____

_____

_____

OCTOBER 15

WORD FOR TODAY: SAUCE

What to do with a lovely bag of freshly picked apples from my daughter-in-law Sharlee Bates? Well, make sauce, of course with some of them.

There are all kinds of sauces out there. I see recipes quite often that look interesting and tempting and then I say to myself, "Why would I want to make that sauce? Yes, it could enhance the flavor

FROM DONUTS...TO POTATOES

of whatever I added it to, but then, wouldn't that just make me want to eat more?"

But then, there is applesauce - pure and only enhanced with cinnamon and nutmeg. How nice is that?

So, I quartered a bunch of the apples and also used my apple cutter on some of them (and ate 7 apple cores). I did not peel the apples. I just simmered them in a bit of water until tender and then put them in the blender - peel and all. I added enough of the water in the pan to make the blender purr into a nice batch of applesauce.

Then I poured the sauce into a plastic container, added 1 T of cinnamon and several shakes of nutmeg and wa la we have nice warm applesauce.

Thanks Sharlee for sharing the apples from your dad's trees. What a gift - and such a healthy one at that.

_____
_____
_____
_____

OCTOBER 16

WORD FOR TODAY: CONSISTENT

After listening to one of the helpful interviews on YouTube, I was reminded of the importance of being consistent. Change can occur over time, but it happens even more efficiently when we are consistent with the choices that lead to our success.

If we are "good" one day and then slip the next and then have a 3rd day where we are compliant with our healthy food choices, the teeter totter effect does not give us a chance to re-establish changes in our palate which in turn will increase the likelihood that the new foods we are eating will be satisfying and tasty.

We are normally resistant to change. We like what we like and don't want to feel deprived but when we enjoy the volume of food allowed on a whole food plant based diet, we get all the nutrients we need, we get plenty of starch for satiety and lots of flavors. It is just when we go back to our old foods that our tongues are reminded of how exciting those highly processed foods excite us and then we have to start being compliant all over again.

Success comes as we make our change permanent and daily become consistent with foods that are healthy. As we all know, seeing a parent being inconsistent in teaching their children creates chaos and they will certainly play one parent against the other as they seek their own pleasure. We too can play one idea against another but when we learn the value of being consistent, the road becomes smooth and we are more likely to arrive at our destination.

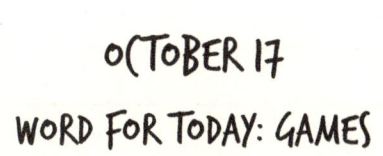

_____

_____

_____

_____

OCTOBER 17

WORD FOR TODAY: GAMES

There are so many games played in what I refer to as life. I remember reading a book called "Games People Play" by Eric Berne, I believe. It must have been from the 70's.

It was interesting to examine the number of psychological

FROM DONUTS...TO POTATOES

games we play to defend our position or why we do (or don't do) what we do.

One game was called "broken leg" in which we get out of doing what might be expected of us. We might use our "broken leg" as an excuse to explain why we are limited.

This could take a form like "Well, how do you expect me to adhere to a plant based diet when I have a "broken leg" i.e. a spouse who won't comply or I have children who need their snacks and I can't resist (or eliminate them)?

Sometimes we play a game where we engage someone in a conversation about some insignificant idea on eating this way. To the extent that we dwell on whether or not something is compliant, we avoid discussing the real impact of meat and dairy in our diets. Diversions can slow us down from doing the important parts.

And then there are the people who explain in the recent Netflix movie how even the ancient gladiators were plant eaters and I think men in particular will benefit from learning how we do not have to be meat eaters to be strong and virile. It is time for the men in our lives to wake up and realize there is a new game in town that will benefit everyone.

_____

_____

_____

_____

ESTHER LEBECK LOVERIDGE

OCTOBER 18

WORD FOR TODAY: BRAINWASHED

This word goes back to my childhood. When someone had a new idea or even challenged the acceptable way of thinking, "Have you been brainwashed" was often a part of the conversation.

What does it mean to be brainwashed? We wash our clothes, we clean our homes, we shower and get refreshed but somehow, we have forgotten to cleanse our minds of past negative thoughts, thinking or even belief systems.

How do we cleanse our minds of erroneous thinking? First of all, it helps to be prompted by having a questioning mind. It helps to realize that we are evolving all of the time and need to take time to rethink what we think and evaluate to see whether or not the way we are thinking still works for us.

Not all thoughts must be dismissed but when we have a question about something, we need to test it to see if it is still true. For years we have been taught we need to get protein from animals and calcium from milk but whom or what was pushing that agenda?

I can say I have put that idea to the test and for the past 3 years have eliminated both from my diet and have actually regained my health and lost 130 pounds as a bi-product.

What is in your brain that no longer serves you? Can you replace erroneous thinking with truth? Can you clean out the cobwebs and learn for yourself what is true for you?

Sure. Be your own experimenter. Be your own judge. Have fun cleaning the beautiful mind you possess.

OCTOBER 19
WORD FOR TODAY: WORTH

We evaluate the worth of everything we touch - especially when we are trying to de-clutter. (This is an on-going lesson for me).

But what I want to talk about is how well we see ourselves as having worth. I am not talking about our net-worth or the fact that corporations talk about the bottom line and often ignore the needs of the people they serve while they try to maintain their profits.

But what are you and I worth? If we were striped of everything we own, would we still have value? I often think about Dr. John McDougall who seemingly lost everything in the Santa Rosa fire two years ago. To me, he didn't lose a thing because he is still himself, spreading the word about enjoying a starch based diet and saving the lives of many people who have not suffered loss through a fire but have lost their way on how to be healthy and respect their bodies.

We are all worthy of good. The sky is limitless, as far as we know, and so are we when we respect ourselves and know that we can prosper as we take time to nourish our bodies with the best food available.

Know your value. You are okay just the way you are. We all have strengths and weaknesses but the bottom line is that we are worthy of having a happy, healthy life. The choice is ours.

There is no guilt...only learning.

OCTOBER 20

WORD FOR TODAY: WAGON

The question is not "Are you on the wagon" or "Have you fallen off the wagon"? What is certain is that we will fall off the wagon from time to time. We are not seeking perfection (or so I claim), but we are seeking excellence.

The wagon is our friend. It is our transportation into a future with a healthy destination. It is also our source of food as we travel and it also contains those who are sharing this journey with us -our community.

It is the place where we sing songs of deliverance as we travel the rut filled roads of life and it lifts us above the potholes that shake us up from time to time.

The solution to falling off the wagon is to get back on as soon as possible. It is too tiring to walk alone. It is too easy to lose our way

What I have noticed on my journey is that for the first time in my life, getting back on the wagon has been an almost immediate response. No longer do I adhere to faulty thinking of days gone by i.e. "Well, I've already screwed up this day so I might as well go whole hog". Now I think about making my next bite a potato.

The past is gone and every moment counts. Decide this moment on how to get back on the wagon and enjoy the safety it provides. Embrace the wagon as your friend - not your jailer.

FROM DONUTS...TO POTATOES

_____

_____

OCTOBER 21
WORD FOR TODAY: AFFIRMATION

What we affirm (say is true) guides us because what we think about... we bring about.

Sometimes our affirmations state a fact about where we want to be. Maybe we are not quite there yet and that is okay. Our minds respond to what we say.

Here is something I keep on my refrigerator.
I AM HEALTHY

I honor my body and am grateful for the work it does for me. I nourish my body through self care. I rest when I need to rest. I eat nourishing meals when I need to eat and exercise when I need to exercise. I am healthy.

Make up your own affirmations such as:

I am worthy
I am made in the image of God
I am divine
I am strong
I am able to learn new eating habits
I am willing to change
I am learning all about food of value
I am providing a safe environment for myself.
I love myself - right where I am today. I am enough.

OCTOBER 22

WORD FOR TODAY: FAST

It is easy to be preoccupied with "fast". We want to be in the fast lane, eat fast food, get in the fastest aisle in the grocery store or at the gas station or at the ATM machine and how could I forget "lose weigh fast"?

But what would happen if we considered another kind of "Fast". This morning I was reflecting on the religions I am familiar with who endorse fasting. My Jewish friends "fast" from pork. My Mormon friends "fast" from alcohol and caffeine. My Catholic friends used to fast from meat on Fridays and eat fish and often fast from something during the LENT season. My Muslim friends fast for Ramadan and my Seventh - day Adventist friends fast from meat. Some Christians have also been advised to fast and pray.

In the Book of Daniel, Daniel's fast is described and basically, it is what I have done for the past 3 years. He demonstrated that his strength was superior to that of those eating the King's meat and drink. Even Jesus fasted so what's the big deal?

Some of these fasts are limited for a certain period of time and some are extended for a lifetime.

When Dr. McDougall runs into a very difficult case, he might recommend sending the patient to True North for supervised medical water fast. Stories of healing abound. It is an opportunity to break bad food habits and re-start our engines with good fuel.

FROM DONUTS...TO POTATOES

Is any form of fasting helpful for everyone? I don't know. People are on prescriptions that require them to eat first or take the drug with a meal so that certainly is a consideration but I believe that fasting from animal and dairy products is what has led to my new life - physically and spiritually.

_____
_____
_____
_____

OCTOBER 23

WORD FOR TODAY: RESOURCE

Years ago, I worked as a counselor at the Women's Resource Job Center where we were funded to help older women re-enter the job market. We taught interviewing skills, did mock interviews, helped them fill out a resume and tried to connect them with job openings in the community.

I too, was a "retread". I finished college later in life and re-entered the job market after having been a stay at home mom.

As we make changes in our lives, we depend on resources to help us. My primary resource for having regained my health is Dr. John McDougall. It was his book "The McDougall Program for Maximum Weight Loss" which taught me the secret to regaining my health and losing 130 pounds. He is a food doctor. I proudly wear his T Shirt which states "It's the food". I value him as a resource so much - primarily because of his heart. All of his information is free on his website drmcdougall.com and that is impressive.

I recently posted about the word FAST and have been asked

if Dr. McDougall recommends fasting. No. He is a food doctor. He keeps it simple. He does not believe in what could be considered FAD foods or ideas. He does refer people to True North's fasting program, but he doesn't get involved in it EXCEPT, his does reference Daniel's Fast in the Bible and basically, that is what he promotes and I follow.

Resources abound. There is lots of "noise" out there and it is hard to decipher what is true and what is a gimmick. Look for examples of long term success. Look for truth. It will win.

___

OCTOBER 24

WORD FOR TODAY: WHOLE

I am actually writing this on October 26 and I'll tell you why.

You know, we often say we are on a whole food plant based diet and there is a reason for that. Whole food allows us to eat the food intact. That is one reason we do not use oil. It is extracted and unprotected from its original "environment".

Sometimes I experiment and sometimes my experiments succeed and sometimes they fail and I learn.

Boy did I learn this week. I thought it would be "fun" to try a day with just water but then I added 2 cups of pomegranates just because they are so healthy. On day 2, I juiced a bunch of pomegranate seeds and hated to throw away the remains and so I ate 2 cups of UNWHOLE pomegranate seeds and water. On day 3,

FROM DONUTS...TO POTATOES

I ate 2 cups of whole pomegranate seeds and water but the damage had already begun.

Most people need more fiber but NOT THIS MUCH.

The spiritual lesson I learned after several hours at the emergency room was...elimination is painful - whether it is de-cluttering or just plain removing a blockage. Our bodies are a temple...not a garbage can.

_____

_____

_____

_____

OCTOBER 25

WORD FOR TODAY: PAIN

I was so happy to list constipation as one of the ailments I have not suffered from ever since I started "The McDougall Program for Maximum Weight Loss" 3 years and 3 months ago.

But then, thinking I was invincible and my wonderful body could process 2 cups of just the pomegranate seeds (after the juice had been extracted), I decided to experiment.

Yes, I did also drink copious amounts of water that day but I found out those seeds, by themselves, just were not digestible.

Well, I am thrilled that I have a healthy body and the staff at Kaiser Hospital was surprised that I take no medication. It was another opportunity to spread the good news about a plant based diet and I also told them this was not a result of the diet - it was a careless experiment and that I hope they continue to spread the good news of eating this way.

Without any pain medication I managed to work my way through it, so to speak.

I finally added 1/2 cup applesauce and 1 small potato to my food intake. I'm making progress.

OCTOBER 26

WORD FOR TODAY: HELP

Ben has been the best help as I "moved" through this experience of constipation.

He continued to fill my water bottle, check on me every few minutes as I spent most of 3 days in the bath tub. He went to the store for medical supplies, the grocery store for prune juice and of course took me to the ER.

Today he made me potatoes and sweet potatoes and boy did they taste good. He did the grocery shopping, washed clothes, brought me my phone so I could listen to podcasts to keep me distracted and was so concerned.

He saw me at my worst and still loves me. (It's a good thing that what he always loved about me was my mind and spirit), ha.

When I was a child, my grandmother asked me "What is your gift?" I never knew what to tell her and finally came up with "The Gift of Helps". Now I realize what a great gift it is to offer help to a loved one. Thank you, Ben.

And now I am back…

FROM DONUTS...TO POTATOES

_____

_____

_____

_____

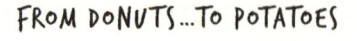

OCTOBER 27

WORD FOR TODAY: HEAL

We all want to be well. Most of us want a magic pill or a quick fix and that is normal. However, some healings take time. Sometimes we get help from the medical profession, prayer, and support of friends but sometimes the ability to heal ourselves resides within us and our own food choices.

Once we learn that so many diseases are food borne, why is it that our resistance to change is so strong? Do we not have enough information about the benefits of eating a whole food plant based diet or are we not totally convinced that it is what used to be a normal diet or is the change back to that way of eating too drastic?

I certainly understand. The abundance of food that is available to us is overwhelming. I have heard that there are 60,000 food items in some grocery stores and why would we not assume they are all healthy, available and safe to consume? The ads on TV suggest that drugs are the answer but are they only a way to maintain and not heal? The food ads touting the processed and fast foods do not help clear our minds from what we have become accustomed to as tasting so good and let's face it, pleasure is fun. Habits have become ingrained.

What to do? If the power to heal ourselves is within us, what does it take? Does it take reading "The McDougall Program for Maximum Weight Loss", watching Netflix movies like the new

"Game Changers", "Forks over Knives" and "What the Health" or maybe all of the above?

Deciding to change how we eat often takes a crisis but if we really think about it, we do not have to wait for the heart attack, stroke or diagnosis of diabetes. We can think. We can realize our bodies need good nutrition. We can eliminate the foods from our homes that are sustaining bad health and have at least one safe place to be.

Is this a big change? You bet. But I am talking about our lives. We are worthy of the best fuel possible. We can let food be our medicine.

_____

_____

_____

_____

OCTOBER 28

WORD FOR TODAY: VEGAN

I want to have a little talk about being (or not being) vegan.

I am "vegan" when it comes to telling a travel agency, a cruise dinner waiter and airlines about my food preferences. Sometimes saying I lost 130 pounds by going vegan is my first introduction to someone I may never see again - especially if it would take too much time to explain that I am a Starchivore, a follower of Dr. John McDougall, an adherent to his Program for Maximum Weight Loss or that I follow a whole food plant based diet.

Sometimes that is just too much for someone to "digest". I recognize that many of you may be "vegan" for ethical reasons and

FROM DONUTS...TO POTATOES

that is to be applauded. Going vegan saves our environment, helps the forest, saves the planet and the animals BUT going vegan may not be enough to save our lives and our lives matter too.

So, what is the difference, some may ask? You see, we could be vegan and not be giving ourselves the healthiest food. As a vegan, one can drink, eat processed food, consume oils, sugar and salts and even eat fake food.

Dr. McDougall says "The fat we eat is the fat we wear" and of course eating all of that fat does not prevent heart disease and diabetes.

So...if you really want to do it all, you can continue your efforts of being vegan and in addition, take care of yourself by going the extra mile.

Always ask yourself - Is there any way I can get back to eating whole food? If you will notice, almost everything I eat is identifiable. What you see on my plate is something you recognize. Now you can get fancy and make exciting, complicated, time consuming menus but you don't have to.

Keep it simple and let your tongues get acquainted with real food and soon that is what you will be craving.

_____

_____

_____

_____

ESTHER LEBECK LOVERIDGE

OCTOBER 29

WORD FOR TODAY: MILESTONE

When driving down the road, we used to see what I would call paddle boards along the road which posted the distance in miles to the next post.

We also have milestones in our lives which denote a change in our growth.

Myah, my youngest granddaughter, will turn 13. I can imagine becoming a teenager is a big milestone in her life.

When I was growing up, the elders would always ask us when we were dating, "When are you going to get married" and then it became "When are you going to have a baby"? It seemed like there was always a push to get us to the next stage of development.

Going plant based is often done in stages as well. First we think about it and then decide to put it to the test. Some people say they are going to "try" it for one meal a day.

I often tease (or challenge) those who try by saying "When you got married, did you say "I do" or did you say "I will try"?

Some treat changes like making a New Year's Resolution. They try. If they don't succeed, who knows or cares?

Success is more likely if we face changes with determination and by declaring our goals and setting up milestones to measure the distance to our destination.

Milestones mark our progress but to have any, we must move or take action. Milestones then become markers of how far we have come.

Getting off all of my medications by July of 2018 was a big milestone for me. The distance was two years.

Set your sights on where you want to be. Visualize it. Dream about it and set in motion a plan of action.

FROM DONUTS...TO POTATOES

_____

_____

_____

OCTOBER 30

WORD FOR TODAY: CONFINE

Confine is a word which implies limitation. We might be confined to our room, to a jail cell or stuck in a relationship or job.

But setting limits can also be freeing. Having too many choices may be time consuming and make decisions more difficult.

Just think of the options which are eliminated when we switch over to a plant based menu. We never have to think about what meat we are going to buy. We don't have to even look in the dairy case at the grocery store. We can just breeze by, knowing there is nothing in it for us.

As I pass the bakery section, I say "poison" to myself and do not even take the time to lust after baked goods I once enjoyed. They are no longer a part of my life.

We have also eliminated alcohol from our home so going down that aisle in the store frees me up to spend more time in my favorite place - the produce department. Here, I am not confined. There is so much to explore. New foods I have never eaten await me.

Am I confined or set free from foods which kept me either sick and/or were never satisfying?

I am free. I am free of many food borne diseases. I am free from so many food addictions. I am free from 130 pounds and pressure on my knees and perhaps best of all is freedom from being numbed down through food which kept me dull. I can think. I can make healthy choices and I am free to be all I can be. I am no longer confined to the past.

_____

_____

_____

OCTOBER 31

WORD FOR TODAY: MESSAGE

What kind of message are you sending to your world? At some level, we are all messengers.

Some of us whisper, some come up with songs to share and some speak their truth from a pulpit or use a megaphone while standing on a street corner.

Some messages are sent by text and some are delivered in person especially when someone has died.

It is true that I have felt like an evangelist at times - wanting to share my story of "salvation" with everyone - even to those who might prefer to turn a deaf ear.

What's kind of funny to me is that people don't seem to turn off their TVs when the drug companies send us messages incessantly on the evening news. They extol the virtues of their products which falsely imply healing when maybe they are only offering a band aid while also warning of possible dreaded side effects. Who will counter these messages with the truth of healing which comes from eating a plant based diet?

Are we then the ones that must be silenced or is our lesson to learn to be sensitive to those who are drawn to hear? Timing may

FROM DONUTS...TO POTATOES

be the key but holding back is a challenge when we see suffering and when living by example seems too slow.

Regardless of the question, I know the answer is love.

_____

_____

_____

_____

NOVEMBER 1

WORD FOR TODAY: PRAISE

I used to have a T shirt which read "Praise the Lard" right across the bust line. It was from a meat company and did generate some attention as people tried to figure out if "Lard" was misspelled.

I had another T shirt from my cousin's yogurt shop with "The Udder Delight" printed on the front but now I wear one from Dr. McDougall which simply states "It's The Food". It's an "attention getter" too.

We praise what benefits us. We recommend good documentaries, books and podcasts and extol the virtues of eating plant based food. We tell our friends about restaurants which are supportive and help us make healthy choices while eating out.

Last night we were invited to join family members at a Mexican restaurant. The actual menu warned us that they use lard. I let the moment override my good judgment. I had previewed the menu online, didn't see that and had decided to have a veggie burrito but in retrospect, I would have done better to have ordered a salad. I'm still learning.

Praise requires scrutiny.

_____

_____

_____

_____

FROM DONUTS...TO POTATOES

NOVEMBER 2

WORD FOR TODAY: TRIAL

I have never been on "trial"; however I have had trials come my way over my lifetime.

But were they really trials or lessons? Was I a victim or a student?

It's all about perspective. Every day we have an opportunity to learn and adapt as we evolve into a newer person...one who faces each circumstance knowing that the answer lies within.

I was talking to my brother about a maintenance problem he had, He revealed to me the answer often comes to him in the quiet moments of the night.

When we take time to know our bodies, I think we intuitively know what is best for us. That doesn't mean that we always follow that path. We might be stubborn, rigid or downright resistant but that doesn't negate the fact that the answer is still within.

What marvelous, "wanting to be healthy" bodies we have. We can co-operate or resist and suffer the consequences until we learn to stand trial, be examined and be our own judge.

_____
_____
_____
_____

ESTHER LEBECK LOVERIDGE

NOVEMBER 3

WORD FOR TODAY: FULL

What am I "full" of? How do I know when I am full? Does my stomach stick out? Do I have that overfed feeling? Do I want to lie down and sleep?

I remember 3 years ago how I felt after the traditional Thanksgiving feast. I would moan and groan and feel miserable but I knew I was full. Was that what I needed to feel satisfied?

So, now that I eat a plant based diet, how in the world do I know when I am full and need to stop eating? The truth is, I don't know. It seems like no matter how much easily digested food I eat, I never have that stuffed miserable feeling any more.

I think my stomach "feeling full" receptors don't speak to me anymore. I cannot rely on that full feeling to stop eating. So, I just prepare a reasonable meal and know that at the end of it, I will BE reasonably full whether or not I FEEL it. I can always eat more if the hunger pangs signal that I need more food.

I love being able to eat when, why or how much I want. The key is "what" I eat. As long as I stick to vegetables, grains, fruit and legumes, my bodily needs will be met and I will have that feeling of satiety without the miserable feeling I used to have.

Be full of joy, unspeakable joy.

_____

_____

_____

_____

FROM DONUTS...TO POTATOES

NOVEMBER 4

WORD FOR TODAY: SOLACE

Twenty years ago, when Ben and I were caretakers for my mother, I remember she loved to soak in this very same bathtub. I am not sure of her reasons but I do remember her loving to spend time here.

One day she called me in because she needed help in getting out of the bathtub. I'm sure she, like me, sat here for a long time and would continually let some water drain out as she added hot water to maintain the temperature. The problem on this particular day is that she had used up all of the hot water and had also drained the bathtub and she laid here naked in this tub at 90 years of age and wanted to be lifted out.

I did not have the strength to lift her out of the tub and the only solution that came to me was to fill the tub with more water so that she would be buoyant. Unfortunately, the water was now cold.

A place of solace was now very uncomfortable.

We can linger in these comfortable places for awhile, but the time comes when we need to move on.

Lesson: get out of the hot water before you run out of resources

ESTHER LEBECK LOVERIDGE

NOVEMBER 5

WORD FOR TODAY: MUSIC

Ah... Music and all of its forms is such a blessing to us. It's kind of like a smorgasbord. There are so many selections, so many styles, so many genres out there and we get to choose what is helpful at any given moment.

I thought it was interesting that this morning I woke up with the song about all being well with my soul on my mind. When I told Ben, he told me he woke up with the song about saints marching in on his mind. It would be interesting to explore where these songs come from...kind of like the dreams which come to us.

Sometimes music makes me want to dance. Sometimes it makes me want to clean house (not too often). Sometimes it makes me want to reach out to a loved one. Truly it is a universal language.

And at times like this...are you ready for a drum roll? Being able to pass gas without pain or fear is music to my ears.

Being kind to our bodies for its healing powers is the best form of gratitude. The best prayer may be as simple as what we put on the end of our forks.

Today I choose to be kind.

FROM DONUTS...TO POTATOES

NOVEMBER 6

WORD FOR TODAY: FAIR

My mother taught me an interesting lesson. At first I thought it was a silly cliché, but as time has passed, I see wisdom in it.

I guess within every group of people, there's often one who is difficult to know how to handle. Sometimes love is extended, sometimes boundaries are set up and sometimes we just feel inadequate about not knowing the answer.

How are we to handle difficult people? My mom's answer was using the 3 F's: be firm fair and friendly. But how do you do that when someone is obnoxious? I'm still searching for answers.

We often hear it said that life is not fair but that has nothing to do with US not being fair. Sometimes I have separated myself out from this difficult person.

The next time I have an opportunity to be together I hope I will have better techniques and tactics to spread more love.

I think I'll continue to risk and test my own evolution. Just maybe I'll have less judgment the next time.

ESTHER LEBECK LOVERIDGE

NOVEMBER 7

WORD FOR TODAY: STONE

I have heard about people wanting to get stoned. Perhaps it elevates them above their current circumstances. It might even be a way to think creatively. Perhaps it numbs pain, but what if you're the one getting stoned because of the rocks hurled at you by others?

That puts an entirely different slant on the word.

I have never thrown a stone at anyone but what about the times I have looked down on someone just because they viewed a situation differently?

What about the times I have thrown criticism at a friend? Even if I didn't voice it out loud, I think the message got sent.

These stones separate me and often build a platform where I might feel elevated...standing tall and feeling superior.

Eating a plant based lifestyle has done wonders for me but it still requires that I eliminate stones of self righteousness by leaving them at my feet.

No one will grow and learn if they are pelted with my well meaning stones.

I want to remind myself that changes occur when we decide to honor everyone's path and let them search for their own answers from within.

FROM DONUTS...TO POTATOES

NOVEMBER 8

WORD FOR TODAY: OWNERSHIP

Ownership is kind of like taking charge of my life. I can dwell on past failures, hurts and disappointments and focus on what others have done "wrong", or I can decide that this moment is all there is in moving forward with my life.

This day I get to choose how to spend it. This day I get to choose what I will use to nourish my body. No one else holds a fork over my head and threatens me. I am the sole person that gets to choose what I think and I have the power to choose thoughts that nourish me as well.

When I take ownership of my life, I realize that I am the one who keeps up with the maintenance guide, keeps it clean and makes sure that safety measures are taken into account.

I can visualize what I want in my life and make plans accordingly. I own my own body. I get to choose who will accompany me on my journey. I get to choose the path that best suits my needs. I get to make adjustments as I learn and go along. I am the one who gets to feel the joy of continually learning and becoming my best self.

I own the past, the present and the future and accept the "mistakes" which actually have become my tutors. I get to embrace the evolving me with love and kindness as I also accept the responsibilities of ownership.

_____

_____

_____

_____

NOVEMBER 9
WORD FOR TODAY: REST

At first, I was thinking about the importance of rest and then I came up with Release Every Stressful Thought!

By doing just that, we do give our body the rest and time it needs to regroup, recuperate and renew.

Taking time out from our busy schedules gives us time to think, reflect and plan our strategy for successful living.

When we rest, we have time to listen to motivational talks, read or just go within and listen to our body which sends us signals as to what we need if we just take the time to listen.

Sometimes our body sounds an alarm and we are tempted to drown out the alarm through medication or distractions. But if we get quiet, we can get in touch with our selves and learn a lesson or two.

_____
_____
_____
_____

NOVEMBER 10
WORD FOR TODAY: HEALTH

It is possible to lose weight a number of ways, but if we lose our health in the process, what good is a skinny body?

FROM DONUTS...TO POTATOES

While it is true that reducing our weight does help conditions such as high blood pressure and diabetes, as long as our arteries are clogged with fat, even with a skinny body our heart is still in danger.

When I focus on healthy food, I know I will achieve my ideal weight. When I strive to get my weight down, I often sacrifice my health. This is a lifelong journey and every step we take towards our goals strengthens our resolve.

If I had it to do it all over again, I would stress my improved health over my impressive weight loss. Within health we have the word heal. Within the word diet, we have the word die.

I have learned over the past three years and three months that when we focus on health, weight will take care of itself.

As long as we are focusing on weight, we are looking at external appearances. Perhaps our message is missing the biggest audience which is all of us wanting to be healthy even when we don't have weight to lose.

This is not a message just for fat people. This is a message for all people as we strive to be our healthiest selves.

_____
_____
_____
_____

NOVEMBER 11

WORD FOR TODAY: DECEIVED

Ah, that is an old word which denotes being led astray, being misguided even if not directly being lied to.

When we are conceived, we get a blueprint of our lives which can be nourished and promoted by following a plan for good health.

When other mammals are born, they stick close to their mother for sustenance and protection. It is the mother's milk which gives them what they need for rapid growth and the ability to become independent.

When my son was born, I was fortunate to be able to offer my breast milk as his first food for five months. As I introduced solid food to his diet, he continued to grow but still retained the desire to nurse until he weaned himself. There are substitutes for this process but there comes a time when we all get weaned.

Well, that is until the food industry plants the seeds in our minds that we need their product.

Once I became aware of this seduction, I realized that as mammals, we are the only ones to drink the secretion of another mammal.

That no longer makes any sense to me and eliminating dairy from my body became an easier choice.

One could see the milk industry in a number of ways but I just choose to see it as a way to sell a product through what may have been convincing evidence to many of us.

So the answer to this promotion lies within each of us. We can accept the ads which do not enhance our health or we can wake up, wean ourselves and grow into maturity and independence.

_____

_____

_____

_____

FROM DONUTS...TO POTATOES

NOVEMBER 12

WORD FOR TODAY: STILL

We can command the swirling ideas and thoughts in our mind to be still.

It is often in the still of the night that healing thoughts come to us

There are many voices out there swallowing up our time and energy as we attempt to sort through what is right for us.

My grandmother Kearns used to say to me "I love you still and the stiller you are, the better I love you". Perhaps this thought came to her out of her Quaker heritage when they often sat in a service where no one spoke unless they were guided by spirit to do so.

Words can be so cheap and often silence is uncomfortable for some of us so we attempt to fill the void with more words.

I had a hard time being still in school or in Sunday school. I wanted to talk with my friend Diana Shelton Lewis because our times together were so limited.

In the sixth grade, Victor Brownell, my first male teacher wrote in my autograph book "You'll grow up to be a fine woman if you learn not to imitate other women by talking so much". Years later, I was able to relate that story to his widow.

And so it is that I am continually learning when to be still and when to speak out. We all have a voice and our truth needs to be shared.

In the stillness of the night, I want to listen and learn.

_____

_____

_____

_____

FROM DONUTS...TO POTATOES

NOVEMBER 14

WORD FOR TODAY: RELAX

We live in a world of stress, hurry, fast lanes and impatience yet we are advised to let go, relax and be in the flow.

Often we want to control situations and outcomes as well. We think we know best and to take on another line of thinking is not easy

Forcing our way or insisting that we are right and refusing to compromise may lead to a hardened position.

Ben's dad used to say "Son, you can be right...dead right."

Being flexible and willing to learn goes a long way in advancing whatever cause we have. It doesn't mean we have to go along in order to get along.

Be true to yourself, be willing to adapt and continue to grow into your best self. Be willing to exchange self righteousness for enlightenment as you climb to new heights in self awareness

Relax and know the best is yet to be.

NOVEMBER 13

WORD FOR TODAY: ATTENTION

In school, we were told to "Pay attention".

In some circles, we are told "What you think about, you bring about".

We are also encouraged to pay attention to our bodies. Our bodies do "speak" to us in numerous ways. When we have pain, it is like our body is screaming "pay attention to me...how much louder do I have to speak"?

We can often drown out that voice because it is most likely going to suggest making changes and who wants to change?

Being comfortable in old eating habits is just that - our comfort zone. Change often elicits a sense of insecurity. We might ask "If food has been my refuge, how am I going to handle stress and my discomfort with life"?

My truth is that it took a crisis before I was willing to pay attention to a new way of living. Repeating old solutions no longer served me and I was finally ready to reach out for a radical approach to renewed health.

My body has been thanking me in many demonstrable ways and I am continually amazed at its ability to continue to whisper in my ears.

Three years and four months ago today, we formed a new partnership and I love paying attention to my inner voice as it continues to speak to me.

ESTHER LEBECK LOVERIDGE

NOVEMBER 15

WORD FOR TODAY: BALANCE

It is important to have balance in our lives. Dr. Dean Ornish talks about the four areas of our lives that need to be in balance: nutrition, exercise, meditation and community or love.

It is easy to get carried away in any one of these four contributors to our health. Extremes in any of these areas affect our ability to work towards our wholeness.

Three weeks ago, my system got out of balance when I went overboard by eating 2 cups of pomegranate seeds (pulp) after I had strained out the juice. This is just another reminder that we need to concentrate on "whole" food. Yes, fiber is important in our diet but come on, two cups?

Getting back in balance has been a very painful experience for me. In order to reduce the frequency of continued trauma, I was advised by a non plant based doctor to reduce the fiber in my diet. Adding food that I normally don't eat such as white rice, white bread and white pasta caused the scales to be tipped out of balance in the other direction.

I returned to my favorite food - sweet potatoes for relief and after 3 days of potatoes I had longer periods of relief. Yesterday I woke up feeling wonderful and decided to delay eating until I got hungry. I never got hungry and my systems had a full day to rest and heal. I had so much energy and was able to get out of the house and resume normal activities. Wow did that feel good.

Today I have a follow up appointment with my plant-based doctor who will advise me on the best way to continue my healing.

This has not been an easy topic to discuss but it has opened the doors for us to speak about something that affects many people... constipation. Without this good discussion I would not have had your prayers and your support. Thank you so much

FROM DONUTS...TO POTATOES

_____
_____
_____

NOVEMBER 16

WORD FOR TODAY: FORTY

Forty is a number which has been said represents a "period of time"

Stories like the flood report that it rained for 40 days and 40 nights. The Israelites spent 40 years "wandering" in the wilderness and Jesus, I think, fasted for 40 days, if I remember correctly.

But for me, 40 months is literally the actual time I have been following "The McDougall Program for Maximum Weight Loss".

This period of time has brought me so many benefits. I have been able to eliminate my dependency on statins, sleeping pills, pain medication, and levothyroxin for my low thyroid, get rid of high blood pressure and pre diabetes as well as a low dosage of lithium as insurance against manic episodes.

Oh yes, and the prospect of needing to have my knees replaced was also eliminated. My eyes improved to the point I no longer have my driver's license restricted requiring me to wear glasses to drive.

Now that I have outlined just some of the medical improvements, I will also mention that my weight dropped from 257 to 122 (usually closer to 127) and I have re-gifted my size 24 clothes (I did have one dress that was size 26) and now I slip into a size 6! My all time high weight was 282 in 2011.

These past 40 months have passed so quickly and the best part is learning that eating this way has weaned me from my lifetime of food addictions and set me on a path that is sustainable for the rest of my life. I have found my answer and am thrilled.

It is my joy to spread the word about how eating a plant based diet can reverse disease and lead others to a more fulfilling life of peace and clear mental health.

And, finally, I learned at the ripe old age of 72, that it is never too late to create a new life.

___

NOVEMBER 17

WORD FOR TODAY: FEAR

Fear is a very limiting emotion because it can keep us tied to things that will never happen unless we create it.

It has been said that what we fear has come upon us and could that be because we actually made it happen by focusing on it? We know that what we think about, we bring about and so it is that what we fear can consume our thoughts and actually reinforce events that would lead us to that fulfillment.

I remember, when I went through a divorce back in 1978, I was afraid of getting back into the dating game. I think that fear, in part, may have been what led to me putting on more weight - thinking that guys would not be attracted to me with that extra layer of "protection". As it turned out, there was another band of single men who just happened to be attracted to fatter women. Fortunately for me, when I met Ben, he was attracted to my mind and spirit.

FROM DONUTS...TO POTATOES

We may think that being afraid of falling may cause us to be more cautious as we age. Maybe we hang onto stair railings, use a cane, a walker or even a wheel chair but actually we do not need fear. We just need to be wise, know our strengths and act accordingly.

There is no boogie man out there to get us. Life is much simpler than that. There are just decisions and choices that we make that have consequences. There is just cause and effect. If we overeat, don't get out in the sunshine, get our rest or our exercise or have a support group, we just pay a price in our mental or physical health.

Keep it simple. Fear not. There is good news. We can create our new lives. I dare you.

_____

_____

_____

NOVEMBER 18

WORD FOR TODAY: FREE

People used to say "there is no free lunch" but I want to tell you that all the information you need to succeed in changing your life IS free.

Sure, effort will be required and it will take time to learn how to change your mind and your old lifestyle but if funds are limited, that is no problem.

It cost nothing to take advantage of Dr. McDougall's website where all of the information you need is free. At www.drmcdougall.com, there is a search bar where you can enter any topic that concerns you and get answers posted there. He has a free newsletter that is available as well as the recipes of his wife Mary McDougall.

You can also go to YouTube (free) and enter his name in the search bar to view his podcasts which help to educate all of us as he leads us down the path of sustainable health and weight loss.

There are many other plant based doctors who also have free information and YouTube lectures/interviews but at first, I found having a singular source kept me focused.

Many Face book groups offer support on a personal level and are free including "Esther's Nutritional Journey".

It is free to walk, get out in the sunshine, listen to music, call a friend, attend church/mosque/synagogue/temple or simply sit in the silence at home.

Lack of funds will never limit your personal growth. In fact, you can actually increase your spendable income by choosing whole food and letting the processed foods stay on the shelf.

Being free from food addictions is a plus I never imagined would be possible. Enjoy the free stuff.

_____

_____

_____

_____

NOVEMBER 19

WORD FOR TODAY: TRIP

Today we are planning to take a trip to Apple Hill. It is just up the road a way but puts us in the foothills with the chance to see more colors and see the apple orchards.

Taking a trip is a bit different from being on a journey. It is a

FROM DONUTS...TO POTATOES

slight deviation from our daily routine and offers a fresh look at our surroundings.

Breaking out of our habits opens the door to meet people and change our view of life. It is also a chance to share the trip with a friend and enjoy the companionship along the way.

When it comes to changing our daily food routine, adjustments might be more easily made by thinking of taking a side trip instead of being overwhelmed with the thought of a life long journey.

If making a radical change seems daunting, just think of being on a side trip. Who knows where that will lead and it just might lead to a new lifetime journey.

Baby steps work for some people who are less inclined to take giant leaps. We all get to choose what trips we want to take and consider the length and difficulty level of our adventure.

Whether this is your trip of a lifetime or simply a change, make it yours.

_____

_____

_____

_____

NOVEMBER 20

WORD FOR TODAY: FAT

Dr. McDougall says "The fat you eat is the fat you wear". It is just that simple.

So, what are the ways we can clean out our arteries, improve our circulation, reduce our risk of a heart attack, eliminate type 2 diabetes and lose the fat we are carrying around?

The obvious answer is to eliminate the fat. A pound of olive oil (and other fats) contains about 4,000 calories per pound compared to fruit, vegetables, starches and grains at less than 600 calories per pound.

It is possible to eat a whole pound of a salad (100 calories) for what 1 T of oil would cost you if you were counting calories and you would be giving up lots of nutrients in the process.

Oil is highly processed and when extracted from the plant, has no nutritional value but it can certainly be the difference between a weight loss stall and successfully achieving your goal.

There are other healthy fats which also slow down weight loss: they are nuts, seeds, avocado, soy and olives and that is why they are eliminated from The McDougall Program for Maximum Weight Loss until a person reaches goal and sustains that goal for 6 months.

Being vegan is a good start to eliminating fats by abstaining from meat and dairy but the silent kicker is the oil which can sabotage the best in us.

Check it out for yourself if you want optimum health. We get all the fats we need from plants.

_____

_____

_____

_____

NOVEMBER 21

WORD FOR TODAY: SELECT

Not every decision we make is in our best interest. There are many influences on our lives and the choices we make often reflect the opinions of others.

FROM DONUTS...TO POTATOES

But there comes a time when we take ownership of our lives and accept responsibility for our selections. Call it what you like - maturity or maybe just getting tired of repeating the same lessons.

In school, our goal is to learn, pass the test and move on... regardless of how much we like the teacher!

Yes, we can select to stay in our comfort zone and blame others and that may buy us some time, but I don't like repeating courses.

It is not easy to stand out from the crowd when we make difficult decisions but with practice, they become easier.

Good habits are the culmination of repeatedly making good selections. Practice, practice, practice.

_____

_____

_____

_____

NOVEMBER 22

WORD FOR TODAY: FAN

I have just been designated as a "Top Fan" of Dr. John McDougall's website. What an honor. What does it mean? How did it happen? Why was it done? I don't know and I don't care. It just represents the truth of my life.

I became a FAN of him 3 years and 4 months ago when my friend gave me his book "The McDougall Program for Maximum Weight Loss" at precisely the moment I was trying to decide how to lose the 70 pounds I needed to lose in order to be referred to Orthopedics for knee replacement(s). Talk about serendipity!

Reading his book changed my life forever. It taught me a whole new way of looking at how to lose weight and keep it off forever. It taught me that starch is what we are meant to eat to sustain satiety so we never have to be hungry again. There is no need to count calories or measure portions (although I do love to weigh my food because most people would not believe how much I eat),

Not only did I lose 130 pounds instead of 70, I went from one size 26 dress to size 6 but that is all outward appearance. What I really want to stress is that all chronic on-going issues listed on my after office visit report from Kaiser are GONE. That included so many health issues such as GERD, Diverticulitis, Low thyroid, high blood pressure, pre-diabetes, taking statins, sleeping pills, pain pills and lithium. There were many other issues as well, but suffice it to say that at age 76, I am medication and fat free and no longer need glasses to drive. I eliminated the need for knee replacements too. I am a whole person, full of life and eager to spread the good news of what brought me to this place.

As a thank you to Dr. McDougall, I took his Starch Solution Certification Course and attended his 3 day weekend seminar in order to thank him in person and have him autograph my book. The best part is that all of his information about how to achieve your optimum health is free because he received it freely from those people on whose shoulders he has stood for nearly 50 years. Talk about paying it forward! He is my role model.

Yes, I am a FAN.

FROM DONUTS...TO POTATOES

NOVEMBER 23

WORD FOR TODAY: RIGID

I got to thinking about this word this morning and wondered if is from the same root word as rigor mortis? Rigor mortis is what sets in when someone dies but can being rigid also be a form of stiffness while we are still living?

I can hold onto my beliefs in a hardened way. Sometimes I think I am just so right and then later learn that I wasn't so smart after all.

We can get all uptight when events in our lives unfold in a different way than expected but what if we could let go and let the best be the outcome whether or not it is what we would have thought would be the best.

To be in the flow of life allows new, exciting outcomes to be made manifest. Yes, I do think it is good to imagine what we want in our lives and add our emotion to that process but if we become rigid, we just may be limiting other good from coming into our lives.

I want to hold the future in my hands in a gentle way. I want to allow for surprises, serendipitous outcomes and an acceptance that what is best will materialize.

_____

_____

_____

_____

ESTHER LEBECK LOVERIDGE

NOVEMBER 24

WORD FOR TODAY: THINK

How often do we think before we "swallow"? It is easy to be spoon fed information that is believed to be true, but do we check it out? Do we question what used to be an authority in our lives or do we just take the pill and go on.

It is so important to pause and think before we eat. Some say we need to be mindful of what we eat. Where did the food come from? How was it made? Who was responsible for either providing it or creating it?

How many times do we chew before we swallow? How many times do we do a double take and think before we put something in our mouths? Just because something is on a menu, does that mean it is edible, digestible or even healthy?

Taking a pause is important. It gives us time to be thankful for what is set before us. It gives us time to think and evaluate for ourselves what our bodies and minds need.

Take time to think. It just may save your life.

FROM DONUTS...TO POTATOES

NOVEMBER 25

WORD FOR TODAY: MOVE

My dad was a great player of the game checkers. His strategy was well thought out so when it was his time to "move", it was quick and decisive.

He set the standard high and never "let" us win but we would strive to beat him even in the midst of many defeats.

There are all sorts of things in my life that move me. It may be an inspirational movie, a love song or an act of kindness.

Sometimes hitting bottom or having a crisis is what moves us to change our direction in life and take steps which will move us towards improved health.

We can move these prompts to the back burner of our minds or we can plan on how to make the next move to take us to the winner's circle.

I have only moved to a new address four times in my life but the best move I have made is switching to a plant based way of eating. It is a move that has changed me forever.

Now it's your move.

_____
_____
_____

ESTHER LEBECK LOVERIDGE

NOVEMBER 26

WORD FOR TODAY: RECEIVING

Mr. Fred Rogers, in one of his interviews, talked about "graceful receiving" as being one of the best gifts we can give to another person.

In this Thanksgiving week, we are reminded to give thanks, to give help to those in need, to remember those who through whatever reason, are in need of receiving.

But the idea of us who have so much receiving gracefully is a concept that I had not thought of. When someone wants to give me something, I often resist and in that process, I just may be robbing them of having a wonderful giving moment.

It has been said that it is better to give than to receive and I can understand the joy of sharing some time, a special gift or even a thought with someone else and seeing the joy on their face.

So, during this week, I want to be aware of how well I can receive as I attempt to give to others. It just may be that it's the ying and yang of life as we learn to receive and give.

Dr. McDougall shares his knowledge freely because he received it freely from those who pioneered this work long ago. That is his joy - not to profit from it in material ways, but to profit through the joy and health he brings to others.

In everything give thanks.

FROM DONUTS...TO POTATOES

NOVEMBER 27

WORD FOR TODAY: PROGRESS

Patience is a virtue and it helps to use that when we are in the middle of making progress.

We are all a work in progress and we are continually adapting to our changing world. We often take two steps forward and then a step or two or even three backwards as we continue our journey.

Yes, it would be sweet if we could push a button and have the desired outcome immediately but evolution takes time whether we are changing our lifestyle or even remodeling a part of our house.

Since change does take time, it gives us an opportunity to make adjustments during the process. What a relief that can be since we are continually learning and can change our minds on what we want in our lives.

Along with patience, we need to apply forgiveness for the choices we have made which we thought did not enhance our growth. When we know better, we do better and our work simply continues.

There is no guilt...only learning.

ESTHER LEBECK LOVERIDGE

NOVEMBER 28

WORD FOR TODAY: FULL

Actually, I used this word earlier but my post went to "draft", never to be seen again.

I mentioned that I have a full plate when it comes to my health, my wealth, my happiness and my joy. I love reaching out to my FB family for support and encouragement and am fortunate to have most of my family nearby. I have a church community I enjoy and of course, I love my food and my new life.

I remember in times past, after a big meal, I'd just want to stretch out because I would feel so full, but now I eat to my heart's content and never have that "Oh, my goodness, I am stuffed" feeling.

As a child, I sang a song about my cup running over. I feel that way and am so happy for all of my blessings, gifts and comforts of life.

I also remember those whose plates are not so full. I want you to know that you are not alone in your suffering. But there is a light at the end of the tunnel and as you press on to your own goals, you will continue to grow into your best self.

Be of good cheer. We have the answer to good health where so much of life begins.

FROM DONUTS...TO POTATOES

NOVEMBER 29

WORD FOR TODAY: FIRE

On these cool mornings, it is great to be able to fire up the stove and warm our bodies. Fire can be our friend or our foe. It can be used to cook our food, heat our homes and of course has the power to destroy life and communities.

I have been in a fire as a child and know the power of its destruction even though I lived to remember that day.

Fire can also be within us when we get fired up and ready to take on the day, a new challenge or project. It moves us forward as we determine our goals and how we are going to get there. It is the fuel that gives us energy to stick to a task and get results.

How can we get fired up? How can we become motivated to make the best decisions for our life? I'm not sure how it happens but do know that crises often put us in a position to make some hard decisions. Some people seem to be able to look at a situation intellectually and make some better decisions for their life without having been "at the end of their rope".

For me to make my big change, I had painful knees which were threatening to interfere with my travel plans. Fortunately, I was given Dr. McDougall's book (The McDougall Program for Maximum Weight Loss) and I was ready to put it to the test.

My motivation matched my willingness to learn something new and it led to success - much more than I ever imagined, more than being pain free...medication and chronic health issue free too.

_____

_____

_____

_____

ESTHER LEBECK LOVERIDGE

NOVEMBER 30

WORD FOR TODAY: PROCRASTINATION

I learned a lot today from Dr. Doug Lisle's interview with Chef A.J. on YouTube in which he talks about procrastination.

It is so easy for me to put off what I don't want to do in the first place. What was interesting to me was how he pointed out the three factors which often play a part in that process.

First of all, it is easy to just dilly dally -somehow buying into the myth that if I just put it off for awhile, maybe the need to do it will disappear.

Secondly, we have the ego trap where we might believe that we cannot succeed anyway so why try if in fact we might fail.

And finally, this really hit me because when I look at my office/memory-room, cleaning it up and discarding what I no longer need is just overwhelming. I remember my mother teaching me, when it came to cleaning, to just start in a corner.

We often have this same dilemma when it comes to starting a healthy eating program. To completely change how we eat can seem like just too much change, maybe we have had a history of starting a new eating plan and failed and just maybe we don't want to give up our favorite foods anyway.

His suggestion is to start by determining what we are willing to give up for the rest of our lives - then it becomes a lifetime change instead of a diet.

Release and let go...a continual process.

_____
_____
_____
_____

DECEMBER 1
WORD FOR TODAY: SPREAD

When we go to smorgasbords, we often say "What a spread". Undoubtedly this may have been your experience during the Thanksgiving holiday.

We are blessed with so many culinary options now and often the spread we are presented with creates a spread in our bodies.

One of the best ways to reduce the spread is to dilute the offerings with less calorie dense foods. It also helps if the lower calorie dense foods are eaten first.

But when you experience times when less than best choices have been made, realize that you can spread out any "damage" by making your next meal compliant and continuing your new lifestyle.

We continually make improvements as we learn and go along. Every new bite of food can put us back on our healthy journey as we make the most of every situation.

No guilt -only learning.

_____
_____
_____
_____

FROM DONUTS...TO POTATOES

DECEMBER 2

WORD FOR TODAY: MINIMIZE

This past weekend, we were in San Francisco and I chose to take some sweet potatoes, strawberries and blueberries with me so I wouldn't be so hungry when we went to a nice celebration.

As the appetizers were being passed around the crowd, I chose not to eat any that had fish/meat on them and thus minimized some of the damage. It also helped me minimize my intake of calories when I chose the lime water instead of the champagne.

When we had the opportunity to go through the buffet line, I was so pleased to see many roasted vegetables and I filled my plate to almost overflowing. The corn casserole had me going - I know there was something not compliant in it because it sent my taste buds into high heaven. And then the cookies came, at least 3 different kinds. Once I let down my barrier, it was hard to control how many I ate.

The next morning, we went to Brenda's for breakfast and my first step was to ask the waiter what they had that would be vegan friendly. She suggested the tofu succotash which would include a creamy biscuit, toast or a green salad. Hurray for me - I chose the salad. I gave myself a pat on the back for getting back on plan.

Later, we went back to the AIDS Memorial Grove for a wonderful event of remembering those who we have lost to the AIDS epidemic. Following the stories, the video and wonderful choir, we were treated to a soup line where we had a choice of clam chowder, chili or vegetarian soup. Isn't it wonderful how people love us? There was also a choice of saltine crackers, bread rolls or chocolate chip and peanut butter cookies. Yes, I ate one of each cookie and if I could have gotten my hands on more, I would have. It was then that I knew I had to revisit Dr. Doug Lisle's interview with Chef A.J. where he taught us about the "Cram Circuit".

There will be more on the importance of learning about cramming.

___

DECEMBER 3

WORD FOR TODAY: CRAMMING

Dr. Doug Lisle continues to advance my learning and I am so glad that he is on Dr. John McDougall's team. Check out his video interview with Chef A.J. posted a few days ago.

I remember cramming for finals and what a silly process that was. How much did I really learn as I attempted to remember what I thought would be key questions on an exam, only to have them go into cyber space moments later (no, we didn't have that back then).

So what is cramming on a whole food plant based diet? Actually, it doesn't exist. It only exists for me when I have eaten a healthy meal (and always someplace besides home where I am safe). It occurs when I go to a party and decide that now that I am at goal weight, I should be able to add some nuts back into my diet or sometimes, it may be thinking I should be able to eat a cookie. So, as the story goes, I eat a cookie and then when the waitress comes around with more trays of free cookies, I take another, and then another. Now mind you, I am completely full of good food, but THEN....cramming pops into my psyche and I start thinking I will never be able to have another (at least not at home) and the cramming kicks in. If possible,

FROM DONUTS...TO POTATOES

I would even pick up one that someone else has left behind. I become like a raving maniac although I try to pretend differently.

Cramming can be any high calorie dessert we eat after a full meal when we really are no longer hungry, but wow, cramming in that extra high calorie dense foods are a killer.

Since I have reached equilibrium in my weight by following The McDougall Program for Maximum Weight Loss, the truth is that it is not likely that I can add much back into my diet without experiencing weight gain unless I get back to the gym.

Cramming served a purpose years ago when we were not sure when we would be able to eat again...but now, that is not the case for me.

_____

_____

_____

_____

DECEMBER 4

WORD FOR TODAY: LIFESTYLE

When I first started following "The McDougall Program for Maximum Weight Loss", thinking about lifestyle was the farthest thing from my mind.

I wanted to lose 70 pounds (at first), have my knees quit hurting and be able to continue travelling. Whatever guidelines Dr. McDougall had in his book about improving our lifestyle (sleep, exercise, meditation, spiritual awareness etc) did not even register with me until I read his book a second time with a different focus.

All my life, I focused on weight loss. I had not learned that health also includes changing our lifestyle. Last night, I attended a seminar on cancer with Ruben J. Guzman, MPH, and LMP and had the total picture to health presented in such a way that I more fully understood the need to address all areas of our life if we want our bodies to do what they do best - heal. This lifestyle is not a diet. It is a chance to rejuvenate ourselves for the rest of our lives.

Our attitudes, our ability to forgive, get enough exercise, sleep and maintain good relationships are just some of the areas he pointed out in his free seminar.

I had my mind refreshed about how the protein in dairy is linked to cancer cell growth and that if we want to heal, we need to eliminate toxins in our bodies and give them the best nourishment possible AS WELL AS address our propensity to complain, hold onto resentments, have negative attitudes or friends and by choosing bad habits and a stressful life.

It is time for this message to reach all people - especially those suffering from food borne diseases (heart, diabetes, high blood pressure etc) and to realize that although weight loss is a benefit, it is not the sole benefactor in changing one's lifestyle.

If you are in the Sacramento area, I recommend checking out Coach Rubin for a free seminar on how to enhance your life.

_____
_____
_____
_____

FROM DONUTS...TO POTATOES

DECEMBER 5
WORD FOR TODAY: BACK

We often say we have gotten back into the swing of things, that we are back on track, that we have our back covered and even some say "my aching back". But what I want to talk about is what happens when we get back into our healthy groove.

Going back could also be like going back to the future - not necessarily like living in the past. We do want to move forward and embrace all of the good ideas we have been exposed to and in doing so, we often go back to what we know has worked for us.

Today, I went back to the gym after being away for several weeks. It felt good to put my swimming suit on and do some exercises in the hot tub and of course to reconnect with some friends.

This afternoon, I will go back to my ophthalmologist to have my eyes examined.

So, no matter where you are on your journey, going back may be just what you need to reinforce your resolve to be your best. Go back and re-read the books which have led to your success and certainly go back and watch the documentaries which inspired you in the first place.

Going back just may push you into a healthier future.

ESTHER LEBECK LOVERIDGE

DECEMBER 6
WORD FOR TODAY: VISION

I have heard that without a vision, the people perish.

Yesterday I had my annual visit with my ophthalmologist, who has been following my vision for many years. He had informed me that I have a macular pucker and a condition called pseudo defoliation which makes it a bit trickier to remove cataracts.

Three years ago, he was going to refer me to a surgeon for possible surgery on the macular pucker. I explained to him that I had recently (3 months prior) started a whole food plant based diet and I believed eating such great food could also have a positive effect on my eyes. He agreed to check me six months later and indeed my eyesight did improve and continued to improve over subsequent checkups. Yesterday I was told that my condition was stable and that he'd see me in another year. I no longer am required to wear glasses for driving. The best part is that I gave him my card and he listened to my whole story.

I envision a world where we are realizing the answer to our health issues is dependent upon the food we eat. Is it an easy journey? No. But neither is it easy recovering from a stroke, a heart attack, diabetes or taking medications for years which may only manage a disease and never cure it.

Can we see into the future? Yes... and we get to choose how we are going to get there. We cannot serve two masters. We get to select health or disease. The choice is ours.

"Do you see what I see"?

DECEMBER 7
WORD FOR TODAY: WORRY

Sometimes I spend time rehashing a conversation in my mind. I did that last night. I wondered if I should have spoken up about a difference of opinion or was it really better that I just let it slide.

There is no right answer. It was just a choice. But what did I learn? I learned that during the time I spent rehashing the event, I was living in the past. That encounter was over so why was I giving it so much attention?

I guess having an analytical mind can take up my time and even over-work a situation but when the light does come on and I get a new thought, I am thankful for the opportunity to learn.

We do not have to protest every difference that comes into our lives. These differences just point out that many of us are following a script from the past and haven't learned the joys of reframing a situation.

This same scenario will undoubtedly come up again and hopefully I will unhook my sensitive antenna and sit in that person's shoes for a few moments.

Mr. Fred Rogers was right. We are all special and unique and okay just the way we are. We do not have to be a reflection of each other to be appreciated.

It is a good feeling to be in the company of like-minded people but the test of our love is learning how to appreciate diversity.

"You are my friend, you are special. Won't you be my neighbor?"
Thank you, Mr. Rogers.

DECEMBER 8

WORD FOR TODAY: HEALING

This morning I was asked how I healed myself from anal fissures (and I would add rectum fissures as well).

There will be some people who have not been following this drama but suffice it to say it was not caused by a whole food plant based diet. I have not had a single day of constipation since I began this way of eating 3 years ago and that is just one of its great benefits.

So, before we look for a cure/healing, we should examine the cause. This woody impaction occurred after I had the not so bright idea of eating 2 cups of pomegranate seeds after I had extracted the juice thinking that it would just be good fiber. Lesson #1: we need to eat the whole food as it occurs in nature.

The treatment at the emergency room included enemas and attempts at manual extraction which may have actually increased the damage but it was drinking a magnesium solution which got things moving again.

Now let's go to the healing part. Healing is often a multifaceted experience. It may take prayer where we ask to learn the lessons in it for us, patience as we acknowledge that our bodies want to be well and that occurs over time and I also asked my body parts to forgive me for the damage I had caused them.

I sang joy songs from our former minister Rev. Phil Pierson, I spent many hours soaking in a hot bath, I used a total of three

FROM DONUTS...TO POTATOES

different creams, I tried switching to a low fiber diet on the advice of a non plant based doctor which resulted in constipation and got another appointment with my regular plant based doctor who told me to go back to eating my regular WFPB food. We would manage the process with a stool softener and Miralax. Pain management was attempted with bed rest, hours of trying to relax in the tub, meditation and breathing exercises, using a heating pad and lots of mental work - imagining that my body had been healed and that there would be a time period for it to be manifested. I was advised that it could take up to 4-6 weeks to heal and was so thankful it did heal. I did not want to have to have surgery.

Pain usually subsided several hours after a movement but what made this whole experience almost unbearable was I was having between 4 to 6 movements a day.

Total healing has occurred and I do believe that eating a whole food plant based diet is what our bodies need to give every cell what it needs to heal. I believe it is the answer to disease as well as abuse.

Thanks again to all of you, who offered prayers, sent healing energy and simply gave me good old sympathy.

_____

_____

_____

ESTHER LEBECK LOVERIDGE

DECEMBER 9

WORD FOR TODAY: CREATE

Did you know we are all creators? It's fun to think about. I have relatives like Lynora who is a home decorator and she really knows how to put colors and designs together.

Some creators are like my niece Valerie who is able to paint beautiful portraits and teach others to do the same.

My father loved photography and created a bounty of family movies that we still enjoy.

My brother Leroy is a retired minister and still helps people create peace in their lives.

Ben has a green thumb and instinctively knows how to create a beautiful yard very inexpensively.

We are all part of the larger picture as we do our part to create a healthy environment and families.

There are relationships that need to be nourished and we all participate in that creation too.

Know your creative power. Make good food, music, art and whatever are your talents, spread your gifts and joy wherever you go. We need you.

_____

_____

_____

_____

FROM DONUTS...TO POTATOES

DECEMBER 10
WORD FOR TODAY: WANT

Want is the word I am thinking about today. Before we can get what we want in life, we must identify what it is that we want and then comes the big question - what price are we willing to pay to get it?

When we make a list of the things we want, we might have to prioritize them if funds or even energy is limited. Then we might eliminate some things we can live without and focus on what is really important to us.

It is not always easy to be honest with ourselves when it comes to health. Yes, we all want to be healthy but then someone tells us we can't have our cake and eat it too and we realize, if we are fortunate, that choices must be made.

When we decide it is time to make a change, it is helpful to figure out what we are willing to release in order to achieve the results we want.

As Dr. Doug Lisle says every decision involves a cost benefit analysis. What weighs heavier on your scale - the cost of the energy it takes to make changes or the huge improvement in your health?

Only you can determine if the joy of successfully finding the solution to your disease or weight issue exceeds the cost of putting forth the energy to make it happen.

Be truthful about what you want in life. Being mediocre may be good enough, but, if not, going the extra mile may just put you over the top.

DECEMBER 11
WORD FOR TODAY: BLAME

To blame may simply be to b - lame! We have the power to change our lives, our thinking about food, how much value we put on it and decide the path we are going to take.

The default position is to blame others. Some say "the devil made me do it". Some say "Obesity runs in my family".

It is easy to blame restaurants for not providing us with compliant food and we even blame our young children thinking that they need some junk food around and then it becomes just too hard to "be good". We blame our spouses for making this change difficult by not going along.

But when do we actually get to grow up and make our own decisions about the path we want to take? I think it happens most easily when we get desperate - maybe at the end of our rope - at which time it doesn't matter what others think or what they choose to do.

We finally can become resolute and decide to give up the "Oh, but it tastes so good" excuse that keeps the ball and chain of food addiction attached to our bodies and keeps us in the jail called failure.

We can change our minds once we actually believe that this is not just another diet to lose weight but it is the answer to restoring our body and mind to wholeness. If we do get to the place where we really believe it, then the next question is "Do we love/respect ourselves enough to give ourselves the best fuel"?

We are the ones who choose what to put on the end of our fork. We get to B - lame or not.

FROM DONUTS...TO POTATOES

DECEMBER 12

WORD FOR TODAY: ENABLE

What we enable, we promote.

I usually think of enabling as perhaps condoning less than healthy behaviors in another.

It can be so subtle. I remember Thanksgiving dinner in November 2016. I was only 3 months into following The McDougall Program for Maximum Weight Loss when I was confronted with the dilemma of what to cook for our family. I questioned my years of serving a traditional meal - one our extended family had become accustomed to being served.

I was the only one eating this way and I did not want to "rock the boat". My solution was to maintain the tradition. I simply set aside a portion of the sweet potatoes, green beans and salad for myself before I added the sugars and fats. I could enjoy the fresh fruit platter and skip the turkey and dessert.

Leftovers were sent home with others to keep them out of my environment. The same dilemma resurfaced again on Christmas and Easter.

As time went by, serving my family what I had come to believe was toxic food became somewhat of a moral issue for me. Why would I send milk and chocolate milk, whipped cream and cheese home with my granddaughters?

Eventually, Ben switched over and we didn't even want to buy those foods.

We still wanted to share holidays but what would be a reasonable solution? We ended up combining Ben's birthday with Christmas and treated our family to dinner at a vegan restaurant. For Easter, we treated them to a Mexican dinner at a restaurant which also had a no oil vegan menu and everyone was able to make their own choice.

I use to rationalize that when I sent food home with my family that they were eating that kind of food anyway and at least I was saving them money but would I give alcoholics liquor I no longer wanted to drink or give meds to a person having drug issues?

Who would have ever guessed the issues that would arise when we chose a different path?

_____

_____

_____

_____

DECEMBER 13

WORD FOR TODAY: SUPERSTITION

Today is Friday the Thirteenth. What does that bring to your mind? Does it make you think twice about stepping on a crack in the sidewalk or letting a black cat cross your path or maybe it simply means that this is the 13th day of December and the 6th day of the week.

Superstitions may be like taking a placebo. If we put our faith or believe in either, we just might create the outcome we want.

When I read The McDougall Program for Maximum Weight Loss, I chose to put it to the test. We must evaluate everything for ourselves. We hear so much "noise" these days and hardly know what to believe. There are "scientific" studies out there supporting

FROM DONUTS...TO POTATOES

whatever we choose to believe but have they stood the test of time which this program has done?

Dr. McDougall's message has not changed. It has remained the same for over four decades. We are starchivores and "Starch is the Solution". His program has produced amazing results as evidenced in the lives of thousands of people - many whose stories are documented on his website.

At first, I wasn't impressed with the stories - I figured they could be contrived but I was willing to treat his program like an experiment. I had never succeeded in sustaining weight loss on any other program over 50 years of dieting. This was a whole new way of thinking.

Could eating so simply, inexpensively, and never needing to be hungry again really work? Could I actually get all the protein I need from plants? You mean not only could I lose 130 pounds and keep it off but reverse disease and eliminate all medications as well?

The answer is yes. I created my own test and the program gets all of the credit...I only validate the results of the experiment.

Is it a placebo, superstition or facts? What works for you?

_____

_____

_____

_____

DECEMBER 14

WORD FOR TODAY: MIND

Ben is the first one to get out of bed each morning...not necessarily the first to wake up and after our daily chat, he says "Do you mind if I turn on the light"? Of course I always say "That's fine". Up until that time, I usually have my eyes closed so he just wants to alert me in case I want to cover my eyes.

Today that got me to thinking about the word "mind". We mind our manners, we might mind our doctors and of course some of us did mind our parents. We also talked about how much our mind plays a part in becoming successful in following a plant based diet. Our mind or brain is our control center so I asked Google about the difference between the mind and the brain and I learned that our brain is part of the visible, tangible world of the body. Our mind is part of the invisible, transcendent world of thought, feeling, attitude, belief and imagination. The brain is the physical organ most associated with mind and consciousness, but the mind is not confined to the brain.

Wow...now I really have something to ponder. It kind of reminds me of when I try to figure out the difference between my spirit and my soul.

Anyway, suffice it to say what we think about, we bring about. If we have success on our mind, we are capable of producing it. If we focus on past failures, we just might produce more of the same but our mind is not restricted by the IQ of our brain. Isn't that exciting?

No matter how much we have struggled in the past, I think we can change our brain by the renewing of our mind.

Over time, my brain has adapted to my new food choices and satisfaction is my friend. Yes, I know the old way is highly palatable, but the longer I reward myself with healthy choices, the sooner my brain accepts it as being the new normal and the struggle is diminished.

That is my answer to the question posed by Face book each day "What is on your mind?"

_____

_____

_____

_____

FROM DONUTS...TO POTATOES

DECEMBER 15
WORD FOR TODAY: PREVENTION

An old proverb says "An ounce of prevention is worth a pound of cure" but what if the damage is already done?

I have been a life-long sun worshiper. I remember as a kid spreading a towel out on the sidewalk and "laying out" with Joan, my Portuguese girlfriend.

I have been guilty of idolizing the bronzed look and sought it with lots of time in the hot tub and pool.

I also have thought of my plant based diet as being a "cure all" for everything. I have even felt kind of invincible to any food borne disease.

Just as there are exceptions to every grammatical rule, I have learned that sun damage is an exception. It is not caused by eating the Standard American Diet.

In July, I had an area on my forehead biopsied - basal cell carcinoma. My hairdresser had suggested I get it checked out but it didn't appear to be changing so I did nothing about it until it bled.

A few weeks ago, I noticed a "freckle" on my forehead and looked back on my July photos and didn't see it. This week, I went to my doctor to have it checked. He took a photo and sent it to dermatology and it was biopsied a few minutes later.

In two days, I was told it was skin cancer - early stage 0 and will be treated topically after the biopsy wound heals.

Denial, or a plant based diet, doesn't cure skin cancer.

So, at this stage in my life, prevention will not reverse previous damage but I can learn how to reduce the effects of the sun on my skin.

As Grandmother Kearns used to tell me, "You can't stop the birds from flying overhead, but you can prevent them from building a nest in your hair".

In the meantime, consider preventing or reversing food borne diseases in your body by following a plant based diet. That does work.

___

DECEMBER 16

WORD FOR TODAY: FIRST

Who or what do you put first in your life? There are many answers to that question.

I am thinking about the advice we get when we fly:

We are told to put our oxygen mask on first, before helping others. Why is this important rule necessary for ensuring survival? If you run out of oxygen, you can't help anyone.

This advice applies to our food preparation and planning too. If we are not equipped with proper nutrition in our homes, we will default to whatever is available when hunger or an emergency strikes.

My plan of attack is to shop for staples that will sustain me and then batch cook so I don't have to start from scratch each day.

My intention is to always have five items on hand and prepared: potatoes, sweet potatoes, steel cut oatmeal, beans and brown rice.

If I have nothing else in the house, these foods will satisfy me and give me the fuel I need.

Of course I want to have fresh fruit and vegetables on hand too, but they will not take the place of my starches. Life is easier if we have canned or frozen food stored as well.

FROM DONUTS...TO POTATOES

There are stories of people who have gone a period of time eating only potatoes and thrived.

My Grandmother Kearns was poor and was down to having only potatoes in her house when an "angel" left a bag of groceries on her doorstep. When my niece Ruth Paz was a child and heard this story, she said "If all you have is potatoes, God will supply the rest".

These starches are my new "centerpiece". I can plan meals around them just like I did meat in the old days.

Plan and prepare for success and if you really are serious about winning, dump the junk. Chef A.J. says "If it is in your house, it will be in your mouth". Keep your environment clean. Eventually a stressor will trigger you to eat what is handily available. Choose a potato.

_____

_____

_____

_____

DECEMBER 17

WORD FOR TODAY: DILIGENT

I was going to use ".Hang on" as my word(s) today but thought I would use "diligent" since it is just one word.

In the face of having so many friends suffering from food borne debilitating issues/illnesses, how do I hang onto hope? How can I be diligent in sharing what I believe to be the answer to good health as we age? I am still learning.

I recently read a book about when to speak up and when to shut up. I think the line between the two must be very fine because it's hard to find it. I can swing from being compassionate, sympathetic, encouraging and acknowledging how difficult it is to be sick and how difficult it is to change, to wanting to figuratively shake people by the shoulders and say "Wake up people".

That's usually where I remind myself that just 3 1/2 years ago, I too would not have been in a place to hear about how food could be my medicine. It wasn't until pain slowed me down that I was open and receptive to learning how to live.

One of the ways I am encouraged to be diligent in spreading this message is by the many people in "Esther's Nutritional Journey" who have inspired me with their stories of healing and progression as they have adapted to a new lifestyle.

I want to thank each one of you for your feedback which has allowed me to see that change is coming. Not all will hear this message, but some will ...and hope is rekindled.

_____

_____

_____

_____

DECEMBER 18

WORD FOR TODAY: LIMIT

There are speed limits on the roads to ensure safety for all. There are limits on the amount of alcohol a person can drink and still be considered sober enough to drive.

Some people limit meat consumption to once a day and others to once a week or maybe once a year.

Some people can limit themselves to eating just one cookie but

FROM DONUTS...TO POTATOES

how often can we limit ourselves to just one potato chip or just one peanut?

If desserts are such a great thing, why must we limit them?

I have discovered the joy of eating a plant based diet and there is no limit to how often or even how much I can eat of the four basic food groups: fruit, vegetables, grains and legumes/beans. It is true that while I was losing weight, there were some healthy foods which were high in fat that I eliminated from my diet (nuts, seeds, avocado, olives and soy) but what a pleasure it was not to have to weigh my food, count calories, use a small plate or have just one bite.

If limits are required, perhaps we need to consider if they are beneficial to us at all.

It has been said that the sky is the limit...but is it? There is no limit to the light all of us have within us. We can share it freely without ever having less for ourselves. It is renewable.

Give and it shall be given to you. Love abundantly. Breathe fresh air deeply. Sing. Rejoice. Be thankful. There is no limit.

_____

_____

_____

_____

DECEMBER 19

WORD FOR TODAY: AFTERGLOW

There are times in life when the afterglow is as warm and fulfilling as the initial event from which it was created.

Moments come and go in our lives but there are special times we will remember for a long time.

Last night we combined Ben's birthday celebration with an early Christmas dinner for our family. It was so special having our three in town children and their in town children, his sister and her friend and our new friends Peggy Bean and Larry White join us.

We are so fortunate to have loving independent children and growing grand children make the effort in rain and heavy traffic come to share the love.

Yes, our complete family was not all there but the tables were filled with a time of reconnecting.

Last night we enjoyed vegan food while others enjoyed what they chose, but the best part was just being together.

Our blended family combines the best of many people and we give thanks for the joy each of them contribute to our lives. We are in the glow.

_____

_____

_____

_____

DECEMBER 20

WORD FOR TODAY: KEEP

In this current climate, we are encouraged to release and let go of the things that no longer serve us. We are advised to "de-clutter". But what can we keep?

I think it is pretty cool to have kept a size 24 (3X) pant suit. That enabled me to create a "stripping" video where I let go of the old to reveal the slimmer me underneath.

Keeping a list of my beginning body measurements was a good

FROM DONUTS...TO POTATOES

idea too. It is amazing to count up the inches lost even when the scale didn't seem to move.

Another item I advise keeping is a "before photo'. We never know. We just might be asked to be on the cover of Woman's World magazine and a picture is worth a thousand words.

The words that we keep in our heart are important too. They might be encouraging words we have heard, words of a poem, a scripture, or a song from childhood or something whispered in our ear. We can pull them up into our consciousness at any time to inspire us to keep moving forward.

I remember the time my mother was in the hospital and we thought we might be losing her. All four of her children gathered around her bedside. My brother asked her if there was anything special she wanted to say to us. Perhaps he was thinking it would be some kind of a blessing. She kept it simple. She simply said, "Keep on keeping on" and she did the same.

_____

_____

_____

_____

DECEMBER 21

WORD FOR TODAY: SAVE

Lots of things come to my mind as I think of this word. We save for a rainy day, are asked to save the date for an upcoming event and if we are lucky, someone may ask us to save the last dance for them.

Preachers want to save the "lost", environmentalists want to save the planet, vegans are interested in saving the animals and most of us want to save on our electric bill.

We get insurance for our cars and our homes as well as our health in order to save ourselves from the cost associated with loss but the best insurance may actually be prevention.

We can install fire alarms, drive defensively and get our annual check-ups and all of these efforts are helpful but when it comes to saving our health, an ounce of prevention is worth a pound of cure.

Medication is a treatment. It is not a cure. There are two medications I have taken for over 30 years and neither one cured me. I thought I was stuck taking them for the rest of my life until... well, you can guess...until I discovered the healing powers of eating plants.

We can save ourselves much grief. Perhaps that is our biggest mission and it just so happens that all of the other things we all want to save will be affected as well.

This is a real win-win situation.

_____

_____

_____

_____

DECEMBER 22

WORD FOR TODAY: CONNECT

Magnets have always fascinated me. I used to play with them and watched to see if the two different pieces repelled each other or rushed to connect.

By nature, we have a need to connect with one another.

FROM DONUTS...TO POTATOES

Sometimes we are magnetically drawn to people in an almost urgent manner.

Last night I called my high school roommate to wish her a happy birthday. We were also in each other's wedding and after spending two hours on the phone, I wondered why I don't call her more often.

People who enjoy people are the luckiest people in the world. I guess we are all lucky because what would we do without each other? I happen to believe we are the hands and feet of God.

Whether we connect on Facebook or in person, at a conference, church, synagogue, mosque or temple or even a restaurant, these moments are precious.

Belonging to a community is a part of a healthy lifestyle: Diet, Exercise, Meditation and Love. I am thankful for the groups on Facebook which allow us to stay connected.

_____

_____

_____

_____

DECEMBER 23

WORD FOR TODAY: WAIT

We don't like to wait at traffic lights, we don't like to wait in line at the store, children don't like to wait for Christmas and some of us have a hard time waiting to hear the latest news about someone we love.

Having patience is a gift. Sometimes we get anxious and that feels uncomfortable and we desire a quick remedy. What or to whom do we reach out for in those moments? Do we really think that food or drink is going to change the situation? Maybe we reach out to a friend to help us walk through the process as we seek clarity.

Sometimes it helps to wait in the silence as we seek guidance and have our strength renewed.

We used to hear Elvis Presley sing "Fools Rush In" and we are reminded that even waiting serves a good purpose.

Waiting can be a teacher if we are willing to listen while events play out at their own speed.

Sometimes we are just an observer in life...not the director. If we wait, we might be called in to help, but it just may also be that we don't have a part in this play.

_____

_____

_____

_____

DECEMBER 24

WORD FOR TODAY: DECLARE

"Well, I declare!" is something my grandmother and other old timers used to say. Now, we don't hear that very often.

But what we declare is important. "What we think about, we bring about" plays into the equation as well. When Ben initially said "I could never eat like you", he was declaring his desire not to make any changes. I assured him by replying "You don't have to" but in time, he eliminated meat and dairy and lost over 60 pounds.

FROM DONUTS...TO POTATOES

The Declaration of Independence established our identity as a country.

Making our declarations known can also set up a sense of responsibility to follow through on any statements that we make.

Be careful what you wish for...you might get it is another testimony to the importance of what we say. Acknowledging what we want also sets into motion a path to our goals.

What we declare identifies our intentions when we are honest with ourselves. Talk can be cheap but declaring takes it a step further. It is strong and powerful enough to change our lives.

I do declare!

_____

_____

_____

DECEMBER 25

WORD FOR TODAY: GIFT

I love the story about the little drummer boy because for a long time, I didn't know what my gift was but it made me realize that no talent is too small.

Sometimes we compare our talents with others and always seem to come up short.

Some people have gold to bring. Some can sing. Others can paint and then there are those who create masterpieces in the kitchen.

I like those people who know how to give good hugs and then there are those whose smiles seem to spread from ear to ear.

Often an encouraging word fills the bill and gets us through another day.

Holding the hand of someone in pain is a great gift too and of course phone calls are helpful for people who don't text.

Whatever is your rum pum pum pum contribution to the story, do it proudly.

No gift is too small.

_____

_____

_____

_____

DECEMBER 26

WORD FOR TODAY: DIAGNOSIS

Diagnosis is identifying the nature of an illness or other problem by examination of the symptoms.

When we get a diagnosis...especially one from a medical doctor, it is easy to accept it not only as "Gospel" but to so identify with it and claim it that there are times we can perpetuate the condition as our new truth and see no separation between it and us. We become "it". We often say "I have –- instead of "my symptoms are ––"

I diagnosed myself as a "food addict". I had all of the symptoms: I couldn't stop eating See's Candy until it was all gone. It was the same way with Ben and Jerry's ice cream. (At least I had good taste). Or was it because those sweets were so palatable and such a great dopamine hit -more than anything else in my life that I wanted to experience it again and again?

What a great escape. I was in heaven when I enjoyed those

FROM DONUTS...TO POTATOES

orgasmic concoctions. I didn't want to talk to anyone when I was in the middle of ecstasy. Just leave me alone with my "fix".

Moderation? You've got to be kidding. I always hoped that my husband already had enough and I could eat the rest. Sharing was the lie I told myself I could do.

Admitting I was an addict was helpful when I tried to explain to others that I chose not to take one bite because of my fear that I'd be on a slippery path to overindulging once again... with the accompanying feelings of failure since I didn't seem to be able to control what I put in my mouth.

After 3 years of successfully following The McDougall Program for Maximum Weight Loss do I still think I am a "food addict"? It depends. I do use it to explain to others why I choose to resist that one bite and when I have indulged, one is never enough as greed overtakes me but I have found the antidote and keep my prescription handy. I keep it refilled in my "medicine cabinet" - the pantry and refrigerator but there is nothing like taking it fresh off the baking sheet after roasting - my sweet potatoes.

I have found the "Starch Solution". It is my hope that everyone finds their cure rather than the bandage of drugs. We can let food be our medicine or as Dr. McDougall says, "It's the Food"

ESTHER LEBECK LOVERIDGE

DECEMBER 27
WORD FOR TODAY: START

When I was a child and needed to clean my room or do a chore and I didn't know where to start, I remember Mom telling me "Just start in a corner".

In the corners of our minds, we have cobwebs that need to be cleaned out. We need to sweep out thoughts that keep us tied to past behaviors. Think of this: Everything in our brain is in the past.

When we clean "house", we create space for something new. Think about what you want in your life and imagine how you are going to feel when you make it happen.

I am imagining that when I clean off and remove the shelving in our car port, we will have room to put our car in there instead of on the driveway. It is a suggestion Ben made and I didn't resist so it will be a team effort. Get support for the changes you want to make and claim it for yourself.

Each day we can start with gratitude for our many blessings - the ones we have and the ones that are waiting to come into our lives as we create the space.

January 1st is a popular starting point for many of us but each moment of our lives is an opportunity to begin to release what is keeping us tied to the past and move in a new direction.

Start your journey.

_____

_____

_____

_____

FROM DONUTS...TO POTATOES

DECEMBER 28
WORD FOR TODAY: CRAZY

Crazy has often been described as repeating certain behaviors over and over WHILE expecting different results!

Whenever I used to diet, I was also "crazy" because I would restrict certain foods TEMPORARILY while expecting PERMANENT results.

Dr. McDougall uses the word "Diet" in some of his book titles; however, that may be because that is what people are looking for when they want to lose weight.

I call this group "Esther's Nutritional Journey" because following Dr. McDougall's Program for Maximum Weight Loss has been my path to learning how to choose health for the rest of my life.

I have to admit that losing weight was my first incentive but as I have continued this journey, I have come to know that choosing health FIRST is what will give our new direction permanence and the weight will find it's happy place.

We do not want to be slim sick people.

_____
_____
_____
_____

ESTHER LEBECK LOVERIDGE

DECEMBER 29

WORD FOR TODAY: UNDERSTAND

Years ago, after 15 years of marriage and enjoying two wonderful sons, I went through a divorce. It was during that time that I wanted to understand my own mental illness. I went back to school to study psychology. I wanted to understand.

Today I still struggle to understand not only myself but other people.

Sometimes I can't understand. I don't understand why people don't see the advantages of eating a plant-based diet. I don't understand how I can see it as the answer to so many problems and others don't see it that way.

There are probably more things I don't understand than what I do, but what I have come to the conclusion of this morning is our commission in life is not to understand. Our commission is to love. That is the only commandment.

I love Mr. Fred Rogers's song where he assures us that he likes us just the way we are. That is what I want to learn. It is only through acceptance that we allow others to grow and learn (or not) at their own pace

FROM DONUTS...TO POTATOES

DECEMBER 30

WORD FOR TODAY: INQUIRE

I just imagined seeing a sign on the door of a retailer which read: "Help Wanted - Inquire within".

That led me to thinking about how important it is in life to inquire within when we are seeking to find our way.

It is so easy to seek out others for guidance when we are in trouble. Why is it that we sometimes put more value on the insights of others than going into the silence and asking ourselves what would be the best course of action to take?

Talking to people in the know can be helpful. We can learn from the experience of professionals. They can guide us in a positive direction too but if we rely on someone else too much, it could weaken trusting our own intuition.

As we take time to inquire within and test the answers that come to us, we have the opportunity to trust ourselves and own the direction we choose. After all, we are the ones who have to accept the consequences of our own actions.

There used to be a comedian on TV and I vaguely remember his punch line "The devil made me do it" and of course we all laughed. Maybe the program was called "Laugh In". At any rate, if we are going to be held responsible for our actions, we might as well practice the art of going within for direction.

Owning what we want is the first step to being honest with ourselves. If you think it would be nice to be healthy and slim at the same time but you are not willing to pay the price, be honest with yourself. Wait until the need becomes real for you. Then the motivation will come from within. It will be your best motivator and guide.

That just may be the process by which you convert from being a complainer to a doer.

It has been said "What you want, wants you". Check it out. Ask (inquire) and you will receive.

_____

_____

_____

DECEMBER 31

WORD FOR TODAY: CELEBRATE

I like to sing a song about every little cell in my body being healthy It really gets me into a state of celebration.

I love celebrations. Today we have several other things to celebrate. We have my sister-in-law's birthday and my brother's wedding anniversary and of course moving into a new decade is exciting too.

But every day I celebrate my new birth into knowledge, freedom from addiction, and a restored body, mind and soul as I continue to follow the McDougall Program for Maximum Weight Loss.

My cousin asked me why I switched overnight instead of gradually adopting the program and I said it was because I wanted to put it to the test. How would I ever know how well the program worked if I didn't DO it?

I had put many diets to the test over the past 50 years and they all worked...temporarily. The problem was that none had been sustainable for life. This one promotes the way I want to live for the rest of my life.

In the video "Esther Loveridge's Drastic Weight Loss Secret" on

FROM DONUTS...TO POTATOES

YouTube, I vowed to give Dr. McDougall the credit if his program worked. It did... so I do.

Let the celebrations continue.

_____

_____
_____
_____

AUTHOR'S BIOGRAPHY

At the age of 72, I faced a crisis. Pain in my almost bone-on-bone knees was threatening to cramp my style of traveling the world. It was then that a dear friend gave me a book which changed my life forever.

My journey on following a plant-based diet had begun. After adopting "The McDougall Program for Maximum Weight Loss" my passport to the world was renewed.

Success in achieving a healthy body, mind and soul chased me down the street. I was able to eliminate all medications including statins, pain and sleeping pills, Levothyroxin, and lithium (some

FROM DONUTS...TO POTATOES

medications I had taken for over 30 years). I reversed all diseases (GERD, pre-diabetes, high blood pressure, high cholesterol, sleep apnea, low thyroid and constipation). I actually eliminated the need for knee replacements and as a bonus, I lost 130 pounds.

Another friend encouraged me to start a group on Facebook by suggesting I could inspire and motivate others with my story. I created "Esther's Nutritional Journey" on Facebook and it was for that group that I started posting my "Word for today" to share my personal journey, offer support and impart my wisdom and inspiration along the way.

I also posted photos of what I ate each day to demonstrate that one does not have to be a chef in order to transition to a plant based diet. It is as simple as selecting a variety of food from four categories: fruit, vegetables, grains and legumes. Use this book as a helpful tool for weight loss, regaining your health and stabilizing emotional health as you take control of your life and what you put in your mouth.

There is no magic pill but with consistent effort and dedication to the principles of Dr. McDougall's book, I feel like I have found the fountain of youth. It is as close to you as your local grocery store's produce department.

His program is free. At www.drmcdougall.com, you can access all of his information.

It is my hope that you will be encouraged as you read these daily posts.

Perhaps through the daily readings you learn how an ordinary person was able to achieve a drug free life by simply adopting a plant-based diet. It is not an easy journey at first, but as dietary changes are made it becomes a new way of life.

I want you to know that old age doesn't have to be spent in a rocking chair. It is never too late to move towards restoration. The best is yet to be.

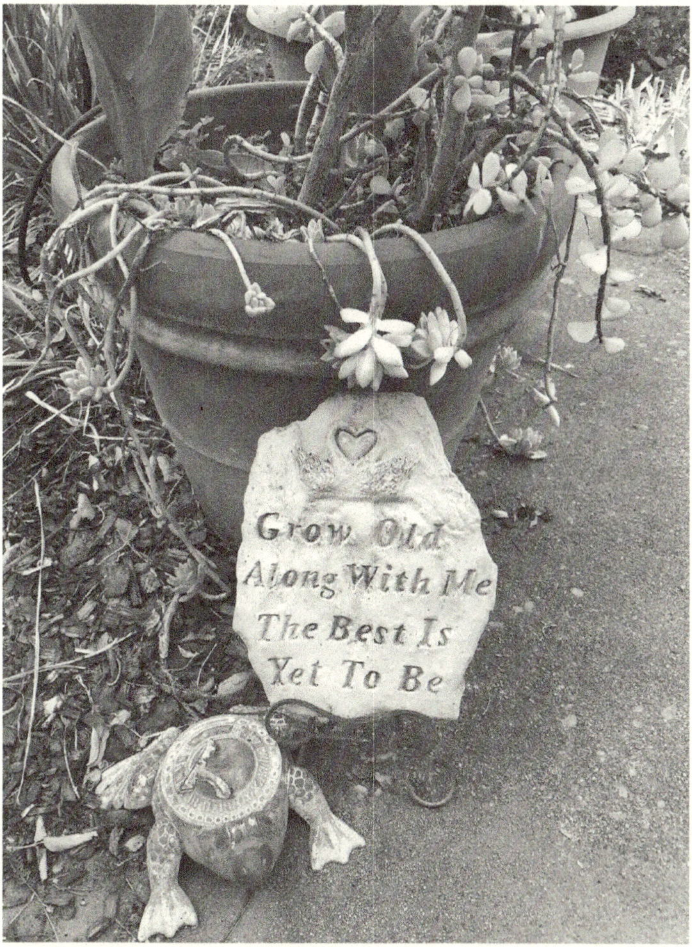
Grow Old
Along With Me
The Best Is
Yet To Be